TWO WHEELS OVER CATALONIA

Cycling the Back Roads of North-eastern Spain

Richard Guise

summersdale

TWO WHEELS OVER CATALONIA

Copyright © Richard Guise, 2011

Map by Robert Littleford

Summersdale Publishers Ltd
46 West Street
Chichester
West Sussex
PO19 1RP
UK

www.summersdale.com

Printed and bound in Great Britain

ISBN: 978-1-84953-144-3

Substantial discounts on bulk quantities of Summersdale books are available to corporations, professional associations and other organisations. For details contact Summersdale Publishers by telephone: +44 (0) 1243 771107, fax: +44 (0) 1243 786300 or email: nicky@summersdale.com.

PERMISSIONS:

p. 20, excerpt from *A Piper in Brazil* by James D. Faulkner (2006, James Donal Faulkner) is reproduced by kind permission of James Faulkner. (The menu quoted in the first chapter of this book was first published there.)

Excerpts from *A Handbook for Travellers in Spain* by Richard Ford (1855, John Murray) are reproduced without permission as it is out of copyright and in the public domain.

Excerpts from *Fabled Shore* by Rose Macaulay (© Rose Macaulay, 1949) are reproduced by kind permission of PFD (www.pfd.co.uk) on behalf of the estate of Rose Macaulay.

To Julie, for her support, her tolerance and her marmalade

Richard Guise is the author of *Over the Hill and Round the Bend* and *From the Mull to the Cape*. He is based in Quorn, Leicestershire, and spends part of the year in Llançà, Catalonia.

Contents

Acknowledgements..7

A Note From the Author......................................8

Map..9

Day 1 Like That?
Portbou to Llançà..11

Day 2 At the Edge of the World:
Llançà to Cadaqués..31

Day 3 Giggling Amigos:
Cadaqués to L'Escala..55

Day 4 Costa Brava for Better or Worse:
L'Escala to Sant Antoni de Calonge..................76

Day 5 Little Britain:
Sant Antoni de Calonge to Malgrat de Mar......93

Day 6 Irregular Situations:
Malgrat de Mar to Barcelona..........................110

Day 7 Old Friends:
Barcelona to El Prat de Llobregat....................134

Day 8 Solo to the South:
El Prat de Llobregat to Calafell......................156

Day 9 The Wrong Shirt:
Calafell to Cambrils..170

Day 10 To the Delta:
Cambrils to Sant Carles de la Ràpita..............190

Day 11 Accidentally in Paradise:
Sant Carles de la Ràpita to Prat de Comte....................207

Day 12 *Vive la Vía!*
Prat de Comte to Tortosa...222

Day 13 Antonio and Xavi:
Tortosa to Ripoll..235

Day 14 Defying the Laws of Physics:
Ripoll to Olot...256

Day 15 740 Steps Before Breakfast:
Olot to Girona..274

Day 16 Down to the Sea Again:
Girona to Sant Feliu de Guíxols....................................293

Notes on Catalan Street Names......................................305

Statto Corner...312

Railway Access...316

Selected Sources...318

Acknowledgements

For creative ideas, thanks to Jim Faulkner, Narcís Genís, Jordi Pellejà, Nuri Pellejà and Mireia Sanuy. For reviews and comments, thanks to Jan Baker, Tom Baker, Jude Gourd, Tim McEwen, Chris Owen and Isabel Ruiz de Conejo. For help in flora identification, thanks to Mary Thomas. For a comprehensive and detailed review of all things Catalan, thanks to Montserrat Castelltort. For invaluable help at the sharp end, thanks to Anna, Jennifer and Lucy at Summersdale. And for inspiration and support way beyond the call of duty, thanks especially to Julie Challans.

Despite all the reviews, any errors remaining in this book are of course my own responsibility.

A Note From the Author

Catalan and Spanish

Many geographical names in Catalonia are different in Catalan and Spanish; for example, Girona (Catalan) and Gerona (Spanish) or Ebre (Catalan) and Ebro (Spanish). Throughout this book I use the Catalan versions, unless there's a different English equivalent, for example Aragon rather than Aragó.

As for other local vocabulary, some is in Catalan and some Spanish, depending on the context – that's just the way it is in Catalonia. I don't indicate systematically which is which.

Some basics:

The Catalan for Catalonia is *Catalunya*.

The Catalan for Catalan is *català/catalana*.

The Catalan for Spain is *Espanya*.

The Catalan for Spanish (= of Spain) is *espanyol/espanyola*.

The Catalan for Spanish (the language) is *castellà*.

The Spanish for Catalonia is *Cataluña*.

The Spanish for Catalan is *catalá/catalana*.

The Spanish for Spain is *España*.

The Spanish for Spanish (= of Spain) is *español/española*.

The Spanish for Spanish (the language) is *castellano* or *español*.

Personal Names and Accommodation Names

Some of the personal names used in this book are not their real ones. Any names mentioned for accommodation and eateries, however, are the real ones.

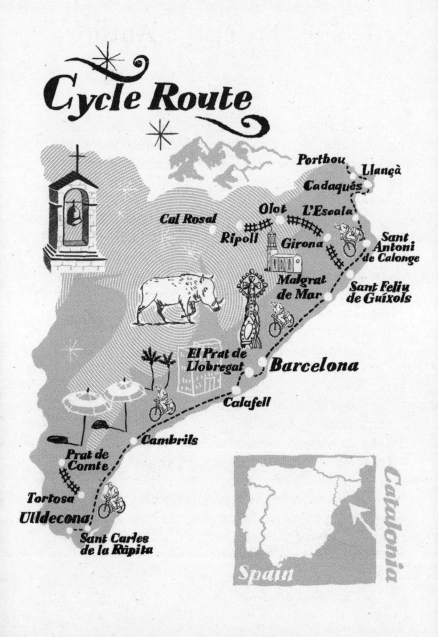

Cycle Route

Portbou
Llançà
Cadaqués
L'Escala
Olot
Cal Rosal
Ripoll
Girona
Sant Antoni de Calonge
Malgrat de Mar
Sant Feliu de Guíxols
El Prat de Llobregat
Barcelona
Calafell
Cambrils
Prat de Comte
Tortosa
Ulldecona
Sant Carles de la Ràpita
Spain
Catalonia

Day 1

Like That?
Portbou to Llançà

It was a calm, misty-blue morning. Eerily calm for a spring that followed the most violent of winters.

Two sheets of identical blue were divided by a distant grey line. Since the lower sheet ended abruptly 200 metres beneath my feet, it must have been the Mediterranean Sea and the grey line the horizon.

Standing alone at the dead end of a dusty track, I strained to hear any sound but the call of a gently wheeling gull, eventually picking out some thin voices, too far away for me to detect their language. After a minute or two the limp, white sail of a small yacht, perhaps a kilometre out to sea, drifted from behind the sharp, black rocks of Punta del Falcó to my right, the south. The voices must have been carried from there on the gentlest of breezes, across the marble-still water.

The track had been unsignposted but might have pointed to 'End of Pyrenees', 'End of France', 'End of Spain' or 'End of Catalonia'. For this was why I was here. And why Benny the bike was here, too, leaning against one of the two green water tanks that evidently justified the track's existence. The ridge of short, spiky bushes running parallel to the track carried along its crest the frontier between France and Spain before this invisible boundary plunged down the vertical cliff face into the sea, and so this weedy spot, just in France, was the nearest I could get to the top-right corner of Catalonia, Spain's north-easternmost region.

Catalonia is a right-angled triangle, its right angle at the north-west, high up in the Pyrenees, and its 300-kilometre hypotenuse forming the region's coastline. Three hundred kilometres if it were a straight line, that is. My objective was to cycle this coast before turning inland to sample the Catalan interior.

Raising a hand to shade my eyes, I squinted along the visible coast to the south and could just make out the light-grey curve that ended in Cap de Creus, a target for lunchtime the next day. In the morning haze, it seemed half a world away.

As if to distract me from any second thoughts that might have crept in, the sound of a vehicle rattling along the dirt track behind suddenly broke the spell. As a small, white van came into view, I prepared my excuses in French for standing on what might well have been the property of Cerbère Council. As the van approached, though, I was surprised to see a logo on the side proclaiming it as the property of Portbou, Cerbère's Spanish twin just south of the border. The driver's window was already down and a chubby face, unshaven and boasting at least a few teeth, smiled at me.

'*Bon dia,*' he said in Catalan.

'*Bon dia,*' I responded, but continued in Spanish – though far from fluent, I was at least confident in that. 'I was just taking some photos. I hope this isn't private land?'

Chubby shrugged. 'Cycling far?'

Having heard my plan, he couldn't prevent a hint of doubt creeping into his eyes.

'You're going all the way to the Delta de l'Ebre?'

'*Sí sí,*' I nodded enthusiastically.

Chubby looked me up and down before inclining his head to take in Benny.

'Like that?'

His eyes had focused on the basket hooked over Benny's handlebars and on my lightly sandalled feet. Of course, according to Continental cycling convention I should have been sealed from head to foot in bright Lycra, but had no intention of charging around the countryside like an elongated bubblegum wrapper. Instead it would be T-shirt, padded shorts and sandals, with boots for the rough stuff and waterproof coat for the wet. My only concession to speed was a rather battered blue helmet – in case my head speed was suddenly reduced to zero.

'Ah no,' I half lied. 'I've got my luggage waiting down the coast. This is just a short Day One.'

Still evidently unconvinced, he changed the subject again. 'I take the photo!'

Which indeed he did, taking my camera and positioning the scenic waterfront of Cerbère's little bay carefully to the side of Benny and myself, a vision of naive confidence. Basket, sandals and all. Wishing me a cheery '*Bon viatge*', Chubby banged back into his van and, shaking his head rather ostentatiously, bounced back up the track. He must have been dispatched simply to take my photo, by Spokey the Cycling God.

The track emerged on the coast road halfway between two large blue EU signs declaring 'France' to be to the right and 'España' to the left. I was surprised no Catalan nationalist had replaced the Castilian 'ñ' with the Catalan 'ny', or even the whole word with 'Catalunya', but perhaps any would-be graffiti vandal had been assuaged by the new sign on the French side that announced in Catalan: *'Benvinguts a Catalunya Nord'* (Welcome to North Catalonia). This reminded me that Catalonia is not only an administrative region of Spain but also a cultural nation that extends some way beyond Spain's boundaries. This double meaning of 'Catalonia' has been – and still is – the source of much angst and would doubtless form an edgy background to this trip.

The Pyrenees are often quoted as forming a natural frontier between France and Spain, one of the most obvious national borders in Europe. Not quite so obvious through all the pages of history, though. At one time the powerful state of Aragon and Catalonia extended as far north as Narbonne, while at another the Frankish-controlled 'Marca' territories reached as far south as Barcelona.

After passing the abandoned frontier post, rarely manned since 1995 when the Schengen Agreement, eliminating border controls, came into effect, I was soon swooping down the curves into Portbou. The population of this atmospheric border town had shrunk dramatically since its geographical and political significance waned, so that fewer people lived here in 2000 than a hundred years before. Apart from

Schengen, the two big events that had transformed Portbou in those hundred years were the construction in 1929 of its monumentally scaled railway station and the destruction of parts of the town, along with, tragically, some of its citizens, in the Spanish Civil War of 1936–9. You can still see what look like bullet holes on the upper parts of some buildings. When Spaniards, including Catalans, refer simply to 'the war', this is the one they mean.

Happily, despite Schengen, significant differences still remain either side of the border, not least economically. The rash of clothes shops and liquor stores among Portbou's shady, narrow streets bear witness to tasty price disparities between France and Spain. My *café con leche* on the promenade was literally half the price I'd just paid for a *café au lait* in Cerbère. This cafe was simpler, the service friendlier, the banter sharper. Definitely Spain.

Before moving on, I checked out the town's plethora of information boards. Many revealed items of genuine interest to the traveller: one explained the causes of catastrophic local forest fires (planning neither to cook or smoke en route, I felt confident of my innocence), another traced the up-and-down history of Portbou's population, while a third focused on the good/bad old days of the frontier up on the hill. It included a postcard in 1960s colour showing the harsh Mediterranean sun blazing on a long line of now-classic small cars queueing at the border checkpoint that I'd just passed.

Portbou's narrow bay ends abruptly and I was soon pushing uphill rather than pedalling. After just a few bends, all other traffic headed through a short road tunnel, opened only two or three years before, which shaved about 3 kilometres – and the wiggliest bends – off the route south. It was especially welcome to the residents of both Portbou and Colera, the next village, which would explain their frustration when, despite its evident physical completion, some administrative obstacle delayed its opening. The story goes that one of the local mayors simply led a determined band of his constituents to one entrance, dismantled the barriers, walked through to the other end and there did the same, declaring the tunnel open – whatever the local road authority might have said.

Benny and I, however, pulled out onto the old, wiggly route to take in its spectacular views. Having muscled their mountainous way eastward across more than 400 kilometres from the Bay of Biscay, the Pyrenees suddenly go indecisive when faced with the Mediterranean, making a late lurch to the south and stretching their bony fingers to form not one but a whole series of sierras and headlands. After a year-long drought, the destructive winter storms had at least brought some rain and the almost treeless landscape was finally blessed with some early colour. In the distance, the patchy green mountainsides were peppered with bright yellow broom, while beside the road and the dirt tracks that joined it, swathes of white alyssum, smaller patches of blue rosemary and even isolated, hesitant, pink rock roses were bringing life back to the land.

Behind me, squashed in a valley between two of the headlands, lay Portbou, its white and terracotta buildings huddled at the seaward end, its vast railway sidings stretching deep into the landward end and there, between the two, the dramatic iron arch of the station itself.

Though I was standing above the southbound railway tunnel, it was in the northbound tunnel between Portbou and Cerbère that lurked a clue to the reason for these out-of-scale installations. In there something magic happens. The Catalan Talgo train from Barcelona enters with its wheels 1,668 millimetres apart and yet emerges in France with the same wheels only 1,435 millimetres apart. While the majority of Continental Europe adopted the standard gauge, most of the Iberian peninsula chose a broader one. Hence the traditional need to change most trains at Portbou. Hence the remarkable size of its station. Hence the extent of its freight sidings. Hence – by the time you read this, but not yet at the time I write it – the demise of the Talgo.

This low-slung rake of elegant, silver and red carriages has been gliding from Barcelona to Montpellier (and formerly onward to Grenoble and Geneva) since 1969, its variable gauge axles noisily nudging to the new gauge down there in the darkness beneath the frontier. But at last the Talgo's time is up. The extensions from French and Spanish high-speed lines, both standard gauge, have already met in another Pyrenean tunnel a few kilometres inland and soon their much faster, but strangely anonymous services will cut out Portbou and Cerbère altogether. The Catalan Talgo will have nudged its last axle.

The various routes across this mountainous frontier between France and Spain seem nowadays to be getting bigger and bolder. Some 25 kilometres inland, the Coll del Pertús, through which Hannibal's elephants rumbled north to challenge Rome and then Roman armies marched south to conquer the whole of Iberia, is now pierced by the dramatic viaducts of a twentieth-century motorway above and the arrow-like tunnel of the twenty-first-century railway below.

Times were when such ostentation would be unwelcome, for these hills were once criss-crossed by smugglers' routes. In Richard Ford's classic 1845 *A Handbook for Travellers in Spain*, he declared that 'many Catalans are not much more than agents for the smuggling [of] French goods', and went on to recommend to travellers crossing the Pyrenees that they take not only a local guide, but also 'a *contrabandista* if possible'.

During and after the civil war it was people who were secretly moving across the border. The English author Laurie Lee, for example, recounts how in 1937 he crossed the mountains alone in a snowstorm to try to join the Republican cause. After the Republican defeat it is estimated that about half a million refugees streamed in the opposite direction, many over the difficult Coll de Banyuls, just a few kilometres from the coast road on which I was cycling. Now even this old track, between Espolla in Spain and Banyuls in France, is surfaced throughout, although the fact that it's not signposted as a route to the other country still gives it an illicit air.

After a few hairpins, a new view opened up ahead, now clearer as the day burned away the mist: the vast southward sweep of the easternmost ranges of the Pyrenees as they skirted another steep-sided bay, formed the sprawling hillsides of Llançà, sheltered the thin white strip of El Port de la Selva and finally reached out into the long, thin grey line of Cap de Creus. Guidebooks will tell you that these settlements form the northern end of the Costa Brava. Don't believe them. This is the southern end of the Costa Vermella, more usually seen written in the language of its northern half as Côte Vermeille, the Vermilion Coast.

The little insect *Kermes vermilio* hasn't had a great impact on the world, but the person who first extracted a red dye from it, calling it *vermiculum*, led to the French using the word *vermeil* for any red dye, the English using 'vermilion' for a brilliant shade of scarlet and the straightforward Catalans using *vermell* to mean simply 'red'. (Not the band. They call them 'Els Simply Red'.) It's the rising sun slanting its dawn caress across these east-facing slopes that gives the Vermilion Coast its name.

The maps produced by the Institut Cartogràfic de Catalunya, which appear in every size, scale and format you could imagine, are invariably excellent. They clearly show that the Costa Vermella doesn't hand the baton to the Costa Brava until Cap de Creus. The Departament de Turisme, however, must occupy a different building, since they pretend (no doubt for tidy administrative purposes) that the Costa Brava extends north to the very border.

Reminding myself that, like the birds and the beasts, geographical features don't know they have names anyway, I remounted, cruised past the unfortunately named village of Colera and into the bay of Garbet, where I hoped to get a coffee at the isolated restaurant on its beachfront. It was closed and wrapped up for the season – literally, with its veranda neatly encased in bubble wrap and parcel tape. And so I sat on the pebble beach, remembering why Garbet was once the funniest place in all of Spain.

Take any language. Some people can speak it fluently, some less fluently, some not at all. When cafe owners get their menus translated into a language other than their own, they usually get someone from the first two categories to do the job. However, to the eternal gratitude and giggle levels of native speakers, they occasionally resort to the 'not at all' category and, among all the resplendent examples of the would-be English form of this art, the most gigglesome I've ever seen used to be on display right here at Garbet's campsite cafe:

INCOMING
Salad of the time
Selection of Catalan Sausages –
quarter note and white
Soup of having cooked
Rape – the fisherman style
Greenness (according to the season)

MEATS
You throw veal to the coal
Chicken to the ember
Catalan sausage with Jewish (Dry)

PROSTRATE
Ice creams 'he/she requests letter'
· Honey and I kill
Tart of the house

COVERS AND APPETIZERS
Veal balls
Small bombs

TOASTED BREAD
'All I smelled'
To the pleasure or half and half

You could probably base an entire term's Spanish class on how this menu came to be but, alas, this classic of the genre disappeared from public view a few years ago. My favourite individual dish to appear on such a menu, at a restaurant in Llançà, is 'Hopeful Duck' ('Don't choose me!').

The reason I'm able to share Garbet's linguistic delights with you here is that exactly the same translations appeared at a restaurant in Barcelona, were noted by my friend David O' Donoghue, lent by him to our mutual friend Jim Faulkner and appeared in the latter's *A Piper in Brazil*, from which I quote above.

Anyway, back to the pleasure (or half and half)...

While I'd been in Garbet, a dark cloud had lumbered over the hill behind, blotting out the afternoon sun and now threatening rain. Hastily pushing Benny off the beach, I scooted sharply over the next hill, past bathers retreating up Grifeu Beach, along Llançà's curving promenade, in and out of a garage to drop off the bike and up a short flight of steps to let my partner Julie know that I'd managed Day 1's twenty-odd kilometres without falling either over a cliff, under a bus or in love with a French woman.

Though I'd called Llançà either home or 'a home' for sixteen years, I'm ashamed to admit that I'd never done that day's little bike ride, until it formed a prelude to the longer one I was about to undertake. While the train journey north to Cerbère had taken less than a quarter of an hour, following virtually a straight line through several tunnels, the return had taken me a gentle four hours and left me feeling fit and confident about what would surely be a jolly jaunt along the coast.

A challenge to such optimism came from our Catalan neighbour Rosa, who, seeing me dismount from the bike, came over for a word.

'Where have you been, Ri-chard?' she asked in Spanish, pushing the stress to the second syllable, as Catalans often do.

'Up to Portbou. And tomorrow I cross Cap de Creus to Cadaqués.'

'Like that?'

What was this preoccupation with my kit?

'Well, I may put my boots on.'

'Ri-chard', warned Rosa, 'that route is *muy duro*. You will be very tired.'

'I hope not. After that there will be at least two more weeks on the bike. I'm going to the Delta de l'Ebre and then inland.'

Immediately regretting this bout of honesty, I knew what was coming.

'*Hombre*! You are not young. You will be practically dead. But why are you going, Ri-chard?'

'Well, I've been here for sixteen years now...'

'I know.'

'... and for three years of that I travelled for work less in Catalonia than in California or Singapore or Hong Kong...'

The shape of Rosa's mouth suggested that she failed to see anything *duro* in this.

'... and in the years that I've come here from England, I've stayed in this little corner of Catalonia relaxing, looking at the sea, drinking a little beer...'

'Getting a little fat.'

'*D'acord*. And there's all the rest of this country to see. I tell people in England that I spend a lot of time in Catalonia, but the truth is I don't really know it. I know Llançà and I know Barcelona, but Catalonia? Not really.'

'But why now? Why all in one go?' asked Rosa, not happy with a justification that would have satisfied less dogged interrogators.

'Well, actually, I'm leaving. We're leaving.' She'd drawn it out of me earlier than I'd planned to tell the neighbours.

'Oh!'

'Not immediately. But next year.'

'Oh.'

I don't know whether I was pleased or sorry to see Rosa's shoulders droop.

'We will put the house on the market next year.'

Suddenly she brightened up.

'Ah, Ri-chard. You will tell me the price before the sign it goes up.'

'You want to move house on the same street, Rosa?'

'No, no. But my family, you know, it is big.'

'Ah, message received. Yes, I'll tell you the price first.'

'Now, be careful on those tracks, Ri-chard. There are wild boars, you know. Did I tell you about my unfortunate grandson? Well, another time. Wear some better shoes. Take a waterproof. *Duro, muy duro.*'

And with that she was gone. All right, I already knew some sections would be harder than others, but the repeated implication that I wasn't up to the challenge was, well, interesting. Anyway, there's one thing I did manage to keep from Rosa: I'd have a support team.

Before I moved to Spain in 1992, I'd never heard of Llançà. As with many Brits, the only places between France and Barcelona that had wandered into my consciousness had done so courtesy of glossy brochures or holiday programmes on TV. I could have named Lloret, Tossa and possibly Blanes before drying up and wondering if Benidorm might be up here too. Not a very positive image then.

However, after my first week at work in the suburbs of Barcelona, my American boss and her husband offered to take me on a day trip to their favourite part of this coast, which turned out to be the southern end of the Gulf of Roses – and my old image of an overdeveloped Costa Brava of crowded beaches and ugly high-rises was instantly swept away, to be replaced by one of lazy coves, whispering pines and windy headlands.

When, after a year, I'd decided to settle in for the long term and finally sold my little bungalow in the English Midlands, I had money in the bank and the Catalan property market at my mercy. The low end of the Catalan property market, that is: churning out user manuals for a computer company was never going to make anyone rich. (What would have done, at the time, was buying up Internet domain names of course, but I'm not that bright.)

Anywhere within commuting distance of Barcelona was out of my price range; Barcelona itself was way out, especially since the 1992 Olympics had launched the Catalan capital onto the world stage. A weekend retreat it would have to be then. (Ho hum.) At this point, the map hit the floor and the brain creaked into gear. It didn't need to get out of first. What I wanted was somewhere on the coast and with a railway station. The line that snaked north out of Barcelona finally hit the Mediterranean again at Llançà before shooting up to Portbou, where most of the services from Barcelona terminated (and still do). A 'no-brainer', as my American boss would have said: it was Llançà or Portbou. A weekend's recce ruled out Portbou as being too darkly enclosed by mountains but, with the help of a well-made pizza and carafe of red wine at a seafront cafe, gave an enthusiastic thumbs-up to Llançà. I'm easily bought.

Like many settlements along the Catalan coast, Llançà's a two-centre affair, with the original town sitting snugly a kilometre inland, safe from the pirates that plagued these seas in the Middle Ages, whether Franks from the north or Moors from the south; while the newer port brazens it out down by the shore. I settled on a small flat on a hilltop halfway between the town and port, where room size was sacrificed for the sake of a breathtaking view from the balcony. Dawn was always my favourite time of day there, as for many of the friends that came to stay, with the sun floating silently up over a headland to the south before turning the sea to a ripply red – to vermilion, in fact – and warming the hands that cupped their breakfast coffee. Once or twice in your life you know you've actually done something right for a change and buying the flat in Llançà was one of mine.

You may have noticed an unexpected past tense in that paragraph, for after twelve years even a spectacular dawn didn't justify the previous evening's long trek up from the bars and restaurants; and so I (or rather we, for Julie had joined me by then) sold the flat to buy a house down in the port. Two purchases and one sale have now given me enough experience of Spain's bizarre house-buying process to make it worth sharing.

Right from the start you notice something odd. Look at those photos in the window of the *immobiliaria* (estate agent: literally, the seller of things that don't move). Tempting? Well, if you're a lavatory fetishist perhaps, or an aficionado of the Spanish skirting board. The agent's photos of one of the homes I bought included a close-up of a rather grubby Mickey Mouse shower curtain, while completely failing to feature the garden, with its pine trees and spectacular bougainvillea.

Even when you persuade them to show you some properties, don't expect any enthusiasm.

'Oh, Señor Guise, that is a very narrow and damp house, you won't like it at all.'

'This room is too dark, señor, no? Who could possibly live here?'

'*!Ostras!* [Blimey!] How this door sticks – nobody's been here for ages.' (I bought that one.)

If, against all advice, you eventually make an offer that is accepted, however, the agent suddenly bursts into life to reveal himself – or, more usually, herself – as a veritable financial wizard. The Catalans, at least, are very precise when it comes to money. Whether you're buying or selling, she will take a blank sheet of A4 and proceed to write a list of exactly what you will pay/receive at each stage and in what format: bank transfer, cheque or cash. Yes, cash. What I'd heard about the black money circulating in the Spanish economy turned out to be all too true.

You see, each property in Spain has two values: the price agreed between buyer and seller and the *catastral* (officially registered) value. The latter is lower than the former, before the recession at least, and both parties tend to prefer that the various taxes be calculated with respect to the lower figure.

For 'tend to prefer', read 'insist'. Add to this the desire of sellers to receive part of the price in cash and you begin to see why the estate agent writes all this by hand – and why her company's name appears nowhere on this particular sheet of paper so vital to the customer.

'Actually,' I said the first time this happened, 'I'd rather do it all legally, with no cash payments involved.'

'Ah,' replied the agent, looking at this innocent foreigner over the top of her glasses. 'Of course we admire the honesty and fair play of the English, but if you do not pay some cash in Spain, you do not buy a house in Spain.'

She was right. Everyone's at it. Even the *notarios* (official solicitors) know about it. In fact, they facilitate it. The official handover ceremony for the flat I sold took place at a *notario*'s office in downtown Barcelona. After the verification of identities, the handshakes and the smiles, the *notario* stood up.

'*Bueno*,' he announced. 'That is the end of the official business. You have the use of this room for ten minutes in case you have any unofficial business.'

And with that he stepped silently out of his own wood-panelled office. With sweat on my brow, I suddenly noticed the ticking of the clock on the wall. Having got the nod from the agent, the stone-faced buyer pulled a briefcase onto the shiny table. My heart missed a beat. Thankfully, instead of a machine gun he produced a plain brown envelope, from which he extracted a thick wad of notes, passing it carefully across the table to me.

Although I was expecting this, and although hundreds of Spaniards must be doing the very same thing every day, I still felt uncomfortable. After wiping the sweat from my hands, I removed the rubber band and, with the agent's assistance, counted out the notes. Some I had never seen before. Hundred-euro notes are green and five-hundreds purple, by the way. My cool-headed agent confirmed that there was indeed 25,000 euros on the table. With hands that I noticed were now shaking, I stuffed the notes back into the envelope and the envelope into my own briefcase.

Five minutes later, I was pulling a stool up to the bar of a nearby cafe that I'd checked out beforehand. Having ordered my *café con leche*, I stepped down again to walk as unostentatiously as I could with a firmly gripped briefcase to the toilets, where, in the privacy of a cubicle, I proceeded to remove half my clothing in order to transfer the readies to a body belt. Emerging just a little fatter than before, I resumed my seat, took one sip of the coffee and then realised I needed to return to the toilet for its more usual purpose.

After several pairs of suspicious eyes had followed me all the way out and all the way back again, I quickly paid up and left. There followed a frantic ten minutes during which I walked briskly in and out of several inappropriate shops, down and up several unnecessary subways and finally onto the platform of Passeig de Gràcia station just in time to catch the train up to Llançà, all the while glancing around me like a first-time thief.

You may think my precautions, though clumsy, to be excessive, but in addition to the fact that I'd previously been the victim of a pickpocket at that very station, just a few months before a couple in exactly the same circumstances, leaving a *notario*'s office in Llançà itself, had been relieved of their cash by a gang waiting in a car park.

What a ridiculous system this black-money business is.

For my own part, the 25,000 euros successfully made it not only to Llançà but all the way to a Leicestershire branch of the HSBC bank, where they were paid in, accompanied by all the required details of their provenance. I'm told by Spanish friends that not only was I supposed to have stuffed the spondulicks in a mattress until required to pay for yet another black-money deal, but had broken some unwritten law in revealing the name of the payer. Well, maybe one day Spain will be dragged into the twenty-first century and its citizens forced to be honest with the taxman; until which time, I feel I've done my bit to bring this day a little closer.

In the meantime, you'd be well advised to think twice before buying a house off Honest Dickie.

Coming back to the matter in hand, it was at the house in Llançà port that I'd popped Benny the bike into the garage at the end of Day 1 and here, that very same evening, that we marked the start of the trip by a meal with our friends Tom and Jan, who have the honour of being, I believe, the town's only American residents.

With the prospect of the inland Pyrenees cropping up later in the schedule, I'd wondered if they'd be interested in joining me, as I knew they had some walking experience up there. Once a beer or two had been sunk, I broached the subject.

'After about two weeks' cycling I should be hitting territory you're both familiar with. Fancy a day's walk to give me a break from the bike?'

'Sure,' Tom immediately offered, his eyes lighting up at the reminder of the great outdoors. 'I could do the whole tour!'

'Well...' I started, but was interrupted by Jan.

'He's talking four hundred miles, Tom…'

'Yeah, no big problem.'

'… and you haven't cycled more than a hundred yards since way back…'

'Oh, a little more 'n that, I'd say.'

'… and we're flying to the States next weekend, honey.'

'Oh, right. Maybe later in the year, Richard.'

The terrace where we were sitting is a great place for discussing travel plans, whether imminent ones or just fantasies. We looked out on busy martins and sparrows competing for nests in the eaves of the buildings down the hill; up to silhouetted swallows circling over the shore; and further up still to seagulls lazily coasting on the evening thermals. At eye level we're sometimes lucky to catch the quick black blur of a bat on its evening business or even the rare sight of a starling on a rooftop, lost and looking for friends.

That evening everyone and everything seemed to be on the move. After some time planning this ride, I was relieved that at last I was on my way as well.

Day 2

At the Edge of the World: Llançà to Cadaqués

The rain promised by the heavy skies had fallen overnight, giving a small boost to Llançà's drought-grizzled – and then storm-beaten – plants. Having packed the car the previous night with luggage for two weeks' cycling, including a second bike, I double-checked that I'd left the car keys with Julie – my support team, who was still sleeping – and walked Benny quietly down to the marina before getting on. His brakes can echo like a screeching hyena between the tightly packed buildings of Llançà's backstreets.

Doing without lights to save weight, I'd waited till daylight's tardy arrival before setting off. The main coast road to El Port de la Selva is my favourite ride around here, twisting and turning between steep slopes to the right and countless rocky coves to the left – a classic corniche route which, because of its views and easy access to the sea, has witnessed literally incessant development for the last two or three decades. As I passed by that early spring morning, most of the properties would have been empty, save perhaps for a few feral cats in the gardens.

Llançà is a permanent home to some five thousand residents, largely Catalan: some fishermen, some commuters to nearby Figueres, but most relying nowadays on the tourist trade. In the peak months of July and August, this number can increase many times over, as the creeping suburbs of second homes and rented property fill with well-dressed escapees from Barcelona, a two-hour drive down the coast, with French holidaymakers seeking a frisson of foreignness and with a fair smattering of be-sandalled, sun-seeking Germans, Belgians and Dutch. There've been occasional rumours of other British residents, but we haven't met any for years and our little terraced house a few streets back from the sea is, thankfully, surrounded by locals – mostly Catalan like Rosa, some Spaniards from elsewhere.

Rosa had recently called me over as I came back with the shopping, beckoning me with her finger to come close.

'Ri-chard!' she hissed. 'You must be careful to close and lock your doors.'

'Why?'

'Some foreigners have moved into the street.'

'But Julie and I are foreign, Rosa.'

'No, I mean really foreign. They have a car with a Madrid registration.'

'¡Madre mía!'

'I think they're Russian.'

The only other British resident I knew mixed two characteristics that rarely go together: he was both English and exotic. With a beautiful Czech wife, a pet python and a sparkling, all-in-one stage suit hanging from the washing line, he was Llançà's only – perhaps Catalonia's only – Elvis Presley impersonator. Unfortunately, his swivel-hipped renditions of 'Blue Suede Shoes', intoxicating though they were, didn't really fit into the genteel Llançà scene as easily as elsewhere in Europe and so Elvis, Mrs Elvis and Python Elvis soon moved on to the loucher nightspots of Berkshire.

Not only 'genteel' but gentle too, Llançà is really a family resort, which is perhaps why it seems to have missed out (thankfully) on the recent upsurge of the Spanish *costas* as a destination for hen and stag weekends from northern Europe, especially Britain. Meeting friends at Girona-Costa Brava Airport, we've had to pick them out at Arrivals among swarms of pink fairies, flocks of Batmen and bands of gorillas. Funny old world. Fortunately, among these crowds, most of our friends stick out pretty well.

If a single scene were to sum up what Llançà is about, then it would be a summer evening on Passeig Marítim, with a group of close-harmony singers entertaining a small crowd sitting on the promenade or in the nearby bars with Catalan sea shanties, while children play on the beach and lovers walk barefoot in the surf.

Although there are plenty of things to do and see in both town and port, some may not be particularly obvious to the visitor. So let me suggest four short walks which will take you to odd corners of this Catalan seaside resort.

First, at the eastern end of Llançà's Passeig Marítim, simply carry on walking, keeping the boats on your left, and you'll come to the fishing harbour, home both to Llançà's fleet of eleven trawlers and to a handful of smaller vessels, which look as though they're made out of old, square caravans, and which practise *palangre*. This involves dropping a connected series of hooked lines, anchored to the seabed by lead weights, and returning to collect the tackle and its catch some hours later.

Between the decline in piracy and the rise in tourism, fishing was the dominant commercial activity along this coast and multilingual information boards up and down Llançà's shoreline explain many of the other methods used over the years – lantern fishing and the use of 'gill nets, trammels, nanses, sepieres' – obscure names to laymen like me. The black and white photo displays give an idea of how physically demanding pre-motorised fishing must have been, with muscular men, young and old, hauling boats out of the water. A stark contrast to the somewhat less lean bodies hauled into their swimsuits on today's beaches.

Certain areas of Llançà's harbour have restricted access, but shortly after the trawlers start returning, usually around five in the afternoon, you can wander right beside them, trying to put names to the contents of the pre-sorted trays being manually lifted onto the wharf: tuna, hake, squid, turbot, sardine, swordfish, conger eel – plus many more we've been unable to identify. Until the great storm of 26 December 2008, the public could also observe the computerised – and extremely efficient – wholesale fish auction, but, as I write this, the building where it took place still stands half ruined by a violent assault from beyond the seawall and the auction has been transferred to a temporary building with no room for public access.

Second, from the other end of Passeig Marítim, walk up towards the bridge but then straight across the road onto a dirt track, until a gateway into a private garden forces you to turn left and onto a very narrow footpath. This leads you into another secret world: the maze of paths and plots clustered around a number of usually dry stream beds that form Llançà's allotments. Bigger than most British allotments, much more in need of efficient watering systems and yet strangely productive, these fields boast tomatoes the size of cannonballs; wavy rows of healthy carrots, potatoes, courgettes and cauliflowers; bushes and trees heavy with apples, oranges, lemons and walnuts; and well-stocked corners of dark-green beans, light-green marrows and shiny black aubergines. At the height of the season, the gardeners can be seen pedalling all over Llançà with trays full of produce strapped to bike racks, supplying temporary outlets squeezed in everywhere the customers may pass: a front porch, the doorway of an ironmonger's or the corner of Plaça Major. Out of season, they're just as busy, securing their boundaries with ready-to-hand bamboo or with an inexplicably large number of abandoned bedsteads.

A wander through the allotments should bring you out somewhere near the old town, where a third recommended call would be the 'pot shop'. A surprising number of Spanish shops and bars bear no actual name at all, but this example, just down Carrer Major from Plaça Major and with its pots bursting onto the pavement, is unmissable. Though some of its ceramics may be unusual, though its collection of wines and sherries from the barrel is impressive (and cheap) and though the sudden descent through the ceiling by a muscular assistant on an unprotected platform can be startling, what makes the Pot Shop an unforgettable experience is the sheer chaotic density of its displays. Its columns of flowerpots teeter on the permanent brink of collapse and its severely bent shelves of spirits will surely one day plummet expensively to the floor. Whatever you do, don't even think of entering this Aladdin's cave carrying an umbrella, a basket or – heaven forbid – a child. That one tiny plate which you knock from its display will surely bring the entire shop crashing around your feet.

And finally, remembering that the sea is what Llançà is all about, head back to the port and there, just before El Racó, a tapas bar right at the seaward end, turn right along Carrer de Miranda and follow the red and white footpath markers up the steps at the end. This gives you access to a splendid section of clifftop path that weaves around for a kilometre or so as far as Platja de les Tonyines ('Tuna Beach'), where the paved, multi-million-euro seaside track to the south takes over. The Llançà end of this route seems untamable and, as several parts of the rough path take you within centimetres of certain death at the bottom of a crumbling cliff, your mother would insist on you wearing sensible shoes. No warning tape or 'At your own risk' notices here. Unlike other mollycoddled nationalities, Catalans are trusted to know that somewhere below a clifftop lies a cliff bottom.

That damp April morning the corniche road was considerably safer than the coastal path beneath it, with barely a vehicle passing me. Now cycling south-east, I could see the reason for the late dawn: a heavy bank of cloud over the hills ahead, from which the sun was only now emerging, to spread its gold on yesterday's headlands stretched out behind me. The unusual sight of silver roadside puddles, the new steel grey of the sea and the sharp, dark line of its horizon all gave the morning a fresh character and told a waking Catalonia that the drought really was over. As I splashed along the corniche I could smell the rich scent of Mediterranean pine, while each little inlet brought a whiff of seaweed and a rush of surf that seemed to have been missing for weeks. After yesterday's little jaunt – which, after all, had ended at home – I felt that I too was emerging from a long drought and starting out on another adventure.

Signs to two more villages hidden from the pirates – La Vall de Santa Creu and La Selva de Mar – passed, before I pedalled into El Port de la Selva, a picture-postcard cluster of white and terracotta buildings gathered tightly around a bay as extravagantly curved as Captain Hook's left hand.

It's easy to see why property prices in El Port de la Selva are a notch or two higher than in Llançà. The old church, the town hall, the shops, the restaurants... all gather closely around the seafront like a classic town on the French or Italian riviera. Though most of the fishing boats now use a newer harbour half a kilometre further out, a few still dock at the old quayside, where nets of blue, green and red are often photogenically spread across the big open space in front of the old fish exchange.

It's perhaps surprising, then, that this quaint old place was at the centre of a political storm in 2010 when the council declared the town independent from Spain – or at least 'morally excluded from the ambit of the Spanish Constitution' (the words of a declaration by the mayor, as quoted at www.elmundo.es on 28 June 2010). The catalyst for this unlikely scenario was the latest episode in the long-running saga of Catalan autonomy. As I understand it, a new definition of Catalonia's self-government within Spain had been thrashed out over several years of toing and froing between Madrid, Barcelona and the Catalan people. The Catalans had made many compromises but finally the new law had been approved, passed and signed by the king. Then up popped the right-wing People's Party to claim the whole thing was unconstitutional, the supreme court agreed with them and, for good (or bad) measure, deleted a few of the clauses that had already been agreed. Cue uproar, a million and a half demonstrators on the streets of Barcelona – and an independent El Port de la Selva. You can't help but think that they might have had a point. It certainly underlines the depth of feeling among many Catalans about their often strained relationship with the Spanish state.

The official route from El Port de la Selva up to the Parc Natural del Cap de Creus follows the coast for a kilometre before doubling back on itself, but I knew a shortcut from behind the Hotel Porto Cristo and dismounted to push Benny past the 'No Entry' sign and up through the winding streets. Soon overtaking me were three noisy four-by-fours, each with a local registration. Road traffic laws evidently don't apply to residents.

At the top, the view back along the Vermilion Coast all the way to Cap Cerbère (just beyond the point where my ride had started the day before) was remarkably crisp, still only half sunlit and, in this damp atmosphere, now less vermilion than grey. Well camouflaged near the peaks of the rocky range opposite sat the substantial remains of Sant Pere de

Rodes, a Benedictine monastery built way out of piratical reach about a millennium ago and now deconsecrated. In many of the intervening centuries, this monastery dominated local administration, land management and especially agriculture, its most visible legacy being the incredible network of old terraces, created with drystone walls, that covers almost every hillside for miles around, once supporting vines and olive trees. One of our Llançà neighbours claims that some individual walls were placed in such inaccessible places that they took over a century to construct. The pest phylloxera hit the vineyards in 1879, destroying most of them and affecting the local economy so badly that widespread emigration followed. Some terraces were later replanted, but many vines were killed off again by the cold winter of 1956. Nowadays most local vineyards are in the lowlands, but in these mountain areas every wild fire reveals miles and miles of old terraces, like the bones of a vast graveyard.

After checking on the flurry of information boards not only the many ways in which I should not start a fire, but also the areas of the park in which I may not trawl, drift or indulge in any other manner of 'commercial or recreational fishing', I set off along the rough, stony track, for which Benny's mountain-bike tyres were ideal. (Incidentally, Benny is so named as he was purchased from the French supermarket, Carrefour, whose name means 'crossroads'. For those who watched British television in the 1960s, no further explanation is needed; for those who didn't, you're probably better off not knowing.)

At once I was deep in the Wild West. Injun lookouts could easily be crouching behind those boulders to the right, their dark-brown eyes following my every move, while, to my left, prickly pears and bristly bushes tumbled down into Deadman's Gulch, where any number of wild critters waited to tear into the flesh of a careless, lonesome cyclist. I could hear the howls of a pack of hungry coyote echoing from rock to rock. Yes, wait a minute – I could! As the beasts got ever closer behind me, their wails were accompanied by the rattle and rumble of another four-by-four. Pulling over to let it pass, I found myself staring at the teeth of four restless, barking hounds caged in the low trailer of a French Land Rover, on whose side was a white line drawing of two dogs chasing a frantic wild boar.

How the park's declared aim of protecting the local wildlife squares with carloads of armed hunters intent on slaughter needs an explanation.

The wild boar is not a lucky beast. This relative of the domestic pig will eat almost anything, including a farmer's crops, is as ugly as hell, cannot fly away from guns and falls into that category of official conservation status called 'least concern'. Weighing in at upwards of 50 kilograms, they are found all over central and southern Europe and can be killed in autumn and winter, with a permit. Here in the Pyrenees thousands are killed every year. Much of the weekend gunfire you hear in the hills is from boar hunters and in many a bar you'll see photos from successful hunts. The word 'coto' painted on roadside walls or scrawled on wooden signs is short for 'coto de caza/caça' (hunting reserve).

Quite what the menagerie in the Land Rover was up to in April I couldn't say. Maybe the hunters were just taking the hounds out for a drive.

From the air, Cap de Creus ('Cape of Crosses') looks like a single piece protruding from the jigsaw of Catalonia as though expecting to slot into a matching piece somewhere out to sea. Its three 'knobs' point north, east and south and I'd entered near the northern one, aiming to cross to the eastern, the cape itself, and then across to the southern by the next morning, via an overnight stay at Cadaqués. However, at the first significant junction of tracks, the fact that the trailer-load of French snarlers – just about under the control of their masters – was heading along my chosen route persuaded me to turn south instead, along a track that my map showed taking a wide curve before eventually rejoining the original route after a couple of kilometres. As you will gather, I am not a member of the Canine Appreciation Society.

Assuming a pedalling posture that I hoped made me look distinctly un-boarlike, I bounced off along the stony track. In the *garrigue*, that dry, thin-soiled scrubland that skirts much of the Mediterranean coast, the underlying rock is never far from the surface. Here it formed a fair portion of the track itself, but the years of passing feet and tyres had worn it down to give me a better ride than I'd expected. The trackside signposts were another matter. It wasn't long before the irritating mismatch between the tracks' numbers and those on the map had me off the bike and up on a knoll, map in hand and puzzlement on face. All horizons looked the same: rolling, wild, dry. It's difficult for any man to admit he's lost, doubly so for an ex-geography teacher. Hell, it was only Day 2 and I was barely 15 kilometres from home. Let's just say I could have been in one of several places. Had a GPS salesman emerged from the bushes I might have succumbed.

Plumping for the track I hoped would return me to the original route somewhere near the deserted bay of El Golfet, I pushed off. Where I definitely did not want to go was to the little settlement of Perafita, back on the main road.

After a quarter of an hour I emerged in Perafita.

OK, Plan B. With a ho and a hum, I rejoined the motor traffic that I hadn't expected to see until the afternoon and gaily freewheeled down the smooth tarmac into the outskirts of Cadaqués, where I took the slightly less smooth, but still surfaced, 6-kilometre road eastwards out to the cape – a route I would retrace with a little more leisure later in the day.

Just as the mass of the cape itself rose before me, the tough man's route that I'd intended to use came in from the left. Some ten years before, on a solitary winter's day ride, I'd taken it myself and my neighbour had been right to warn me it was *duro*. The toughest bit, I remembered, was on a precipitously steep section and involved lifting the bike above my head to inch between the prickly undergrowth down to the remote bay-within-a-bay of El Golfet. Here a ruined stone hut was just about the only sign that other humans had sat on that beach and stared at that empty seascape. Nowadays it may well be covered with information boards. Never mind, other *duro* stages would doubtless be ahead of me. Indeed, I was already off my bike again to push it the last few hundred metres up to the top of the cape, which now loomed ahead like a lost world in a Rider Haggard novel.

I've failed to mention why I was making the effort to come out here at all, rather than taking the more obvious, direct route south across the neck of the peninsula. On the right day, Cap de Creus just happens to be one of the most spectacular places on earth.

It's rare that the axial line of a mountain chain reaches right to the sea, but here, at the easternmost point of the Iberian peninsula, the Pyrenees reach out in a final, fantastic frenzy before diving beneath the waves. A last lunge before the plunge. Bit by bit, as you approach the looming headland, vegetation vanishes. First the trees disappear, then the bushes and then almost all the remaining flowers are cast off to leave just bare, grey rock. Well, mostly bare and mostly grey...

Was it...? Could it be...? I say! Incipient boudinage!

These are not my words, but those of a geologist friend who uttered them on first setting foot on the cape... though he did subsequently revise them. Cap de Creus to a geologist is evidently as a sweet shop to a child.

'Look, pegmatite!' he also called, crouching among the rocks. 'And it's cutting across the schistosity. Ptygmatic folding! And over here, there are tourmaline crystals in it. Gosh, and the hole in this schist is magnificent. Oh, oh, high grade... we're in the sillimanite zone!'

Having reflected a little, he downgraded the boudinage to mere 'pseudo-boudinage' (of course!). As he bounced across the sharp rocks undeterred, it had been hard to keep up, both physically and geologically, but my understanding of all these terms – and of what's been going on here – goes something like this...

The Pyrenees have been created by a number of geological events occurring over a long period of time. Their present configuration is due mainly to the collision of the Iberian microplate (i.e. Spain and Portugal) and the southern part of the European plate (i.e. southern France), but they have also been affected by the separation of the European and American plates (which created the Atlantic Ocean) and by the rotation of Spain away from France (which also created the Bay of Biscay). While some of these events are geologically relatively recent (having taken place a mere 25 to 55 million years ago), the rocks and minerals that have ended up at Cap de Creus are not necessarily so, some being more than 450 million years old.

The majority of the rocks at Cap de Creus are metamorphic, which is to say that, while they were originally sediments, they have been changed in form by intense heat and pressure, and also by multiple phases of deformation. The metamorphic rocks are schists (the darker grey rock at Cap de Creus) and have been intruded by pegmatites (lighter grey 'threads' and larger masses). When geologists refer to the 'grade' of metamorphic rocks, they mean the temperature and pressure at which the metamorphism took place: the higher the temperature and pressure, the higher the grade. The grades fall into 'zones' and many of the Cap de Creus rocks fall into the sillimanite zone, which is very high-grade, the rocks having been formed at temperatures higher than 550 degrees Celsius.

While pegmatite exposed at the surface is by no means as rare as the Cap de Creus literature claims, some of the ptygmatic (chaotic) folding of the pegmatites is very impressive indeed. Just look for the worm-like lines of light grey, white and brown rock in among the darker grey of the schist. (Yes, ptygmatic: how many other English words begin with five consonants?)

And what about 'boudinage'? Where a body of rock has been stretched and deformed, it can break up into sausage-shaped forms, usually connected by thinner strands, rather like linked sausages. They were first described by a French-speaking Belgian geologist – and *boudin* is French for black pudding.

At Cap de Creus some of the pegmatites appear to have been boudinaged – just look for lines of light grey 'sausages', each about 20 centimetres long. However, all is not what it seems, and these are in fact 'pseudo-boudins'.

'The more you look at the rocks,' my geologist friend had explained, 'the more you can see. There are shear zones, sheath folds, mylonites, folded mylonites – the place is a positive treasure trove of geological structures. All you need is a structural geologist to explain them to you – if you are interested, that is.'

'Oh, I am,' I'd stressed.

'Because,' he'd added, nodding in the direction of our respective partners, 'instead of admiring these magnificent rocks, some people prefer to look at the tiny, stunted flowers between them.'

To be fair, the flora that survive on these exposed headlands are fascinating in their own right. Particularly adapted to the wind and the salt are sea thrift, sea lavender and, one new to me and which is apparently found nowhere else on earth: a type of carrot plant called *Seseli farreny*.

In fact, there's a strong sense that everything up here is just a bit special.

What greets those who have braved either the sea, the rough tracks or the narrow, winding road to Cap de Creus is not just the splendour of the natural environment but a lighthouse, an information centre, two cafes – and, for twenty-eight years until it was torn down in 1998, on the very easternmost elevation, a tower dedicated to doing nothing at all. It was built to play the part of a lighthouse in the 1971 film *The Light at the Edge of the World*, starring Kirk Douglas, Samantha Eggar and, as the cruel and dominating villain, Yul Brynner – or, as Cadaqués Council's information board calls him, 'Yul Briner'. The foundations of the faux lighthouse can still be seen.

It's probably the views, however, that draw most visitors. On a clear day, the view to the north stretches way, way into the flat, lagoon-strewn coastline of France's Languedoc-Roussillon region; while a short walk across to the cape's southern cliffs is rewarded by a similarly spectacular panorama from Cadaqués to the nipple-shaped hill of Montgrí, the Medes Islands and beyond. With the prevailing wind being from the north, it's often to the south-facing terrace of the old Restaurant Cap de Creus that I gravitate, but this lunchtime was a quiet one and, having stabled Benny outside the mustard-yellow building, I popped inside to the bar.

It's a large building – in fact it's the old administration block for the real lighthouse – but it was still barely big enough for the wild attempts at map-folding being undertaken by a young motorcyclist at one of the tables. While his arms swung like a Chilean condor riding a thermal, his curses revealed him to be English.

'Damned France is too big, won't damn lie down!'

'Can I help?'

Together we wrestled the awkward Gauls into their folds and then compared travel notes.

'Have you just come here from France?' I asked.

'Nope, just heading back there. Been down in Morocco for a while.'

'Working?'

'Quite the opposite. I took seven months off work in England to do some of those jobs on the house you never seem to get round to… and then decided to head south on the bike before I started.'

'How long ago was that?'

'Um, 'bout six months, I suppose. Looks like I'll be squeezing those jobs into the last weekend.'

Laughing both at his carefree attitude and the idea of simply 'heading south', I asked: 'Why Morocco?'

'Well, it was originally just to pass through, but when I hit the Sahara I realised things could easily start to go very wrong very quickly and well, being no mechanic, I decided to quit while I was ahead. Morocco's a cool place to hang around anyway.'

This certainly put my own, comparatively rigid plan into context and I resolved there and then to follow my nose on any diversions that took my fancy. From that particular bar, though, you have little choice. And so, having washed down my crunchy, brown *tortilla española* (thick, fried potato omelette) with a bottle of refreshing lemon pop, I waved cheerio to the London-bound biker and headed back inland towards Cadaqués.

(Since this visit, a threat to the Restaurant Cap de Creus has emerged. Keen to keep the cape's environment as natural as possible, the Department of the Environment has proposed a few startling measures and these include – rather nonsensically – the demolition of this entire building. The proposal seems nonsensical for two reasons: first, for many visitors, the Restaurant Cap de Creus is itself part of the unique character of the cape, and second, right next to it stands a newer, more garish bar, which is quite OUT of character for the area. Another attribute, however, turns out to be more crucial: while the garish bar is a government concession, the Restaurant Cap de Creus is privately owned – by an Englishman. Support has come forward, however, from a surprising source. The local mayor has pointed out the injustice in picking on a local businessman who, though he may not be Catalan, does have his papers in order. We can only infer that this is a rare occurrence! See 'Sources' for reference.)

The 6-kilometre ride back from the cape to Cadaqués is a classic for enthusiasts of the wild and windy. The thin, grey thread of tarmac seems a feeble and marginal intrusion into this savage landscape of rock, cliff and scrub. Even the carefully tended olive groves have about them a sense of the transitory. It's not difficult to imagine the land here before the arrival of humans – and after our departure, when the bumpy track will be quickly recolonised by plants that seem to grow out of nothing at all. Artists have long come here to capture the savagery of the cape and one in particular made it his home.

There were two Salvador Dalís, the second having been told at the age of five that he was the reincarnation of the first, his deceased older brother. It was while on a family holiday in Cadaqués that Salvador II was introduced to modern art and by the age of fifteen, in 1919, had already exhibited some work in his home town of Figueres. In 1930, after making his name in Madrid, Barcelona and Paris, Dalí returned with Gala, his Russian wife and muse, to rent a small fisherman's hut at Port Lligat on Cap de Creus, having been theoretically banned from Cadaqués by his father, who disapproved of much of his son's erratic behaviour.

Having bought the hut, Dalí expanded it little by little into the home where he would spend much of his life. He died, however, at his Teatro Museo in Figueres (the building with the eggs on the roof) in 1989 at the age of 84. His last drawing had been a gift to one of his fans, King Juan Carlos, who had made Salvador Domingo Felipe Jacinto Dalí i Domènech the Marquis of Púbol – Púbol being the location of another of his Catalan homes.

Nowadays the built-up areas of Port Lligat and Cadaqués virtually flow into one another, but to call at the little harbour on which Dalí's home stands, I turned off the road from the cape where a small new development of tastefully low-profile houses leads down to the sea. Bouncing across the beach and weaving between the boats hauled up there, I found a shady spot on the harbour wall, where I glugged at my water bottle while looking around.

It's not difficult to spot Dalí's house. Except for the Hotel Port Lligat, it's the largest of very few buildings on the seafront – oh, and it has a few eggs on the roof. There are two surprises though. Apart from the eggs, it's built in a very normal, very conservative style: a white-walled, terracotta-roofed villa, with windows and doors in standard Catalan green or blue, the whole structure spilling nonchalantly down the low hillside to the shore. Nice gaff, Sal. The second surprise is that, apart from in the very high season, I've found very few tourists about – perhaps because tours of the house are by arrangement only.

Those that are there, however, come from far and wide and one of today's visitors was a Japanese gentleman, taking photos of the house from every conceivable angle. Giving his shutter finger a well-deserved rest, he sat down on the wall beside me.

'You like the house?' I asked in English.

'Like? Oh...' He hesitated a little. 'I would like very much the house. But I am not rich, rich man.'

I smiled. 'Me neither.'

'I visit the house,' he said. 'You visit the house?'

'No. I'm no artist. What's it like inside?'

'Oh...' Another thoughtful pause. 'Oh, it strange. Rooms strange, furniture strange, pool strange.'

'Outside it doesn't look strange at all.'

'No, outside no. But inside strange.'

'Like some people?' I ventured.

This idea he liked.

'Oh...' He looked at the sky while searching very hard for the right response. 'Oh...' I had all day. 'Oh... like some Japan people in bus with me!' He waved at a knot of people emerging from the Dalí house. 'Strange inside. Good, good. You take my photo, please?'

And so one of his twenty or thirty photos of the stylish villa by the sea featured a broadly smiling Japanese gentleman, for once without his camera. I hope he kept that one.

While the main road from Port Lligat to Cadaqués follows the contours inland, the cyclist or walker can cut across the narrow neck of land between the two, skirting the millionaires' district that culminates in the Illa de s'Aranella, a private island off the very tip of the peninsula. On the short ride around the bay I was obliged to wobble past any number of photographers rooted in the road, for the luscious view of Cadaqués presents a severe risk of 'snapper's finger' for anyone with a camera.

Waiting at the beachside Bar Marítim, as planned that morning, was Julie, sipping a freshly squeezed orange juice.

'Good ride?' she asked, as I dropped Benny onto the pebbly beach and myself onto the seat beside her.

'Not quite as planned, but pretty good all the same. Checked in?'

'Checked in, unpacked, car parked, chilled out,' she said, taking another sip.

Who could ask for a more efficient support driver?

'Are you parked in the river?' I asked. Not a question that makes much sense in northern Europe, but the river beds hereabouts, being dry for most of the year, often supplement the meagre car parking provision and our overnight accommodation at the Hostal Marina overlooked just such a dual-purpose strip of concrete right in the centre of town.

'Nope. Residents only. You'll have to take your bike up to the main car park.'

'No probs. Do any shopping?'

'Looking yes, buying no. It's mostly Indian imports that I could buy for a third of the price in Figueres.'

Julie was talking clothes. As any male partner quickly becomes aware, for women shopping = clothes. Except when shopping = bags. For me, shopping = tedious chore best left to professionals and so, having stashed Benny in the car, I was happy to retire to a late nap in our cool, dark room at the Marina. Pleased to have got one of the 'tough' sections under my belt without feeling much impact on the old body, I felt I was properly on my way.

Before eating we had time for a saunter around the bay – and a better place for a slow saunter in the soft evening light I can't imagine.

If Cap de Creus registered eight or nine on the Scenic Scale, Cadaqués, with its almost unbearably picturesque seafront wrapped around the little sheltered bay like a mother's protective arm, must be pushing ten. Many of the elegant villas were built by *'Americanos'* – the local term for émigrés coming home from Cuba around the turn of the twentieth century – who put part of their fortunes into bricks and mortar. This won't be the last time we see their impact on the Catalan coast. Dominating the scene from the hillside is still the white tower of the town's seventeenth-century church and if first-time visitors experience an unexpected sense of déjà vu, it's because the panorama of Cadaqués from one or other arms of the bay has graced so many thousands of postcards, calendars and chocolate boxes.

The further you walk out of town along the shore, the more clearly you appreciate how entirely trapped Cadaqués is by the severe slopes of the surrounding mountains. For centuries, the only practical way in and out of this fishing village was by sea and it's said that this explains why the local dialect of Catalan, Cadaquesenc, has more to do with the Balearic dialects than those of its mainland neighbours.

Though readers of the tourist literature could be forgiven for thinking that Dalí was the be-all and end-all of Cadaqués, this is far from the case, despite the statue of the half-mad, dripping-digit dauber himself, in typical pose, occupying the most prominent position on the promenade. Other artists to have visited or worked in the town include René Magritte, Joan Miró, Pablo Picasso and Man Ray, while other notable visitors have included John Cage, James Mason, Walt Disney and the Spanish poet García Lorca. Its reputation as 'the San Tropez of the Costa Brava' draws many more here nowadays but the peak season, when Cadaqués's population swells manyfold, is blissfully short and outside of July and August you only have to turn a corner or mount a few steps to have one of the steep, narrow, cobbled streets to yourself. It's also out of season when you're safe from that infernal machine that seems to have inveigled its way into any corner of Europe the tourist dollar may reach: the tractor-towed 'tourist train'.

A scramble down one of these backstreets brought us to the little restaurant that Julie had picked out earlier: Trattoria Al Gianni.

'Doesn't sound very Catalan,' I said.

'No, but look at the garden,' she explained. 'Where better to eat?'

'Can't argue with that. And athletes need pasta, don't they?'

'Athletes? How many miles have you done today?'

'It's not a question of miles, it's...'

'How many?'

'Twenty-two.'

'Small portions, I think. Don't you?'

Day 3

Giggling Amigos:
Cadaqués to L'Escala

Portion control took a back seat at breakfast, where I tucked into a couple of *taps de Cadaqués*, the local version of *magdalena*, a sugary sponge cake eaten throughout Catalonia, but shaped in this case like a cork (a *'tap'*). On our evening stroll I'd seen the track by which I planned to leave Cadaqués rising behind the Hotel Rocamar like the route up Everest from which few return.

Though it looked like I had a tough morning before me, it was in many ways not as tough as that faced some sixty years before by the daughter of a Rugby schoolmaster, Rose Macaulay. The English writer, best known perhaps for her novel *The Towers of Trebizond*, was in her sixties when she tackled the whole of the Spanish Mediterranean coast in the late 1940s, alone in her rickety motor car. For me *Fabled Shore,* the book of her journey that I was to carry with me all the way to the borders of Valencia, opened a window onto a lost world, onto a Catalonia that still licked its wounds from the civil war and looked only hesitantly to a world beyond Spain – but a world that would soon pour over the French border yet again, transforming the character of this coast for ever. The war had been over for less than a decade, its shell holes still scarring the roads, and the sight of a lone, foreign, female driver regularly drew astonished stares – partly, she claimed, for the simple reason that she wore a hat.

In leaving Cadaqués, Miss Macaulay described the coastal route to Roses as 'a good road'. As is clear from her later references, she could have meant only the one that I took that morning, which leaves the main road around the bay near the Hotel Rocamar. And yet, even walking a bicycle, I found it a severe challenge. For the most part, there was no question of actually pedalling. Quite apart from the severe gradients, the surface (for want of a better word) was formed either of loose shale interspersed with granite boulders, or of the underlying rock itself, complete with all its folds and fractures. It had clearly never had the benefit of a purpose-made surface at all.

Of course, such rough terrain virtually guaranteed the blessed absence of motorised vehicles – that and the fact that nowadays, halfway along, a substantial barrier blocked progress to all but walkers and cyclists. Although several muscular young mountain-bikers whizzed past me as though riding on air, to all intents and purposes this was not a track cyclable by normal human beings.

After the three hours I'd allowed myself to get to Roses, I was still somewhere in the hills and pretty much all in. And I'd run out of water. And sweets. And an unseasonable heat seemed to have appeared from nowhere.

So by half past twelve, when I slithered down into the Bay of Montjoi, bedraggled and dry-lipped as a tramp, the unexpected sight of a remote beachside bar open for business on an out-of-season afternoon appeared as an unlikely oasis in the desert. Though no vehicles were parked nearby, three large rubber dinghies flying the Spanish flag were moored in the bay and, staggering in, I noticed that their six crew members were the bar's only customers – sipping beers and glued to a dubbed American spy movie on TV. Having let an *agua con gas* spread its sparkle through my overheated body, I asked the barman for advice on the easiest route into Roses on a bike.

'Why, on the road, of course, señor.'

'What road?'

'The road at the back of this bar, señor.'

'Oh, right. Yes, of course.'

He eyed me suspiciously as I picked out a lemon ice lolly, paid up and walked out to observe that indeed there was a very nice road, of excellent tarmac, heading off in the opposite direction to the track by which I'd arrived. This was a dead end from Roses. The idea of any other route to town was indeed a silly one.

Having luxuriated for a while in the unusual feel of tarmac beneath tyres, I began to look about. The road around Montjoi passed the entrance to a restaurant hidden in the trees, where a well-dressed couple were taking a careful photograph of the information displayed outside. It's not inconceivable that you have to be well-dressed even to approach the gate here, for this was El Bulli, voted by *Restaurant* magazine, for the three years prior to this ride, as the best restaurant in the world. Yes, world – as in the whole planet. Although it was April, the next available reservation was in the autumn. Not the next autumn, but the one after that.

You may need all that time to make your selections. At the time of writing, even if you were to restrict your selection of wine to those over 600 euros a bottle, you'd still have eighty-nine to consider. However much anyone pays at El Bulli, I doubt they'd get any more satisfaction than I'd just had from my 3-euro snack at the bar just a few hundred metres away: ice lolly and water. Same views, too. Despite its audacious cuisine, the restaurant itself occupied a modest building among the trees overlooking the Bay of Montjoi, to all appearances just another desirable villa by the sea.

Having already alerted Julie by text to my likely late arrival in L'Escala that afternoon, I had time to enjoy the broad views across the Gulf of Roses to that very town, and beyond it to the grey headland of Cap de la Barra, which lay in the afternoon haze like a half-submerged alligator advancing on the unsuspecting little island of Meda Gran. Soon after, however, the road turned inland before dropping suddenly into the backstreets of Roses, where I wound my way out to the seafront and scuttled quickly along the wide promenade to a likely looking bar where I could keep Benny in sight over lunch.

With a large cheese-filled baguette inside me, my strength began to return and, relaxing with a second *café con leche*, I sat back to take in the view along the broad, curved, sandy beach to the heavily developed town.

The name 'Roses' is nothing to do with roses, as I'd long assumed, but everything to do with Rhodes. To chip away at my vast block of ignorance on the subject of Catalan history, I'd researched a few highlights before I started the ride and managed to compile...

A Brief (and Irreverent) History of Catalonia

This is inextricably linked with the history of both Spain and Iberia as a whole and is, it seems, all down to who was in charge at the time.
(Most dates are approximate and many overlap.)

1. IBERIANS. From who knows when until after the Greeks. This tells us nothing much, as 'Iberians' is just what the Greeks called the natives. What the natives called themselves we don't know – because, apparently, no one can understand the language they used, in these parts at least.

2. GREEKS. Eighth or sixth century BC (historians are divided on this) to the Romans. With an eye for the main chance, Greek sailors blew into what is now the Gulf of Roses. A clue to their priorities is the name of their first settlement: Emporion ('Market'), now Empúries. They must at least have understood the Iberians enough to cut a deal or two with them.

3. CARTHAGINIANS/PHOENICIANS. Third century BC, briefly. Arch-enemies of just about everyone. Being on the trunk road from Cartagena to Rome, Catalonia couldn't avoid the Carthaginian commander Hannibal, nor his war elephants. Keep your heads down, they'll be gone in a minute.

4. ROMANS. Third century BC to fifth century AD.
Roman General Scipio the Bald skipped into
Empúries, tolerated both Iberians and Greeks for
a bit, but then – 'Oh, what the hell? Why not just
colonise the place? It's what we're good at.'
As well as a few thousand indestructible remains,
the Romans left their recently acquired Christian
religion and their language. The Latin spoken by
the Romans who stayed here became Catalan,
while that spoken by those who charged about
suppressing the rest of the peninsula became
Spanish, from 'Hispania', the Roman name
for Iberia.

5. VISIGOTHS. Fifth century to eighth century. For
Visi read western, for *Goths* read Germans. As
usual, a victory over the Italians in extra time.

6. MOORS. Eighth century to ninth century.
The Goths were not overrun by tracts of heather-
covered upland but by the Berbers and Arabs
from North Africa, who indulged in the usual
invaders' pastimes of renaming the country (to
al-Andalus this time) and telling everyone they'd
backed the wrong god and should switch
allegiance to Allah.

7. FRANKS. Ninth century to tenth century.
The Berber of Seville was pretty soon kicked
out of Catalonia by the Franks – a generic name
of the time for northern Europeans in search of
the sun (the Spanish now call us *guiris*), featuring
the surprisingly mighty Pepin the Short. As well
as Frank and Pepin, Jesus was also back in the
limelight, along with a new and significant
creation, the count of Barcelona.

8.   CATALANS! Tenth century to twelfth century.
     Bit by bit, the counties of the Marca Hispànica,
     the frontier area between the Franks and the
     Moors, merged into Catalonia (probably named
     as the 'land of castles'), under the leadership of
     the count of Barcelona. And the count that
     counted at the time was Wilfred the Hairy,
     reputedly so named because he was hairy in a
     part, thankfully unspecified, where a normal man
     is not. Wilf and his descendents Ramon,
     Ramon, Ramon and Ramon became
     progressively cheesed off with Frank, Frank,
     Frank and Frank, despatching them back over
     the Pyrenees. In 989 Catalonia finally declared
     itself independent. Some are still recovering from
     the party.

9.   CATALANS AND ARAGONESE. Twelfth
     century to fifteenth century. The king of
     Catalonia's next-door neighbour Aragon, a
     former monk not keen on such a worldly
     job, promised the hand of his two-year-old
     daughter Petronila to the latest Ramon of
     Catalonia. Even before he got the rest of her,
     Ramon assumed the leadership of both countries,
     which effectively then became one. Having been
     someone else's colony for so long, Catalonia
     went half mad with power, taking over Valencia,
     the Balearics, Sardinia and Sicily. Imperialism
     was evidently cool after all, so long as you were
     fortunate enough to be the aggressor.

10. CATALANS, ARAGONESE AND
     CASTILIANS... OK, SPANISH. Fifteenth

century to the present day, possibly. The writing was scribbled on the wall for Catalonia's short-lived empire on 19 October 1469, when King Ferdinand II of Aragon and Catalonia tied the knot with an eighteen-year-old girl called Isabella, who just happened to be heiress to the throne of Castile – and therefore an embryo Real Madrid supporter if ever there was one. Power that had previously passed up and down the Mediterranean coast now disappeared decisively over the western horizon. After Cristòfol Colom (aka Columbus) had done likewise, it was to Barcelona that he eventually returned in triumph in 1493, but nearly 300 years were to pass before those darned Castilians allowed imports from Spain's American colonies to be landed in Catalonia.

11. A CERTAIN CORSICAN. 1808–1814. There was little chance that Napoleon could resist having a go at his next-door neighbour. He had a go. He failed. But the diminutive emperor did manage to achieve a rare unity between the squabbling Catalans and Castilians, who found themselves aligned against someone else other than each other.

12. CATALANS AGAIN! 1931–1939. On 14 April 1931 Catalonia declared itself independent again. Well, sort of. This time as a republic. Well, sort of. The new government was called not the government of Catalonia, but the government of the Generalitat. Not a catchy name, but still worth another party for sure. The last one for a while…

13. ANYONE WITH A GUN. 1936–1939.
    The Spanish Civil War. Chaos. Tragedy.

14. FRANK FRANCO. 1939–1975. (The dates are
    from the fall of Barcelona to the dictator's
    death.) Francisco Paulino Hermenegildo
    Teódulo Franco y Bahamonde was a very odd
    cove indeed. While his public relations officer
    was locked in the toilet, Frank banned speaking
    in Catalan, reading in Catalan, singing in
    Catalan, dancing to Catalan music and flying the
    Catalan flag. If he'd have thought of it, he'd have
    banned naming your cat Alan. Unsurprisingly,
    1975 witnessed an even bigger party in Catalonia
    than in 989 and 1931.

15. THE GENERALITAT? MADRID? THE EU?
    1970s to the present day. Who may be in charge
    nowadays seems to be a matter of opinion.

So the town of Roses was founded over 2,500 years ago by Greeks who probably named it after their homeland, the island of Rhodes. Remounting Benny, I pedalled round to gaze at the impressive sea gate of La Ciutadella de Roses (the citadel).

Although the remains of both Greek and Roman settlements lie within these walls, the fortifications were raised in medieval times to protect the town against those pesky pirates. The townspeople pretty soon spilled out of the citadel and into the town which nowadays spreads for several kilometres eastwards along the bay, up to and beyond the Castell de la Trinitat. This tough old fortress, built around the same time as La Ciutadella, had already suffered countless attacks before it was effectively destroyed by Napoleon's troops as they scurried out of Spain in 1814.

Having survived a long and tough history, Roses seemed to be blooming that afternoon and a gentle ride through the town's western outskirts took me past row after row of beachfront bars, swanky restaurants and endless apartment blocks. The Costa Brava, which had started at Cap de Creus, had now got into gear.

It's rare for a coastline to have a birthday but, just a few months earlier, the Costa Brava had been exactly one hundred years old. In the 12 September 1908 edition of *La Veu de Catalunya*, a regional newspaper, Ferran Agulló penned an article entitled 'Per la costa brava', the first published use of the term that means 'wild coast' or 'rugged coast'. Its later association with mass tourism stems from the Franco regime's development policy from the 1950s onwards. The districts I was now entering were later additions, but no less 'mass'. In Santa Margarida, things started to get out of scale. By Empuriabrava they'd gone completely bonkers.

A policy that permitted no development of more than three storeys (plus roof terrace) has been strictly enforced on the Costa Vermella for some time. For example, the construction of a block that was about to exceed the limit in the middle of Llançà port had been halted mid build, and still stands unfinished twenty-two years later. The huge development at Empuriabrava, however, reaches depths of planning vandalism that are hard to comprehend. Right by the beach, dominating the entire Gulf of Roses – as well as views to the coast from deep inland – are several apartment blocks reaching up to an appalling nineteen storeys. It's for this reason that I rate Empuriabrava the ugliest place I've seen in the whole of Spain. On the other hand, a woman standing next to me in an airport queue one day rated it the most beautiful. Thank goodness we're not all the same.

The Germans seem to love it, too. For as well as being host to such remarkable eyesores, Empuriabrava is also the largest residential marina in the world, with 23 kilometres of canals, enabling Günther and Gisela to park the Merc behind the security gate and spend the rest of the summer chugging to the *Bierkeller* from their private mooring.

As I chugged Benny into Empuriabrava from the north, it wasn't very clear from the map how we could find our way to the cycle path that left from the south. After trying several roads lined with mock classical porticos, but which ended in culs-de-sac at the ubiquitous canal network, I pulled in next to a short, middle-aged woman with beefy arms and a pair of industrial-sized shears, with which she was pruning the garden hedge.

'*Bon dia, señora. Conoce la calle al sur por favor?*'

She considered me for a few seconds before answering hesitantly.

'*Morgen. Lo siento*. Have little Spanish.'

'*Ah. Deutsch? Habe klein Deutsch.*'

'*Klein oder kein?*'

'*Que?*'

'English?'

'Yes. South? *Al sur?*'

'*Am Süden? Vögel?*'

'Birds? No, yo. I mean *ich*. *Mich*.'

'*Ichmich?*'

Well, having invented the new, but rather inelegant, language of 'Castalemanglish', and with the help of a few arched arms and climbing hands, we established that I needed to resort to footbridges. Armed with *meine neue*

Freundin's directions, however, I did successfully manage to walk and lift Benny to the other side of town and the access point to the Parc Natural dels Aiguamolls de l'Empordà.

After an energetic campaign that started in the 1970s, the creation of this nature reserve has managed to keep development at bay over nearly 5,000 hectares of flat land near the mouths of the River Muga and River Fluvià. Among those benefiting from these efforts are about three hundred species of bird, many of them passing through on their annual migrations, a lone cyclist bouncing along the bumpy but well-signposted tracks and, the day I passed the visitor centre at El Cortalet, about forty excited six-year-olds who fell silent the moment their guide spoke, only to shout as one when he asked if any of them would care to go inside: '¡Jo jo jo!' I'm not gifted at birdwatching but even I managed to spot some egrets, a flock of white storks and, alarmed by Benny's passing, a noisy, ginger-headed hoopoe.

After emerging on the main road south, more coffee soon called and at the small town of Sant Pere Pescador ('St Peter the Fisherman') I pulled in at a roadside cafe. A few minutes later three familiar faces also pulled in.

Twice since Roses, a trio of middle-aged chaps pedalling in my direction had pulled up to ask directions. Their kit couldn't have offered a greater contrast to my own, for they were Lycra-clad regulars, with proper cycling shoes and pedalling sturdy, well-oiled, heavily loaded machines. Maybe it was the weight of their equipment that explained why, although they'd always cycled away before me, Benny and I had always arrived first. Now it had happened again. One of them, a man of about fifty with the competent air of a scout leader, who always carried the map and always spoke first, did so again now.

'*¡Hombre! ¡Hola de nuevo!* Come, you must join us. Where are you going?'

'Today, just to L'Escala. What about you?'

'Probably L'Estartit. Depends how it goes. Then Blanes, which is home to me. We've come all along the coast, over the hills.'

'*Es muy duro,*' (It's very tough) added the elder of his two amigos, a short, wiry man with thinning grey hair and the friendly face of a greengrocer. 'And I should know – I'm from Extremadura!' The groaning of his friends suggested that this may not be the first time he'd used the pun. I'd always wondered if Spain's western region of Extremadura was as 'extremely tough' as it sounded.

'I know the coastal route's tough. I've come that way myself.' Even as I said it, I knew what was coming next. It came from the scout leader.

'What? Like that?'

'Well, I have the *lujo raro* [rare luxury] of a support driver carrying most of my gear for most of my trip.'

'*Lujo raro*' seemed to make them giggle.

'It is a long trip?' asked the scout leader.

I told them my plan. Instead of yet again questioning the standard of my kit, Scout Leader said: 'Ah, you will pass without doubt through Blanes, the most magnificent town of the Costa Brava.' This set the others off again. 'But why are you doing this ride around my country?'

'Well, for pleasure, of course... and there may be a book from it.'

At this, the greengrocer raised a finger. '*Oye, tío*, you must put my favourite joke in your book.'

And here it is. To get it, non-Spanish speakers need to know that the Spanish for 'building' is '*edificio*' and for 'difficult' is *'difícil'* and that Andalusians tend not to pronounce the last consonant in a word.

An Andalusian to a Catalan: 'Can you speak Catalan?'

Catalan: 'Yes, it's easy.'

Andalusian: 'All right. What's the Catalan for *edificio*?'

Catalan: *'Edifici.'*

Andalusian: 'I thought you said it was easy.'

Shaking their hands, I coaxed a few words out of the third cyclist, a younger, quieter man with the physique of a builder. This drew another comment from the joking greengrocer:

'Ah, he doesn't say much. He's from Montevideo.' (The capital of Uruguay.)

And, for some reason unknown to me, this seemed their favourite joke of all.

After crossing over the low, slow waters of the Fluvià, the coast road weaved through a vast area of apple orchards, just showing the first white blossom of spring, as though a light sprinkling of snow lay, still frozen, a few feet from the ground. Whether much would be still there in the morning was open to question, as a fresh north wind had suddenly got up. Some of these apples would find their way to the little shop in the Leicestershire village where I live the rest of the time and where the gardens are full of English apples I'd be even happier to buy, if only they were for sale. Strange old world.

Just out of sight, beyond empty campsites to the left, lay the long, broad swathe of golden – and often deserted – sands facing the Gulf of Roses, the Costa Brava's longest beach. If you want to get to the beach – and on windy days plenty of kite-flyers and kitesurfers do – one way is to turn off at the sign for 'Camping Aquarius' and then plough on along the dirt track as far as the dunes, where there's just enough room for a few cars or camper vans to park. Beware though: if it's blowing a northerly, you'll come away with a pair of severely sand-blasted legs!

It was at the southern end of the gulf that the Greeks had first landed, on what was then an island, to found the trading settlement of Empúries. This island was subsequently joined to the mainland, and on its site grew a small medieval village called Sant Martí, which Miss Macaulay found in the 1940s to be 'a tumbled, ruinous little pile'. Sixty years on, I cycled into what had now become an exclusive hamlet dominated by a solid, square-towered church and four large restaurants set around a plaza, packed on summer Sundays but today almost deserted.

What many of the summer visitors come here to see becomes clear if you leave Sant Martí on the shoreside cycle path, for stretching inland as far as the eye can see – which is about half a kilometre to the top of a low hill – lies one of the most spectacular archaeological sites you could hope to visit.

Out-growing the Palaiapolis of their little island, the Greek settlers soon built a sizable town here where the mainland slopes gently to the sea and it is this, the Neapolis, that runs right to the edge of the cycle track. However, even this settlement is dwarfed by the city built higher up the hill by the Romans who arrived about three hundred years after the Greeks – and with more than just trade in mind. Blocking land access to their enemies the Carthaginians was the aim and the embryo of Roman Empúries was not a market but a military camp.

Systematic excavation of this vast site began only in 1908 and continues to this day. I've made three visits myself and on each a new area has been revealed. On the last occasion I was startled to see that the previous access road itself had been dug up in the hope of finding evidence of occupation by indigenous Iberians even before the Greek settlement. Well organised and with few restricted areas, Empúries is highly recommended – a recommendation that comes with yet another weather tip: if the sun's out, be sure to take a parasol with you, for there's precious little shade anywhere on the site.

Facing Roses at this southern end of the gulf is the windy town of L'Escala – at least it seems always to have been battered on my visits by northerlies stronger than today's... not unusual on this southern side of the Pyrenees.

The *tramuntana*, a north wind that roars literally from 'across the mountains', can be fiercer than the stranger may expect on a Mediterranean coast and, just like the mistral of Provence, can blow for days on end, to the point where those trapped indoors by its icy fingers and wailing cries may begin to lose a little of their sanity.

What I didn't know until I moved here was that, in this part of the world, winds from all points of the compass have names. A clockwise circuit around the wind rose would rustle up the following (using their Catalan names): *tramuntana* (northern), *gregal*, *llevant* (eastern), *xaloc*, *migjorn* (southern), *garbí* or *llebeig*, *ponent* (western) and *mestral*.

And that's not all. The ever-conscientious Catalans go even further, categorising and naming subdivisions of each wind according to their strength. For example, while the *xaloc* (pronounced 'shalloc') blows from the south-east, if it whispers at only 15 kilometres per hour it is a *xaloquet*, while if it roars up to 60 kilometres per hour it becomes a *xalocada*. The Catalan wind rose actually includes thirty-three words for wind. Fortunately the *tramuntana*, at least, can be forecast, since it's at its strongest when there's an anticyclonic (clockwise) system over the Bay of Biscay and a cyclonic (anticlockwise) system over the Mediterranean's Gulf of Lion, funnelling wind between France's Massif Central and the Pyrenees, from north to south.

Zigzagging through L'Escala's narrow streets, I eventually found my way to today's rendezvous. There was Julie, as agreed, at a spot that's hard to miss: beside eleven green-grey men on the promenade. You can rely on them being there – ten sitting and one standing, all with their backs to the sea – as they're fixed to a concrete platform and made from bronze. *La Cobla*, a sculpture by Francesc Anglès i Garcia, is nothing to do with cobblers and everything to do with music and dance.

The origins of the circle dance called the *sardana* seem to be lost in history, but what is certain is that by the end of the nineteenth century, a number of variants had been pulled together and codified into the de facto national dance of Catalonia. Chief among the popularisers was a musician named Josep Maria Ventura and, if this sounds vaguely familiar to anyone who has visited Catalonia, it's because he is commemorated in many a street name, under his nickname, Pep Ventura. (For an explanation of other common Catalan street names, see the section towards the end of this book.)

The music for a sardana can't be played by just any old band. It is always a *cobla*, a group of eleven musicians, playing twelve instruments: five woodwind, five brass, a double bass and a small drum called a *tamborí*. Yes, one member plays two instruments: a small flute and, strapped to his or her arm, the *tamborí*. This band member always sits front left, as seen from the front, leading each tune with an introductory whistle, a beat on the drum – and then you're away.

The *sardana* itself looks deceptively simple. You can see it in towns and villages all over Catalonia, often at Sunday noon in front of the local church, and at many fiestas. First perhaps six or so people will form a small circle, alternately male and female if possible, join hands and begin. Small, delicate movements of the feet move the circle first this way and then that before a more energetic section starts, with hands raised and the odd little jump.

Unless the dancers are from a *colla* (a *sardana* club), anyone can join in, even during a dance, making some circles very large indeed – but beware of several pitfalls. To keep the male/female pattern, it's best to join as a couple; try not to split an existing couple; a single dance can be quite long and tiring; and, most importantly, you must know the steps – it's not as simple as it looks! In fact, some of the dancers will be counting in their heads the number of measures in the *curts* (the slow sections, hands lowered) and in the *llargs* (faster sections, hands raised) and then leading the others. Watch and learn.

One thing you can say for the *sardana* is that it must be one of the world's least threatening dances – which does make you question Franco's sanity when, like pretty well everything Catalan, he banned it.

Having walked to Dave, our heavily laden Renault Kangoo, and just as we were manouevring Benny into it, Julie and I both heard loud cheers from the road. It was the three amigos from Sant Pere Pescador.

'*¡Oye, Ricardo!*' they hooted as they whizzed by, and then, pointing at Julie and giggling: '*¡Lujo raro! Lujo raro!*'

Almost before I could wave, they were gone. Well, they may mock. While the amigos would have been struggling over the mountain track to L'Estartit, I'd be luxuriating in a shower at the Hotel Voramar before sampling L'Escala's 'World Famous Museum of the Anchovy'.

Yes, that's what we thought too: how could an entire museum be devoted to a single, salty little fish? How ignorant we were.

For a start, the anchovy is not necessarily little. The main anchovy image I'd been carrying around – oh, all right, the only anchovy image – was of the little brown fellow that puts the zizz in my pizza. But an adult anchovy can be longer than the width of your pizza. Scary thought. And black? Well, that's way off the mark too. The anchovy is essentially a green fish, with a silver stripe along its back that sometimes reflects a kind of electric blue.

Salty, though, is on the nail. When preserved in brine and packed in salt, anchovies acquire the strong flavour that gives them an edge in several dishes and makes them, for example, a key ingredient in Worcestershire Sauce. For this reason, the title of the museum is actually 'The Museum of the Anchovy and the Salt'.

The handsome blue and white building which houses it used to be the local abattoir and is on the road into L'Escala from Viladamat or Sant Pere, about a kilometre short of the centre. As the only visitors at the time, we were made exceptionally welcome.

'Where are you from?' asked the keen young man behind the desk. 'How did you hear about us? How did you get here?'

A man with a questionnaire in his head.

'Please, have this guide in English. It tells you everything you want to know about the anchovy. It takes you through our museum room by room.'

We looked around. There appeared to be only the one room. Realising that the 'rooms' in the guide were in reality numbers on the walls, we set off. Personally, I'd take a small museum like this rather than a giant like the British Museum any time. For one thing, you don't get 'museum legs', that nagging urge to take the weight off them after about ten minutes. Ten minutes is surely enough to satisfy anyone's craving for anchovy knowledge, but we gave it twenty out of politeness.

It turns out that the first people to think of salting fish – at least in this part of the world – were the Phoenicians. It also turns out that L'Escala used to have a huge fleet of small fishing boats, fabulous black and white photos of which adorned the walls, and it was the main local centre for salting, storing and distributing the fish. It finally turns out – and I'm glad that one of the 'rooms' told me this, for it had been the question I dared not ask – that the anchovy is not just a sardine by another name. While the sardine is a close cousin of the anchovy, it's the pilchard that's the same thing as the sardine.

Just when I thought I'd been told 'everything I wanted to know' about the anchovy, I found I was wrong. Having asked Señor Keen whether the old fish warehouse was still standing in L'Escala (just for the sake of something to say as we left), I was handed over to Señora Evenkeener, the local – and possibly worldwide – expert on fish warehouses. Indeed it was still standing, she advised me, but only just and not without the sterling efforts of many volunteers who had devoted their precious spare time to the restoration, brick by brick, of the magnificent fish warehouse of L'Escala, which was alas not yet open to the public, but would briefly be made available for a short concert of close-harmony singing in a few months' time, should I be interested in attending the event in my capacity as chief overseas aficionado of the fish warehouse.

Though I had to report my unfortunate unavailability for the event, the enthusiasm of both officials on anchovy duty that day did touch me and I strongly recommend a visit to their museum. Where the 'world famous' tag came from, I forgot to ask.

With the *tramuntana* strengthening, we decided against one of L'Escala's many seafront restaurants in favour of another one tucked a block or two back. Julie had picked it out again.

'Looks fine to me,' I said. 'It also looks Italian again to me. Why this one?'

'Let's go inside and you'll see.'

Indeed I did. Even a card-carrying Philistine like me could see that the decor of the Mocambo restaurant was, well, different. It was as though we had entered a golden cave (the bar), beyond which lay a larger chamber (the restaurant) where purple walls and a high, red-beamed ceiling gave the overall impression of having wandered into a fortune teller's den. These may not be the standard descriptions used by interior designers.

'Yep,' I agreed. 'It's certainly not the standard old photos and football teams you get in most Catalan restaurants. Do you think the food will be purple too?'

'I thought you didn't care what food looked like.'

'I don't. It's the taste that matters. Purple pasta would be fine. Though we will be eating Catalan some day soon, won't we?'

'We will.'

The prices were fine too. You can eat very well for very reasonable prices throughout Catalonia, so long as you stay away from those places where style matters more than content. Of course, some people are happy to pay for fancy presentation – and good luck to them – but, personally, I reckon that for an excellent meal, wine included, there's no need to pay more than 25 euros a head, usually less (2009 prices). Above that the Law of Diminishing Returns sets in: the more you pay, the worse you eat.

These of course are my own crude opinions. Julie, being an outstanding cook herself, has better-informed culinary tastes than mine. Choosing a restaurant by wall colour, though – that was a new one.

The latest plate of strength-building pasta, however, was not purple after all.

Day 4

Costa Brava for Better or Worse: L'Escala to Sant Antoni de Calonge

All muscles and limbs seemed intact as I awoke the next day, despite the heavy terrain they'd encountered between Cadaqués and Roses. Though today would be a similar distance – forty-plus kilometres – it should be relatively plain sailing and as I packed up my gear at the hotel, I found myself whistling 'Happy Days Are Here Again'.

'Haven't you been happy then?' asked Julie.

'What? Oh, yes of course. But there's something about the prospect of a day out on the bike that makes you... makes you...'

'Whistle?'

'Exactly.'

It turned out that L'Escala's striking indoor colours were not restricted to the Mocambo. Our room at the Hotel Voramar, overlooking the by now choppy Mediterranean, had recently been decorated in claret and blue: it was like sleeping in a changing room at Aston Villa. Breakfast was yet another colourful experience, our coffees and hams being consumed between walls of salmon-pink and maroon. What Tobermory and Aberaeron do with outdoor emulsion, the adventurous residents of L'Escala do with indoor emulsion. Adventurous indeed, for until recently you'd be hard-pressed to find anything but white on any Spanish wall, outside or in.

All kaleidoscoped out, I waved another goodbye to Julie from the saddle of a different machine. Knowing the first three days would involve some off-road stints, I'd chosen Benny and his wide, mountain-bike tyres. However, with metalled roads heading off indefinitely over the southern horizon, Benny's big brother Tetley, a 'hybrid' and veteran of previous long-distance touring, would now be more suitable – which is why I'd loaded him into Dave the Kangoo before leaving Llançà. (No, I've no idea why my bikes have always been male – they just have. Cars are another matter. While Tulip the Mini was clearly female, the sturdy, grey Kangoo is so male he just had to be 'Dave'.)

The *tramuntana*, which had passed the night whistling through the balconies of the Voramar and worrying the surf onto L'Escala's pebble beaches, seemed this morning to be a spent force. Progress was therefore pretty steady. Taking a leaf out of the happy-go-lucky Cap de Creus motorcyclist's book, I'd decided to break with the coastal route for the sake of including an inland visit I'd been meaning to make since 1993. Funny how the years slip by. So I set off not in the seaside wheel tracks of the three amigos, but instead south-westwards out of L'Escala on the GI-632.

Local Spanish road numbers are prefixed by letters indicating their province, in this case GI for Girona. With a county boundary coming up just out of town, this seemed a good opportunity to remind myself of the various divisions of Spain – which in some respects resemble more closely, say, the German arrangement than, say, the British or French.

One level below the nation state of Spain lies a mixed bag of regions (equivalent to the German *Länder*), some small like La Rioja, about the size of Norfolk, some much larger like Catalonia, similar in scale to Belgium. In Catalonia's case, its status is officially that of an 'autonomous community', i.e. more than simply a 'region'. Within Catalonia are four provinces: Barcelona, Tarragona, Lleida and Girona. Within Girona province lie seven *comarques* or counties. So the sequence is state-region-province-county. The complication is that 'nation', as a cultural rather than administrative concept, occurs not just at state level but also at the level of some regions, Catalonia being a prime example.

Ever since pedalling across the French frontier three days before, I'd been in the rural county of L'Alt Empordà ('upper' Empordà), whose total population numbers only 135,000 – fewer, for example, than the city of Tarragona. On the long straight out of L'Escala I now cycled into El Baix Empordà ('lower' Empordà). Though there's no systematic link with the medieval 'counties' ruled by the counts of the Marca Hispànica, in this case the name Empordà coincides with that of the counts of Empúries, who ruled from Castelló d'Empúries, inland from Empuriabrava, at the same time as the counts of Barcelona.

The quiet little villages on these flatlands north of the River Ter – Albons, Bellcaire, Ullà – still felt pretty medieval, with their narrow, tight-cornered streets winding between simple, solid, stone-built houses. Even in those days, at least one part of the built landscape would have been the same as greeted me. Montgrí, the 'nipple on the hill' visible from Cap de Creus, had finally assumed the shape of a castle, a construction started in 1294 under the orders of the counts of Barcelona to keep an eye on the counts of Empúries – but never finished. In those days the vast massif on which it perches was surrounded by swamps and marshes but the area I now cycled through was almost all agricultural land, albeit occasionally inundated and until recently partly planted with rice.

Soon after Ullà, the twenty-first century returned with a bang, in the form of market day at Torroella de Montgrí. The old royal sea port – now stranded 6 kilometres inland – was thrumming, as tourists clashed elbows with locals in search of a bargain among the endless stalls. Catalan markets, if not centred on a square or car park, seem to wander down almost every street in town. Without the bike, I'd have sought the sound of the classical guitar that usually emanates from an itinerant CD wagon that frequents most markets around here. Not wanting to add weight, however, I settled for a coffee stop on one particularly busy corner and it was from here that I spotted, high above the bobbing heads, a sign for the Museum of the Mediterranean. With a foyer large enough for me to leave Tetley safely locked up, it justified a small investigation.

Though not quite as grand as it sounded – at the time just a single room on the first floor of a backstreet building – it was unarguably atmospheric. The museum's declared aim was to deliver to each of the visitor's senses an experience of the Mediterranean shore. Sight was catered for by a huge aerial photograph covering the entire floor; sound by ambient ripples and whooshes; and smells by whiffs of seaside herbs. Peering behind screens and into corners was an earnest-looking professor type. He glanced up at me quizzically.

'Have you found anything to feel?' he asked. At least that's what I think he asked – it's not a sentence I'd ever heard in Spanish. Nor in English, actually.

'No. Nor anything to taste,' I said.

'Ah,' offered the prof, with a sudden, child-like smirk. 'Perhaps this is not a bad thing.'

After crossing the wide, brown waters of the River Ter, the southbound traveller has a choice: left to continue along the coast or right to go inland. Until about three years before this ride, the coast in these parts was dominated by a row of radio transmission masts set back from the broad sands of Platja de Pals, but oddly enough it wasn't Spanish listeners they were transmitting to...

In 1950, at the beginning of the Cold War, the United States government conceived a plan to disseminate propaganda (or truth or both, depending on your viewpoint) by radio to the communist states of Eastern Europe. Funded by the US Congress via the CIA, the first to broadcast was Radio Free Europe (RFE), initially in Czech. By 1959 another station, Radio Liberty (RL), was broadcasting short-wave transmissions from here at Platja de Pals, although the station's headquarters was in Munich. Having made a significant contribution to the fall of communism in many states, RFE/RL was even nominated for the 1991 Nobel Peace Prize and still broadcasts to countries without a fully free press. However, transmissions from this site ended long ago and the masts themselves were removed around 2006 – though you can still see a photograph of them in the Bar Les Dunes at the northern end of the beach.

This time, however, I turned right from the bridge over the Ter, heading further inland past deep-green fields speckled red with poppies and alive with swooping black dart shapes – martins, I think – to a junction just north of the village of Ullastret, where a brown sign directed me down a bumpy track to the objective of my diversion.

When, over two and a half millennia before, Greeks landed at what was to become Empúries, this was by no means an uninhabited coast. Nor even an undeveloped one. The indigenous peoples along this Mediterranean littoral are nowadays generally referred to as Iberians, or sometimes Celtiberians, since they are thought to have originated from the Celtic homeland north of the Pyrenees. It may be tempting to think of the Greeks (or the Phoenicians, who established colonies further south around the same time) as bringing the first advanced civilisation to the Iberian peninsula. How far from the truth this would be I was about to find out, for down this track lay the recently revealed remains of a complete Iberian town, occupied for about four centuries.

Feeling pleased with myself at having whizzed here in pretty good time, but looking perhaps a little shiny for my effort, I pulled up at the ticket office.

'*Pensionista?*' asked the jolly attendant after a brief appraisal.

'Certainly not,' I retorted, paying my full dues before pedalling away out of the saddle just to show the cheeky pup. Knees pinging from this unwise bravado, I locked Tetley to a post in the car park and set off, leaflet in hand, to examine the site.

Excavated only over the last sixty years, it was far bigger and better preserved than I'd expected. Puig de Sant Andreu – St Andrew's Peak – was a fortified hill town and my entrance was the same as it would have been for a visitor in the sixth century BC: through a massive gateway at the bottom of the hill. To left and right ran the impressive town walls, built from neatly cut blocks and reinforced at regular intervals by deep round towers. Ahead stretched the settlement's main street, with very clear side streets, along which lay the foundations of individual rectangular houses, with carefully sculpted, round storage chambers and even more carefully constructed, elongated cisterns for retaining rainwater.

The higher I climbed, the more of Puig de Sant Andreu's townscape came into view, including a large area to the north still being excavated – although today's workforce comprised just two young people kneeling in a corner, tooled up with a trowel each and a wheelbarrow between them.

At the top of the hill, near two excavated temples, stood the museum and here I discovered just how much is still to be learnt about the lives of Puig de Sant Andreu's residents, members of the tribe referred to in subsequent literature as the Indikets. Though the main gateway and nearby walls have a distinct and purposeful horizontal groove, no one knows what this purpose was. Though they had a religion, no one knows which gods they believed in. Though their written language used a very clear alphabet – writing both left to right and right to left – no one has managed to decipher its meaning.

Settling down under a pine tree and tucking into my packed lunch created from surplus breakfast items, I reflected on the case of a museum that left more questions than answers. Though it may have been less grand than the Greek and Roman remains 20 kilometres north at Empúries, this relatively small site occupied by their predecessors somehow spoke more eloquently to me about the careful lives of a neat and tidy community, here on a low hilltop above the Daró valley in a town hidden from view for centuries.

Having tidied up my crumbs, I eventually snapped myself back into the current century and spread out the map, some of whose folds had already begun to develop ominous holes. This evening's target was the seaside resort of Sant Antoni de Calonge. Between me and it lay the heavily forested hills of Les Gavarres and, to avoid these, I chose a south-easterly, cross-country route that would eventually throw me back onto the coast beyond Palafrugell.

Initially the countryside was dominated by row after orderly row of orchards: apple trees to the left of me, peach trees to the right, most with their awnings neatly tied up but ready for deployment in summertime. When brown 'Xarxa Ciclisme' (Cycling Network) signs started appearing, I happily followed their recommended route, although within each village this official advice seemed to dry up, so that I was always happily surprised to spot them again on the other side.

Despite my diversion to Puig de Sant Andreu, I still had plenty of time to get to Sant Antoni and so decided to go for the hat trick of three museums in twenty-four hours. Thus it was that, turning a corner in the backstreets of Palafrugell onto Carrer de la Tarongeta ('Little Orange Street'), I dismounted to walk the last few steps to my target: the Museu del Suro, the Museum of the Cork. Just as with the Museum of the Anchovy and the Salt, I'd been intrigued as to how a whole institution could be devoted to such a seemingly simple item. In this case, however, the mystery was to stay unresolved, for I'd fallen foul of the Spanish Problem With Time.

Whatever its virtues, every nationality seems to have some failing that puts it out of sync with the rest of the world. With Americans it's maps (they've never produced even a half decent one), with Italians it's hotels (where are they?) and with the French it is of course the lavatory (do they even know what a civilised toilet is?). Being a Brit myself, I'm not qualified to decide on the British equivalent, but I suspect it may be related to the temperature of our beer.

In the case of the Spanish – including the Catalans, though they'd probably deny it – the problem is time. As in time of day. For a start they've managed to merge two quite distinct concepts into one Spanish word: '*mañana*' means both 'tomorrow' and 'morning'. How did that happen? With a completely straight face they'll describe 'tomorrow morning' as '*mañana por la mañana*'. And it doesn't end there. With only three other parts of the day left to name (afternoon, evening and night), they go and do it again! Afternoon and evening have been merged into a single word: '*tarde*', literally 'late'. How vague is that?

But that's only the start of the problem. Well known to anyone who's visited Spain from the temporally normal parts of Europe (i.e. everywhere else) is the vexed question of when the *mañana* ends and the *tarde* starts. Noon of course, you say. Oh no. In Spain the *mañana* seems to end whenever you want it to end. So when the plumber, who'd promised to turn up in the *mañana*, knocks on the door at 1.45 p.m. and you raise the obvious question, he says:

'But it is still the *mañana*, señor.'

This despite the fact that the shops have already closed for the *tarde*.

My guess, for what it's worth, is that the *mañana* becomes the *tarde* while you're having lunch and that, in turn, the *tarde* becomes the *noche* (night) while you're having dinner. The obvious flaw in this system – that people tend to eat at different times – doesn't seem to bother the Spanish one bit. The invention of that handy device, the clock, seems to have passed them by.

It's perhaps no coincidence that so many sundials have survived on the walls of older Spanish buildings. As Ford wrote, more boldly than I dare, 'the sun and shadows are the primitive method of counting the flight of time in countries where it is of little value'.

Combine these problems with a labyrinthine system of national, regional and local fiestas and you often end up with a list of opening hours so complex that a degree in logic would be a reasonable entry requirement for anyone attempting to decipher them. All of which constitutes my excuse as to why the Museum of the Cork was closed when I was convinced it should have been open. After staring once more at the opening hours, I concluded that today could well have been the evening before a fiesta on an otherwise working day within those months loosely defined as off-season. Or maybe the curator was just poorly.

Whatever, my cork education would have to wait. A pleasant bar in an even pleasanter square nearby tempted me to take another break and there I pulled out Miss Macaulay to see if she could educate me on the subject of Palafrugell.

It was the location, she told me, of an ancient 'Palace of Fruits', Palaz Frugell, and, as a walled town, acted for a while as a safe haven from pirates, to which the inhabitants of the nearby fishing villages could hasten when necessary. She compared the layout of the town to a starfish and a glance at the little street map I'd picked up in the bar confirmed that this was still the case, the radial streets continuing as a wide arc of roads reaching out to the coast.

From Fornells in the north to La Fosca in the south, these villages nowadays form a classic stretch of the Costa Brava. Each aficionado seems to have a favourite. Miss Macaulay's was Fornells and, sixty years later, that of the young man who installed our satellite dish in Llançà was Llafranc. My own is the almost impossibly perfect little bay of Calella de Palafrugell, where the sunlight reflecting from a kingfisher-blue sea lights up the vaulted ceilings of shoreside verandas and where lunch at a shady beach cafe could last from an hour to an eternity, with no sense of time passing at all.

Calella lies at the end of what is effectively a cul-de-sac, however, and so, looking at my own map, I picked out a cyclable route directly to La Fosca. It ran from a square at the centre of the 'starfish', but whether this square was one and the same I knew not and so asked the portly middle-aged couple at the next table if they knew the name of the square where we sat. They turned out to be French.

'Bof,' said Monsieur, puffing out his lips, 'J'en sais rien.' He looked a bit crestfallen.

'Oh, it's of no import,' I said quickly, switching to very rusty French.

'Ah, but we should know,' said Madame. 'We come here every year, sit in this very cafe every year. Thierry, go and and look at the nameplate on the wall for le monsieur.'

'No, really...' I started, but Thierry was already on his mission. Madame waved away my protests.

'It gives him something to do,' she whispered. 'He is tiring a little of Palafrugell, I think.'

'Are you staying on the coast?'

'No, no. The Parisians, they go to the beach. We're from Narbonne and we find our interests elsewhere.'

'Palafrugell seems a pleasant town. What do you do here?'

'We sit, we read, we eat of course. We tour around, we shop. And we go to museums...'

At this I risked interrupting her catalogue of adventures with the tale of my failed attempt on the cork museum.

'Ah, the Catalans,' she said loudly. 'Yes they can be a little, er, *ennuyants* [tiresome].'

Before the young Catalan at the next table could raise a second eyebrow, I quickly changed the subject.

'Have you been to the Museum of the Anchovy at L'Escala?'

'No. Now that sounds fascinating. Thierry...'

Her husband had just returned, quite out of breath.

'Thierry, the *monsieur* has discovered a new destination for us: the Museum of the Anchovy.'

Apparently underwhelmed by this prospect, Thierry turned to me, panting, hands on hips.

'I'm desolated, *monsieur*, but – oof! – all the nameplates are hidden by building works.'

'Oh, Thierry,' tutted his wife, 'You're quite hopeless. You must ask the waiter.'

Enough. The poor man was turning redder by the second.

'No, no, please sit down, *monsieur*. I will ask the waiter myself as I pay the bill.'

After doing so and assembling all my bits and pieces at some distance from the tables, I was just about to pedal off when Thierry waved over to me.

'So what's the *plaça* called, *monsieur*?'

'Apparently it's called La Plaça. *Au revoir les deux*.'

I'm not aware of any systematic antipathy toward the Catalans on the part of the French – and should stress, of course, that my own little mickey-taking is not intended seriously. Indeed, I've become rather fond of the Catalans over the years. One thing they seem to share with the English, in fact, is our stereotypical view of the French. A Catalan estate agent once made a telling remark to me:

'The French,' she said, 'are a special people. They come from a special country. And how do we know? Because they tell us so incessantly. Because their country is, it seems, quite perfect. But what we ignorant Catalans do not understand is why, if France is so perfect, they spend so much of their time in our country.'

Touché.

After a quiet, suburban run down to the coast at La Fosca, I suddenly found myself in a noisy seaside world of bars, campsites, ball games, dogs and children – not Parisian children outside August, I would guess. One of the campsites, Camping La Fosca, announced itself as 'The oldest campsite in Spain', dating from 1954. From here I pointed Tetley southwards along the shore once more, plunging straight into one of those stretches that gave – and still occasionally gives – the Costa Brava a bad name.

First up was Palamós, the choice of Pere III of Aragon as a royal port when Torroella had silted up in the thirteenth century, thereby picking up the valuable role as Girona's official outlet to the sea. When Rose Macaulay passed through sixty years ago, she found it lying 'pleasantly along its bay', but nowadays, with cruise port and marina added to the fishing harbour, Pere's town has become a right royal eyesore with apartment blocks, both enormous and anonymous, casting long, broad shadows over earlier, human-sized developments.

The good news was that a cyclable Passeig Marítim had appeared, the first of many continuously paved promenades that would make my southbound navigation simpler – or so I thought. It was therefore an easy task to track down our hotel at the southern end of the next overdeveloped town, Sant Antoni, into which Palamós had imperceptibly merged.

Booking a place to stay here a few days before had proved surprisingly tricky, not because of a shortage of hotels – Sant Antoni seemed to be awash with them – but because many didn't open until summer, in fact until St John's Day, 24 June, which the Spanish tend to regard as the start of summer. (The solstice is actually on 20 or 21 June, depending on the year.) Bucking the trend, however, was the seventy-room, seafront Hotel Reimar and it was here, by the pool, that Julie was waiting.

'You look whacked,' she said. 'Do you want to put the bike in the car later?'

'No, I'm OK...'

But we were interrupted by the very keen receptionist, emerging from within.

'Señor, I will have your bicycle taken to a store room. *Por favor...*' Like a mother hen, he flapped us into reception, placing Tetley gently against the wall.

'The señora has already checked in. Please go...' He waved at the stairs. *'Por favor.'* Wave, wave.

Re-emerging half an hour later from what we'd realised by then was a very empty hotel, we just caught sight of the receptionist himself carefully steering Tetley into a side room as though the machine were made of crystal. We waited at the desk until he returned.

'Thank you for that,' I said.

'Is nothing, señor.'

'Could you tell us where the bar is, please?'

'Certainly, señor, is through that door and turn, er, this way.'

Following his directional wave, we found ourselves in another empty room and waited for the barman. Five minutes later we were still alone and so I returned to reception.

'I'm sorry, but there is no one serving in the bar.'

'Ah, you want to take a drink, señor, I come. *Por favor.*' Flap, wave and double wave.

It did indeed seem that not only was the waving receptionist the most enthusiastic member of staff at this large hotel, but he was also, this early in the season, its only member of staff. Receptionist, porter, barman and waiter, he was also to serve us – and the three other guests that we eventually came across – an excellent breakfast the next morning. Good for him. Dinner, unsurprisingly, was not currently available.

Nor were most of the town's restaurants yet open. Sant Antoni is essentially a summer-only resort, which is a shame actually, for the April weather was perfect, the seafront spotless and yet the beach almost completely deserted.

After ordering food in the only beachfront restaurant open (actually Catalan, for a change), and starting our bottle of *tinto*, Julie and I compared our days. She was surprised I hadn't gone down to any of the beaches beyond Palafrugell.

'I've got a new favourite,' she said. 'Tamariu.'

'I've heard of it, but never been. Is it like Calella?'

'Better. It's an old-fashioned resort squeezed into a little cove and there were some old-fashioned people living there too.'

'What do you mean?'

'Well, at one private house right on the front, a family was being served lunch on their own terrace by staff in starched blue uniforms at beautiful broad tables covered in white linen.'

As she was speaking, our own food had arrived. Julie waited until the waiter had gone before resuming.

'And it was better food than this looks,' she whispered, screwing her nose up.

'Maybe it'll taste better than it looks,' I suggested.

I was wrong.

'How's your steak?' asked Julie.

'Fatty. And your chicken?'

'Frazzled.'

Finishing the wine outside on the terrace, though, raised our spirits again.

'Never mind, we'll eat better tomorrow night,' I said.

'The forecast's fine too. No sign of the *tramuntana* returning.'

'Just as well. Tomorrow's cycling will be tough enough without having to battle against the wind.'

Day 5

Little Britain: Sant Antoni de Calonge to Malgrat de Mar

The world's biggest sporting event, in terms of live spectators, is not the Olympic Games, nor the football World Cup, but an annual European event regularly attended by an estimated ten million spectators. Some eighteen years before, in the Vercors mountains of eastern France, three of those spectators were myself and two cycling chums from Leicestershire. For us, as competitors sped past in a blur, the event lasted about five minutes. It is of course cycling's Tour de France, which lasts three weeks, covers about 3,500 kilometres and nowadays includes stages outside France itself.

The reason *le Tour* was in my mind as I did my daily stretches before a mirror-flat sea the following morning was that within an hour or two Tetley and I would be tackling one of that year's toughest stages ourselves. So, with hills ahead, it came as a special relief that the day had dawned without a breath of wind: one natural enemy at a time is enough for any cyclist.

Having agreed to try to meet up with Julie for lunch, I pulled away to the sound of various creaks, from both bike and body, through the steep backstreets of Sant Antoni to the C-253, the main road south. (In Spain, a 'C' road is the next level up from a local road, the C standing for *comarcal* or 'county'.) Still within a heavily overdeveloped zone, I sped through Platja d'Aro without my feet leaving the pedals. Surprisingly, however, this grim stretch of the Costa Brava ends in an oasis of charm at the smaller, older development of S'Agaró. (*Sa* or *s*' means 'the' in some Catalan dialects.)

This is another result of Catalonia's classic age of elegance, which I'd encountered at Cadaqués and which peaked in the modernist movement of turn-of-the-century Barcelona. Money – and taste – spread up and down the coast and here at S'Agaró in the 1920s Josep Ensesa i Gubert, the son of a rich Girona industrialist, together with architect Rafael Masó i Valentí, began building a number of villas featuring traditional Catalan themes and tasteful, low rooflines – an attribute guaranteed to this day by strict local planning policies. At the heart of the development, on the headland of Punta d'en Pau, lies the exclusive Hostal de la Gavina (Seagull Hotel). Guests that have signed in here include Bacall, Bogarde, Bogart, Borbón, Chaplin, Connery, Cocteau and Carreras... and that's just the Bs and Cs. Señor Borbón is better known as King Juan Carlos of Spain. In case you're tempted, the Royal Suite costs 1,500 euros a night.

When Miss Macaulay passed by here in the late 1940s, this relatively new establishment was one of the very few large hotels along this coast, prompting in her a vision of the future which clearly did not appeal, but which, in one respect, was to prove starkly inaccurate.

'Life there must be very comfortable, sociable and classy,' she wrote of the Hostal de la Gavina, stressing that she didn't fancy such a lifestyle herself. This stirred up a fear that there might come a time, 'still remote' in the 1940s, when the Costa Brava would be 'rich and prosperous' and boast 'a line of such fine hotels all down it'. Had this coast been in Britain, she conjectured, luxury hotels and villas would already be everywhere.

Well, though her forecast of wider wealth and greater development proved pretty accurate, her prediction as to which end of the social scale would form the market for the area's larger hotels was some way off beam. That the working classes, especially perhaps the British working classes, might one day be able to afford travel to such destinations was apparently beyond the conception of Miss M.

It was in the next town of Sant Feliu de Guíxols that my brief dalliance with the Tour de France route started – and a more abrupt start you couldn't imagine.

Sant Feliu, of which I was to learn more later in the ride, had lost out to Palamós as the royal choice for Girona's port over seven centuries ago, but seems to have survived the setback and is nowadays a busy, pleasant and – at least down by its little harbour – perfectly flat town. Hard against its south-western edge, however, lies another range of hills – L'Ardenya – and it is across these that the 21-kilometre coast road to Tossa, the GI-682, winds its wiggly way.

Feeling in need of a coffee to set me up for the climb, I pulled over at a corner cafe where another bike, older and rustier than mine, was leaning against the railing.

'Going far?' a man's voice asked in Spanish. It came from the shadows of the terrace where a chap of about my age, dressed in checked shirt, denims and trainers, lolled back and took a swig of what looked like brandy. Sitting at the next table, I ordered my coffee.

'Over the hills to Tossa and beyond,' I replied.

'Ah, why so many cyclists do the hills I know not. For me, the flatter is the better.' While speaking, he moved his forearm up and down to indicate the preferred gradient. 'Is better also for my machine.' The arm waved at the old bike.

'Oh, it's yours. You don't wear the usual cycling gear, I see.'

'Bah! They all think they are Miguel Indurain, these men with an age that should know better.' Grumpy Old Cyclist looked me up and down. 'You, señor, it is not bad, your clothes.'

'You're the first to say that! But tell me, here in the middle of these hills there are not many flat routes to cycle. Are you from Sant Feliu?'

'Me, I live in Gerona, señor,' (he pronounced Girona the Spanish way), 'and to my home I return today on the same gentle route I have arrived yesterday. Ah, I see it interests you. You know the Vías Verdes?' I shook my head. 'You can save your legs which, I am guessing, have the same years as mine.'

Grumpy had been fumbling in his back pocket and now placed a crumpled map, evidently part of a free leaflet, on the table between us.

'Please take it, señor. I know my way home. And now I must use Pepe's facilities before I leave. Good luck on the hill. You will need it.'

Even as we shook hands, I felt Grumpy's advice might well be crucial and carefully placed his gift deep inside my bag for later scrutiny.

The Tossa road started just around the corner from the cafe. Only once before had I travelled this route: by car, when we were obliged to pull over at the side of the road more than once to let our friend's car sickness pass. Having removed a layer of clothing in the gathering heat, I began the climb immediately on leaving town – and shortly thereafter began my long walk too, for, of the 21 kilometres, I would say I pedalled at most 1 kilometre: the rest was either walking up or freewheeling down. You pretty soon get into the walking rhythm and indeed, as any rambler will tell you, when there are views to be had, Shanks's pony offers the ideal form of transport.

After the initial steep trudge through dense forests of Mediterranean pine (a Category 4 climb, according to www.letour.fr – the easiest category in *le Tour*), vistas started to open up over the shore to the left. Rising almost vertically from the mottled blue sea were extensively faulted cliffs of pale red granite, which, as soon as they presented anything but the sheerest of faces, were colonised by a dense layer of scrub. From my high vantage point among the pines, it was impossible to identify any individual species, but the tough vegetation occupying these perilous sites featured every shade of green, speckled here and there with purples, whites and especially intense points of bright yellow. I began to look forward to the pedestrian pleasures of the uphill stints. Plenty of cyclists passed in both directions, all crouching low in bright Lycra, most pedalling furiously and raising a hand to each other as they passed, but usually not to the short figure walking his bike through the hills. No problem. As they whizzed and whooshed their way along, these 'proper' cyclists missed rustling lizards, echoing birdsong, yellow butterflies and the noonday sun sparkling in the fig leaves.

Julie would tell me later that, driving this route, she was unable to enjoy any of the views as a constant eye had to be kept on the bends of the road, on other vehicles and on speeding cyclists, one of whom actually overtook her. Sixty years before, Miss Macaulay too had had a nervous drive, but reports that between Sant Feliu and Tossa she encountered only two policemen and a mule cart.

After a little over two and a half hours, and after crossing the border into the county of La Selva, Tetley and I bounced along a suddenly bumpy section into Tossa de Mar. Three months later, the winner of this stage of *le Tour*, Thor Hushovd of Norway, managed the same route in about half an hour.

Through all the stages of Catalan history, there's been a settlement at the little bay of what is now Tossa de Mar. In Roman times the village then known as Turissa was home to several villas, the remains of one of which is now open to the public on Avinguda del Pelegrí. Turissa had become Tursia by the Middle Ages, when the 'Moorish Tower' which still overlooks the town was built as a lookout for threats from the sea. The line of the old town from this era can still be picked out – perhaps more easily than in any other settlement along this coast – by the remains of other towers, walls and turrets.

As I cycled into Tossa, the scent of the pine woods was replaced at first by the exhaust fumes of the busy main road and then, as I approached the seafront, by the familiar smell that means Catalan lunchtime: fried fish. For my part, having failed to make mobile contact with Julie, I settled down to a takeaway cheese roll, rather uncomfortably under a hot sun on the sandy beach, and gazed in some admiration at modern-day Tossa. Now a small, attractive town of about five thousand residents, it certainly doesn't deserve the image it has among those Brits who have not actually been there (including, until recently, me) as one of the more lairy Costa Brava resorts. Huddled around its small bay, Tossa's skyline is still dominated by the coastal forest, though nowadays with small white villas half hidden between the branches. Below this the terracotta roofs of the old town and occasional glimpses of its defensive walls make it easy to imagine the place before the hotels and restaurants filled the seafront. Even these more modern developments are relatively modest in scale and, with lunchtime having left the beach temporarily underpopulated, a surprising sense of calm prevailed.

What impressed me particularly from beach level was a stunning white building, whose arched windows and curved roofline peeked seductively through the palm trees to the south. As it happened, a late text from Julie directed me that way and the curvy building turned out to be the Hotel Diana, which I learnt had been built in 1906 as the home of one Joan Sans, another of those returning 'Americanos'.

Julie had found a shady cafe terrace with room to park Tetley in view. Over coffee we compared notes on the bendy road from Sant Feliu, agreed that Tossa deserved a longer stay one day and ruminated on more immediate overnight possibilities, settling on Malgrat de Mar, a town that neither of us had ever visited, some 25 kilometres to the south.

The coastline had now turned almost due west and it was into a blazing afternoon sun that I approached the next resort. Approached, entered and rapidly exited, for a greater contrast with genteel Tossa could hardly be imagined than that offered by Lloret de Mar. Competing with Palamós for ugliness but easily outstripping it in garishness, Lloret is a reminder of what the Spanish used to do thirty or forty years ago to attract north European money: sombreros, straw donkeys, chip shops and *Bierkeller*.

One of those visitors had been Julie herself and I'd just heard the tale. She'd been working at the time in the head office of a renowned clothes retailer in London.

'It was coming up to some royal jubilee or other,' she said.

'1977?'

'Yes, must have been. There was going to be a big street market in Pimlico and three of us from work spent weeks making stuff to sell.'

'What kind of stuff?'

'Oh, skirts, shawls, bracelets, trinkets. Cheap stuff, but on the day the punters lapped it all up and we made enough for six of us to fly to Spain on a winter package holiday for a week. Twenty-five quid each it cost. We flew to Girona airport – it would have been called Gerona then – and before they'd let us into the tiny terminal building, the one that's just been knocked down, they herded us into cattle pens out on the tarmac. Then we were bundled into a bus for the trip down to Lloret.'

'What was your hotel like?'

'It was a scream. A kind of Butlin's de Mar – huge dining room, ghastly food. All the guests were English, I think, and lots were oldies staying all winter to save fuel bills at home. Half of them came down to breakfast in their dressing gowns and fluffy pink slippers.'

'Even some of the women?'

'Ha – closer to the truth than you think. Two of our friends were a gay couple, blokes I mean – not unusual in the business in London, but pretty risqué in Spain at the time.'

'Was one of your crowd that film star friend?'

'Indeed it was, but she'd retired from movies by then.'

Julie's work colleague Jude had appeared in just the one film – and 'appeared' turned out to be an accurate description. It was in the 1960s, she'd told us, that she and her friend had been on an even earlier trip to the Costas, to Benidorm in fact, when they were 'spotted' at a bar by one of the casting team and given roles in a Spanish film being shot on location right there in their resort. Naturally, Julie and I – and Jude's husband – were a tiny bit sceptical of this story and so, at her request, I tracked down in Barcelona a DVD of the film in question: *Un Beso en el Puerto* (*A Kiss in the Port*, 1966), starring Manolo Escobar, a crooner and heart-throb of the time, a sort of Spanish Cliff Richard.

It was in a Cornish village that the four of us eventually settled down for the viewing, wine and snacks to hand. Half an hour had passed with no sign of Jude.

'You're sure it was this film?' asked her husband John.

'Shut up!' said Jude, eyes fixed on the screen.

Another fifteen minutes.

'Do you come on and sing?'

'Ssh!' she hissed... and then: 'There!'

'What?'

'Where?'

'Run it back... look, those two girls.'

As Manolo passed by in the foreground, two young women turned, one pointing, the other craning her neck...

and were gone. Jude had indeed appeared in a movie – and then rapidly disappeared. We burst into applause.

'That turning of the head was something special, Jude,' I said. 'Could have been Sophia Loren.'

'You're just jealous because you weren't in it.'

It had been less than twenty years before Jude's dramatic turning of the head that Rose Macaulay had rattled down this undeveloped coast, turning heads herself with her 1940s hat. At about the same time another Briton was settling in for a longer stay. Norman Lewis spent three years living and working with a Catalan fishing community and his evocative account of the sojourn, *Voices of the Old Sea*, captures the flavour of a society still clinging to ancient ways but on the brink of the irrevocable changes brought by mass tourism. The villagers' lives, loves and labours followed patterns laid down generations before, with the timing of the annual tuna fishing – so crucial to the community's economy – determined by the whisperings of a mysterious witch-doctor figure called the *Curandero* ('the quack'); the naming of fishing boats subject to censorship by a fanatically religious police captain; and most financial and domestic issues coming under the jurisdiction of a dominant female known simply as 'the Grandmother'. One of the more surprising facts the book revealed to me was that most of the fishermen of those days didn't swim, a choice often made, apparently, out of respect for the sea. The folk referred to their own community as 'the Cat Village', to distinguish themselves from 'the Dog Village' a few kilometres inland, and Lewis calls the place Farol.

Though the experiences he recounts were, we are led to believe, quite factual, the name Farol is not, and a long-running debate has followed as to the village's real identity. Since *farol* is Castilian and *fanal* Catalan for 'lantern', the community of Fenals, just west of Lloret, seems to be a favourite contender (the declension from 'a' to 'e' notwithstanding). I intended to investigate.

The road down to Fenals turned off the main drag between Bar El Cid and Club Erótica. It was quite a relief to get away from the truck and bus fumes and trundle instead down relatively quiet side streets. Pulling up on Fenals' wide promenade above a broad, sandy beach, I looked around. More tower blocks, more huge hotels, more fancy restaurants. Not a boat in sight. If there were any signs of anything from the pre-tourist era, they might be hidden among the pine woods at either end of the beach, but all I could see there were modern villas. If the village of 'Farol' was ever here, it had been long gone by now.

Traditionally the Costa Brava ends at Blanes, in fact at a rocky outcrop just offshore called Sa Palomera, a few hundred metres before the small delta of the River Tordera. Historically one of the most important fishing ports north of Barcelona, Blanes has now grown into a bustling town of nearly 40,000 people, dominated by the tourist business. Its fishing fleet has survived, though, despite the events of Boxing Day 2008. The same great storm that caused so much damage in Llançà wrought similar havoc here, especially in the relatively exposed harbour. Online videos show the night-time destruction of two vessels on the shore and, the next day, a Blanes beach covered not with sunbathers but with piles of wreckage as far as the eye can see: boats, huts, walls, awnings – all battered into so much firewood by the forces of nature that have always threatened this coast. Just as at Llançà, a new outer breakwater to protect the harbour was planned but, at the time I cycled through, not yet started.

Though featuring a standard Costa seafront of high-rise blocks, Blanes hasn't quite plunged to the depths of Lloret and Palamós and markets itself as simply 'the best place to spend your holiday'. Indeed, I recalled, according to the Scout Leader of the Giggling Amigos it is 'the most magnificent town of the Costa Brava'. Certainly the beaches (when cleared of shipwrecks) are magnificent and the tourist is also offered two botanical gardens to visit, which the town council's literature (www.visitblanes.net) boasts are both 'globally recognised jewels'. One of them, the Marimurtra garden, occupies a particularly spectacular setting on the clifftops and specialises in the conservation of endangered species of local Mediterranean flora.

My route in took me off the main road onto the older Carrer de la Vila de Lloret, down through a jumble of four- and five-storey blocks, probably from the 1960s, some renovated but many pretty dilapidated, their grey walls in dire need of new render and a coat of paint. The nearer I approached the shore, the smarter the town became. Newer glass and steel constructions looked down on carefully cultivated roundabouts, around which swished shiny Mercedes saloons and the odd open-top sports car, hinting at a rather upmarket resort. In another context the relentlessly developed promenade, Passeig de Pau Casals, would seem overpowering, but the hills, cliffs and rocks that frame it, along with the deep-blue Med and the golden beaches, seem to keep it to some kind of human scale.

Leaning Tetley against a convenient bench with a view of Sa Palomera, and while taking in some gulps of by-now warm water, I contemplated this 'Wild Coast', from Cap de Creus to Blanes, that I'd spent four days traversing.

Twenty years before I'd never set foot here, nor indeed in mainland Spain, taking it to be a relentless line of high-rise hotels in low-class resorts. Well, they're still there – Empuriabrava, Palamós, Platja d'Aro, Lloret – but relentless they ain't. Long stretches, including much of Cap de Creus and the Gulf of Roses, still have barely any development at all, while others retain the small-cove charm that characterised this coast for centuries – if 'charm' is an appropriate word in the context of the daily struggle to survive that dominated the Catalan coast for so long. It's to these villages that the well-to-do of Barcelona and Girona now tend to gravitate, buoying the property market with their demand for second homes and yet ensuring that their favoured hideaways retain an essentially Catalan character. My own, slow journey through the Costa Brava had also shown me that there's a third type of town: one that manages to combine a traditional atmosphere with the seasonal influx of foreign tourists. Into this category I'd put L'Escala, Sant Feliu and Tossa, as well as the Costa Brava's 'last stand', Blanes.

Although I was only passing through and although, like any other Spanish town of this size, it has its ugly suburbs, I could see that Blanes has something about it. Its seafront has happily retained some character, with a number of elegant old mansions still remaining intact, and there was the odd sign of a slight shift upmarket – new benches, a spotless promenade, the occasional trendy boutique and a general impression that the folk of Blanes do care how their home town appears to visitors.

Feeling pretty upbeat, therefore, I pedalled inland and uphill, to cross the Tordera near Blanes's busy little railway station on the N-11 main road. (An 'N' road is the next level up from *comarcal*, the N standing for *nacional*.) Though the narrow river bridge was constructed some time after the invention of bicycles, its designers evidently didn't consider them, for the heavy traffic squashed Tetley and me tightly up against the parapet. Any who follow in our wheeltracks would be well advised to do what we did and turn left immediately after the bridge to take the scenic route into Malgrat.

This is the start of what Miss Macaulay called 'a flatter, duller country'. The scenery in this instance was a vast area of the Tordera flood plain devoted to market gardening and whose smallholdings were full to bursting with potatoes, spring onions, broad beans and lettuces, many of the latter being individually protected by small, white plastic 'hats'. Such a lettuce accessory I'd never seen before – nor since – and whether they protected the produce from sun, snails or something else I couldn't say.

Just as I turned onto the long, straight road that separates Malgrat's hotels from its railway and beach, all neatly parallel, raindrops had begun to patter on my helmet. So when Julie, waiting in the car at our agreed rendezvous point, wound down the window to report that she'd found three hotels with both vacancies and views, we were quick to select the nearest and get ourselves unpacked and inside before the weather deteriorated further.

A few months before, in a queue at East Midlands Airport, I'd got into conversation with a couple who were headed for Malgrat de Mar, this town whose name seems to mean 'Despite the Sea'.

'I've never been there,' I commented. 'What's it like?'

'Oh, we love it, don't we, Arthur?' responded the wife. 'We've been going to Malgrat for two weeks every year for the last twenty-four years.'

'Goodness. What keeps you going back?'

'Oh, it's got everything we need, hasn't it, Arthur?'

Arthur's stance on this, as on every other opinion expressed by his wife, was to remain a mystery, since he simply stood and smiled.

'Do you catch the train down to Barcelona?'

'Oh, we've never been to Barcelona.'

(Catalonia's throbbing metropolis lies less than 60 kilometres away.)

'Not at all? That's unusual. Why not?'

'Oh, there's nothing there we can't get better in Malgrat, is there, Arthur?'

As Julie and I, now washed and scrubbed, descended to the bar of the Hotel Planamar, it was clear that English was the lingua franca and, as far as I could tell, all guests were British, just like all those years ago in Lloret. It was as if, in crossing the threshold of the establishment, we'd stepped out of Catalonia and into a small British enclave left behind on a foreign shore when the Empire had crumbled. After causing something of a stir at the bar by asking to pay for our beers by cash rather than an all-inclusive wristband, we were sitting quietly at a corner table when a short, muscular man wearing a black trilby approached us.

'Romantic weekend, is it?' he asked, with a London accent and a much-practised wink.

'Could be,' I replied, raising an eyebrow.

'Aha! Does the wife know you're 'ere?'

'Or does the old man?' asked Julie, joining in the conspirational theme.

'Ooyer! Message received,' said Trilby. 'Got on the mobile to my old gel and told 'er I'm up north. Well, you jus' gotta get away now an' then, ain't yer?'

Let's hope there were no Spanish voices in the background of his call. Probably not.

Having supped up and stepped back onto a pavement now smelling deliciously fresh after the rain, we found it took a hundred yards or so before we'd re-crossed the invisible frontier into the real Spain, the real Catalonia. A couple of streets back the original, pre-1960s Malgrat was still there, with some elegant, if faded, old buildings, including a magnificent old school whose subjects – *'Religion, Ciencias, Letras, Artes'* – were listed in maroon and sandy ceramics above a shield bearing in its quadrants a lion and castellated tower.

Although we were both pretty peckish, we were not surprised that, at about seven-thirty in the evening, there was no sign of life in either of the two restaurants we came across in Catalan Malgrat. As it was impossible to know whether they were simply waiting for the standard Catalan dinner time of nine o'clock or still closed for the season, our simple aim of having a decent Catalan meal (which, I should stress, we achieve easily and regularly in Llançà) was deferred for yet another day. And so it was that Julie and I found ourselves once more in Little Britain, this time in a shady bar with, set before us, two helpings of sausage and mash and one expat landlord eager to talk.

'Hayatoo binta Mawlgra bifoor?'

'No, we haven't,' I replied, a veteran at deciphering lowland Scots English. 'What brought you here?'

'Oh, I jus' started moving south frae Leith,' explained our host, 'didna fancy Scarborough nor Paris and sorta stopped here.'

'How long ago was that?'

'Ooh, musbe thirrrty years ba' noo.'

So little Malgrat de Mar beats not only Barcelona but Paris too. Mind you, the jolly émigré from Leith had at least made it as far as Barcelona, for he'd worked on the city's 1992 Olympic Stadium, which, he revealed before retiring to the kitchen without further explanation, was actually built 'back tae front'.

And on that bombshell...

... his sausage and mash was pretty sensational too.

Day 6

Irregular Situations: Malgrat de Mar to Barcelona

The next day brought an unexpected new goal, one that should be easily achievable with the destination being Barcelona. After the culinary experiences of Sant Antoni and Malgrat, we simply wanted to eat a Catalan meal in a Catalan restaurant.

Bursting out of the Anglo-Saxon bubble of the Hotel Planamar, Tetley and I set off under blue skies and with renewed energy, looking forward to a spin down the Costa del Maresme, that 60-kilometre stretch of coastline between the River Tordera in the north-east and the River Besòs in the south-west. Although much of El Maresme is visible from Barcelona, I knew little of it, other than its reputation as a Mecca for sunbathers and sailors.

Malgrat de Mar's hotels and apartment blocks soon morphed into Pineda de Mar's, which morphed into Calella's. Up to five storeys between towns, a few more in the urban centres, the blocks rose and fell on my right like a jagged reflection of the low swell on the sea to my left.

While most were rendered in white, some were cream and occasional rogue blocks a kind of butterscotch. Narrower balconies meant hotel rooms, wider meant apartments; open rails older blocks, glass-filled rails newer. Although none plumbed the ugly depths of Palamós, it has to be said that the overall effect was nevertheless a little monotonous. Indeed, a feature of El Maresme is the frequent absence of any clear distinction between one town and the next.

This Calella, not to be confused with the calmer Calella de Palafrugell, had been another popular destination for 1960s package tours, including the school trip which brought Julie to Spain for the very first time. She'd told me about it the previous evening:

'We came through France on the train, sleeping upright in ordinary seats, and, as if that wasn't enough, we had to endure wooden seats in the Spanish train from Portbou to Calella. And when we got here, the town seemed to be one giant building site. Even now, whenever I smell wet plaster, it takes me straight back to Calella.'

Well, at least the seafront buildings I crunched past on the sandy Passeig Marítim seemed to be finished now, albeit in need of some replastering in many cases.

As the N-11 leaves Calella, it is squeezed up against the shore by a small range of low hills. Peering into the jumble of pine trees that cover these slopes I tried to pick out a pair of ruined stone towers. They were built in the mid nineteenth century and formed part of a long-distance communication network that, until I read about it just before this ride, I hadn't even known existed.

Before the advent of the electric telegraph another form of telegraph had for several decades been proving much faster than the fastest horse rider for carrying simple messages. Technically named the 'optical telegraph', it was what we'd more readily call semaphore. A series of hilltop towers conveyed urgent messages via various forms of mechanical blades or shutters in recognised configurations – often of a military nature – over enormous distances. Napoleonic France had been the driving force behind this, but the Spanish state later adopted its own system too. With the obvious disadvantage of a certain lack of privacy, such semaphore lines were never going to last for long and the two towers just outside Calella were among the last to be built.

Although I failed to spot them from the main road, I've subsequently discovered that a better route out of town for the 'semaphore spotter' would be up Carrer Mestral, left on Torrent de Vall d'en Guli and left again on Carrer de Llevant.

After nearly two hours of fairly anonymous resorts, I was relieved to pull into what looked like a proper town: Canet de Mar. I'd pencilled it in as a place to investigate.

Central to the rise and rise of Barcelona as a late twentieth-century holiday destination has been its reputation as a town awash with the luscious, art nouveau architecture from Catalonia's modernist movement of a century before. Many visitors could be forgiven for thinking that the movement started and ended with Antoní Gaudí, he of the fantastical Sagrada Família cathedral and whirly ceramics at Parc Güell. A number of his contemporaries, however, were admired as much – or even more. One of these was Lluís Domènech i Montaner, whose achievements in Barcelona alone include the elegant Hospital de Sant Pau, the ornate Palau de la Música Catalana and, for the city's 1888 Universal Exposition, the extraordinary Castell dels Tres Dragons (now the Museu de Zoologia). While these buildings include plenty of fabulous ornamentation, their designer never reached the indulgent excesses of Gaudí; his creations, mixing slender Arabic columns with the seductive curves of the modernists, all have a certain lightness about them, despite their often vast dimensions. Domènech i Montaner was born here up the coast in Canet de Mar and it was to see some of his more modest creations that I turned off at this neat little seaside town.

First, however, in case the architect's name seems a little odd, a short explanation of Spanish surnames may help.

Domènech i Montaner is his surname – or surnames. As in the rest of Spain and much of Latin America, Catalans have two surnames: their father's followed by their mother's. In Catalonia they add 'i' ('and') between them. So, for example, the full name of the Catalan footballer Cesc Fàbregas is Francesc Fàbregas i Soler; and the famous Catalan opera singer is, in full, Montserrat Concepción Bibiana Caballé i Folch. Among non-Catalan Spaniards more often known by their first surnames only are Formula One world champion Fernando Alonso Díaz, film director Pedro Almodóvar Caballero and actress Penélope Cruz Sánchez. Both the inherited names are the respective parents' father's first surname, which means (unless

I've lost the plot) that all surnames are ultimately passed through the male line.

All of this makes form-filling for foreigners a creative art of its own. I've received official letters variously addressed to me with my mother's surname or with my own middle name as a surname. We can all work out these Hispanic versions of our own names. My favourites, though, are the letters I've received in Spain addressed to Don Ricardo Guise. Don (together with its feminine equivalent Doña) is a courtesy title used as a prefix, rather like 'Esquire' or 'Esq.' as a suffix in English. If ever I'm signed up as the romantic lead in a Hollywood musical (although, to be frank, time is running out), I think the name to go up in lights had better be 'Don Ricardo'.

Leaving the busy coast road and the rattling railway that had run alongside the beach all the way from Malgrat, I was soon on the calm of Canet's Riera Gavarra, a semi-pedestrianised street of small shops and cafes. And there, immediately on my right was a classic Domènech i Montaner creation: a pink-brick, two-storey, corner building, whose curved balcony, with its jet-black railing, seemed to thrust the extraordinary, blue-topped conical tower that dominates the structure right up to the morning sky for approval. Originally a home, now a restaurant, this was Casa Roura, built in 1892. Just a few metres further up the street, looking back downhill to the sea, was another: a three-storey building of delicate columns beneath an ornate, overhanging roof and whose two-toned exterior reminded me of a creamy cappuccino topped with dark chocolate. This was the architect's own workshop of 1920, with his own home in an older house at the back.

Nowadays it's a museum dedicated to his work – alas closed at the time of my visit.

Domènech i Montaner was not only a leading modernist architect, but also one of the driving forces behind the Catalan nationalism of his day. His architectural style is more to some people's taste, including mine, than the gaudy efforts of Gaudí. His buildings fit more easily into their environment, their fine lines and colours make their structure so much lighter and they tend to possess a feature that buildings should abandon only with good reason: they are – more or less – symmetrical!

On the terrace of a street cafe, making notes in my old, dog-eared grammar school exercise book, I felt a presence at my shoulder.

'*¡Qué escritura!*' (What writing!) said the presence, who moved round to reveal himself as an elderly street sweeper taking a two-minute break.

'Well, thank you,' I said in some surprise, since my handwriting, neat as it may have been when I was issued with the book more than forty years before, had long since degenerated into a ropey scrawl.

'No,' he explained, 'I mean it's good to see a young man writing in a book nowadays, instead of tapping away at a screen.'

Easily warming to anyone who saw me as a young man, I said: 'You don't like computers then?'

'Bah! They are just games, aren't they? My boss he plays games all day at his desk while I work here in the heat to pay his wages. Look at my skin. At my hands. *El jefe*, he has the hands of a baby.'

'And the brain?' I ventured.

At this, the disgruntled sweeper roared loudly and waved his besom in the air. Treating me to a broad, mischievous grin that took a whole generation off his weather-beaten face, he replied: 'Ha! I must continue my day's work before we start the revolution, you and me, señor. *¡Buena escritura!*'

Having paid up for my coffee and *magdalena* cake and checked my map, I pulled out of Canet de Mar. Offering a sharp contrast to the ins and outs of the Costa Brava, El Maresme's coastline appeared long and smooth on the map I kept propped on my handlebars, and featured four almost parallel lines snaking the 60 kilometres or so all the way to the outskirts of Barcelona: the thick blue *autopista* up in the hills, the red main road, the black railway and finally the thin blue line of the shore itself. However, my assumption that this would be a day free from navigational decisions was soon proven false.

Catalans are in general extremely efficient in the signage department – even informative to excess, you might say. In Llançà, for example, fingerposts had recently been sprouting faster than runner beans, giving detailed directions and distances for walkers, cyclists and drivers to every conceivable destination. Official mapboards, too, had suddenly sprung up, locating every imaginable feature – including all the other mapboards. Along the Costa del Maresme, however, information for cyclists was a rarity – and, where present, as likely to misinform as to inform. In Calella, a signposted cycle track had led literally into a brick wall, forcing me to negotiate a maze of ramps and tunnels before braving the N-11 as the only way south. In Canet de

Mar, exactly the same type of sign had indeed successfully led me to the next town. In Arenys de Mar, the little bicycle symbol led me into what the regimented French call a *situation irrégulière*...

The route south from Arenys began well enough with the wide Passeig Marítim doubling up as footpath and cycle path. This started to narrow, however, then to lose its surface and finally to sink into the beach where the railway line prevented access to the rest of the world. A low headland lay not far off and, rather than retrace my pedalling, I chose to push Tetley optimistically through the sand. The morning had warmed up, the sand was deep and soft and I was sweating profusely as I trudged past sunbathers of both sexes wearing progressively less and less as I struggled south. Just short of the headland, a low cliff in the sand presented a small obstacle and, as I scratched my head, weighing up the risk of having to lift Tetley back up the same cliff, a nearby sun worshipper caught my eye. I caught his, then his bare stomach and then his very bare nether regions. As Testicle Tomás gestured 'Can I help you?' (at least I hope that's what he gestured), I quickly gestured 'Ah, thanks all the same, mate, but I think I'll go back'. The last thing Tetley needed was an alien member caught in his spokes.

And so it was back past the rows of shiny brown bosoms that I hotly meandered, to the safety of a shady spot where I could recover my composure and consider the situation. The shade was provided by the entrance to a large drain under the railway. I considered the drain, considered the kilometre or so back along the beach and then considered the drain again. There was light at the other end and I reckoned it was just high enough for me to push Tetley through at a crouch.

A few sun-worshipping heads turned as I disappeared down the hole. The trickle of water turned into a definite stream and the light whiff into a definite pong, but through the sewer of stink squelched the staunch cyclist.

For staunch read stupid. For the light at the other end of the tunnel came from a roundabout comprising, in its centre, a rain run-off area leading to a wide, low-angled concrete sump, at the bottom of which a by-now bedraggled cyclist stood in damp shoes, his eyes blinking at the row of hub caps in front of them, hubcaps which periodically moved along as the traffic lights changed. Trying a sheepish smile at the drivers, I received in return only unbelieving stares.

Well, it was either drain, boobs and sand again or an ungainly scramble to safety. Scramble it would have to be. Although the height of the concrete slope was only about a metre and a half, propelling both Tetley and myself out of the sump of no return proved a scramble too far and it was with grazed shin and bruised pride that I settled once again at the bottom. However, with relief I'm able to report that my frazzled brain finally cranked into gear and set me the task of untying all Tetley's bits and pieces – bag, bottle, map and so on – placing them carefully beside my helmet at the edge of the inside lane of traffic (accompanied by a confident 'thumbs up' to the now fascinated motorists), pushing the lighter bicycle up to lean against the crash barrier and finally climbing up beside it.

Two among the latest line of drivers actually applauded me as I dusted myself down and reassembled the equipment before wheeling Tetley, head and handlebars held high, to the far side of the road, where I mounted and pedalled off, hoping I looked more than a little like James Bond after another successful mission. A vain hope.

Through Caldes d'Estrac I stuck to the busy but safe N-11, which ran inland on a raised section alongside the shiny dome of a church and the third-floor balconies of several unfortunate old villas. Rounding a corner as the road skirted a headland, I squinted into the hazy sunshine at a new view ahead, past the cluster of buildings that must be Mataró, as far as the outline of what looked like a grey whale bursting through the blue sea, but which I knew in fact to be Montjuïc, the site of Barcelona's Olympic Stadium.

Mataró is yet another old Roman settlement, the birthplace of yet another modernist architect – Josep Puig i Cadafalch, designer of yet more of Barcelona's crowd-pulling decorative buildings – and yet another town surrounded by extensive areas of market gardening. I have to admit that, soon after passing through most of these towns on the Costa del Maresme, they began to merge in my memory into a single amorphous mass. One attribute does, however, make Mataró stand out: with over 120,000 inhabitants, it's easily the biggest town on the Catalan coast north of Barcelona. Two factors contributing to its growth are its role as the administrative centre of the county of El Maresme and its location at the northern terminus of many cross-Barcelona commuter trains.

That spring morning, as I whizzed along its Passeig Marítim, Mataró came as a welcome relief from the samey suburban sprawl of Marseme: a city bustling with businessmen and skateboarders, shoppers and joggers and beach volleyball players. As I travel around, I can't stop images of places visited years ago floating unbidden into my mind's eye, sometimes not even remembering where they were. Mataró's seafront immediately conjured up similar images of Californian coasts populated by earnest young people in sunglasses indulging in miscellaneous healthy activities. One difference, perhaps significant, was that here in Catalonia, the volleyball players were all laughing. Not quite so earnest, the Catalans.

At Vilassar de Mar, the atmosphere changed yet again. In the absence of any cycle path signs, I followed the sign of a walking man – or rather, a strangely mincing man – as far as a quiet little beach with a selection of old sailing boats to lean against. Which is exactly what I did, unwrapping a packed lunch that I'd assembled in Canet, giving my pedal-weary feet a spell in the sand and generally chilling out. This part of Vilassar's beach, beyond the reach of the waves and therefore comprising as much weed as sand, was today quite deserted. Whether this collection of *llauts*, the traditional, curved Catalan fishing craft, was still seaworthy or beyond use and simply left there for their picturesque contribution to the scene, I couldn't say. The hull of the one I'd chosen was of dark-blue and white, its peeling paint fluttering into the sand as I rubbed my hand against its bows.

I was now into territory I'd occasionally visited, when work had brought me to Catalonia many years before and my boss lived out here in the hills at Vilassar. Wriggling my toes in the cool sands, I recalled, as many of us of a certain age must do, those endless days trapped in an office, shuffling papers about goodness knows what, worrying about goodness knows what else... what on earth was it all about? Though I let the sunlight warm my closed eyelids, I came up with no answer – other than work being a means of paying my way to this sandy spot on a sunny spring afternoon.

Acknowledging my good luck with both the weather and my safe progress – and not forgetting the continuing watchful eye of Spokey the Cycling God – I eventually gathered up my bits and pieces from Vilassar Beach to resume the ride south, now with Barcelona's Montjuïc firmly in my sights. Apparently at the point where Montjuïc plunged to the sea (but actually at the Port Olímpic), a speck of gold sparkled in the afternoon sun, a speck that I knew would grow little by little into the queer but familiar shape of a matador's hat... or half a carafe... or, well, even though they say that Frank Gehry's sculpture is supposed to be a fish, personally I'm still not convinced. Where's its head?

Two other large shapes on the horizon were not familiar. A little to the left of the fish/hat/carafe stood what appeared to be a wonky table for giants, leaning at an angle that would see all the giants' food sliding into the Mediterranean. And some way to the right, amid a rash of new tower blocks, a giant's oil can poked into the sky, its dispensing tube by far the tallest object on the horizon.

I'd slid into Premià de Mar, where the parallel threads of beach, railway and main road squeezed ever more tightly together. With the N-11's heavy traffic belching out more fumes than ever, I decided to dip inland for a break both from the pollution and from the strengthening afternoon sun. As with Malgrat and most other settlements on El Maresme's coastal strip, the normal, dignified Catalan town lies just one block back from the hectic commerce of the seafront. I'd turned off on Carrer de la Carretera ('Road Street') and soon found myself among neat old houses, dated 1823, 1803, 17... well, that plaque's last two digits had worn away. All houses and villas looked rather well-to-do and many boasted imposing doorways, 3 metres or more high and with an unusual offset inner door.

All shops were closed for siesta, but in one small square a waiter carried drinks out to a few tables set beneath an old eucalyptus, where two or three couples were finishing their lunch. Here I leaned Tetley against the tree and, as a treat, downed a real beer – a local Estrella in fact – and picked up the bar's copy of *La Vanguardia*, a leading daily paper.

'Constitutional committee rejects statute'

Turn page.

'Cork industry decline overstated'

Turn.

'Generalitat to reconsider retirement policy'

Turn. Whatever happened to:

'Sex-change mayor in donkey scandal'?

Although these headlines are made up, the point is true enough: Catalan newspapers really are dire: tedious stories, bland prose and photographs so excruciatingly dull you wonder why the papers employ photographers at all. Here's a man behind a desk; here's a group of politicians in suits; here's a group of businessmen in suits who look just like the politicians but have been forced to smile. You may argue that my view is coloured by the poor standard of my Spanish and Catalan, but occasional English translations are just as grim. You may argue that *La Vanguardia* is an exception, but its competitors *El Periódico de Catalunya* and *Avui* are equally doze-inducing. Even stories with genuine news value seem to have had their points of interest systematically removed before publication:

'World to end Thursday. Inaugural meeting of Local Action Committee set for Wednesday afternoon.'

With the combination of good Catalan beer and poor Catalan newspapers beginning to weigh on my eyelids, I briskly paid up, remounted and resumed the haul south.

Still humming resolutely alongside me were the frequent passenger trains between Mataró and Barcelona. Whether humming, chugging or puffing, they'd been doing it for over 160 years, as this was the first railway line in the whole Iberian Peninsula, opened in 1848. There are a number of stories as to why they chose as its gauge six Castilian feet (1,672 millimetres, later adjusted to 1,668 millimetres), i.e. broader than 'standard' – to cope with Spain's mountainous interior, to obstruct a French invasion, to be consistent with Brunel's broad gauge – but, whatever the cause, the effect of the decision for this short line was to have millions of passengers alighting at frontier stations to this very day.

At Badalona, while the railway heads straight across the River Besòs where it flows into the Mediterranean, all road traffic, including cyclists, has to head inland. Passing through in the 1840s, Richard Ford found the coast hereabouts to be 'charming, dotted about with pines and sweet groves tenanted by nightingales, and filled with fruit and corn, with the sweet blue sea gladdening the eye and tempering the summer heats'. The Badalona of today certainly presented a stark contrast, as I was buffeted by 40-tonne trucks thundering through mile after mile of industrial suburbs.

Were a nightingale around, he'd have been hard-pressed to have his song heard even by a mate on the next branch.

The only other time I'd visited Badalona was to act out the final scene in the long, labyrinthine – and actually true – tale of my attempt to get a British Toyota Corolla registered in Spain. The plot's unlikely twists and turns, including among its hours of form-filling an unexpected stint of brass-rubbing, is too exhausting to recount here, but the final nail in the bureaucratic coffin was hammered at Badalona's ITV (MOT) garage, where a vigilant official eventually noticed that the steering wheel of a British vehicle is to be found on the opposite side of the car to that of a Spanish vehicle. He gave me the bad news:

'Es imposible, señor.'

'So what can I do?' I asked.

After much scratching of the head: 'You could move the steering wheel to the other side of your car, señor.'

'And you could move the brain to the other side of your head, Pedro,' I thought, but restricted myself to:

'Ah, I think not. Good day.'

Being already £650 poorer for the attempt, I'd felt I was being impressively restrained. Sutty the Corolla was eventually driven unregistered, untaxed and uninsured across Spain to Bilbao, where I sneaked him onto a ferry bound for Portsmouth – and eventual legality.

It was getting late, and the afternoon beer had sunk to my legs as I finally crossed the River Besòs into the sprawling metropolis of Barcelona, home to over three million of Catalonia's seven and a half million residents and an even greater proportion of its jobs.

Arriving here from England near the beginning of the Industrial Revolution, Richard Ford, having already characterised Catalonia as 'the Lancashire of the Peninsula', identified Barcelona as 'the Manchester of Catalonia'. As the city is still often seen as 'the powerhouse of Spain', Mancunians may nowadays be the more flattered by a description of their town as 'the Barcelona of Lancashire'.

The north-eastern access point I'd used puts you in the district of El Poblenou, not an area I was familiar with. While the giant's oil can had resolved into the three chimneys of the Besòs power station, the giant's wonky table turned out to be an enormous set of solar panels angled towards the sun at the heart of a new development apparently built for, well, giants. It was quite ghastly. Even modern architects can occasionally display some style, as in Barcelona's dramatic Port Vell complex or the Torre Agbar, a gherkin lookalike at Plaça de les Glòries Catalanes, but El Poblenou is just massive anonymous block after massive anonymous block and could be anywhere from Los Angeles to Shanghai.

At the Port Olímpic, I was on more familiar ground. When I first arrived in Barcelona, about six months before the Olympic Games in 1992, the whole of the old port area was one giant building site. For those six months I hardly saw the sea from the city, but it turns out that this wasn't unusual. For much of the twentieth century Barcelona seemed to have almost forgotten its maritime past, the old port being largely a jumble of cranes and warehouses where no one who didn't work there would ever have ventured.

The impetus of the Olympics changed all that. One of the last zones to emerge from the building sites was the Port Olímpic itself, an area of trendy bars and restaurants set around a new marina and right next to the newly (or, as I understood it, barely) completed Olympic Village, home to the competitors. During the games fortnight it was off limits to hoi polloi and we could only peer over the barriers in the hope of glimpsing Carl Lewis or Linford Christie.

Emerging just before this, I remember, was the next area I now pedalled through, Port Vell ('Old Port'), where a swanky new promenade had been built in place of old warehousing and railway sidings, giving citizens and visitors a brand new quayside at which glitzy yachts were berthed for the duration of the games. At the southern end of this stands the ornate Port of Barcelona building and here I swung to a brief halt to watch the new pedestrian bridge swing open to let a shiny black, two-masted vessel glide through. It's seaward of here that, since the Olympics, another vast development of bars, shops and cinemas has risen up, right in the middle of the old harbour. Today's Barcelona, far from turning its back on the port, seems to be diving head first into it.

Pointing out to sea over 80 metres above my head stood the statue of a man who'd sailed into this very port over five hundred years before with news for his sponsor Queen Isabella of new lands found beyond the Atlantic and claimed for Spain on her behalf. The Genoese explorer we call Christopher Columbus is known in Catalonia as Cristòfol Colom. This monument, then, is the Column of Colom. Unfortunately, if he's supposed to be indicating America, he's pointing the wrong way.

A glance at my watch told me I needed to get a move on to make a date with Julie and Dave the Kangoo. After a day more or less on the level, my last fifteen minutes would be uphill: first up the busy Rambles (Catalan plural of Rambla – 'boulevard'), across Plaça Catalunya – appropriately the heart of the city – and then up the elegant shopping street of Passeig de Gràcia, across Avinguda Diagonal and into a small square where sits the Hotel Via Augusta. As if the gradient wasn't enough, the regular clanking down and up of gears at traffic lights had left me breathless.

'Getting too old for this?' asked Julie as she skipped down the steps, fresh as a daisy.

'Forty miles or so is quite a whack.'

'Plus the odd beer?'

How could she tell?

We'd chosen the Via Augusta for a two-night stay because of its quiet location ('quiet' is a relative term in Barcelona) and its access to a nearby car park (a perennial issue here).

With Tetley stored away and the day's dust and sand blasted off me in the powerful shower, we were soon out in the street again. Wherever I've come from, I still find it takes a few minutes to adjust to the buzz of Barcelona. Business people scuttling along, late for appointments, tourists stepping backwards as they gape up at the facades, shoppers swinging their oversized bags as they walk: all swirling around on the same pavements, but managing to miss each other by inches. Black and yellow taxis, battered old Renaults, shiny silent limousines and noisily whining mopeds: all engaged in an incessant mechanical dance that looks manic to the newcomer but in which each participant knows his moves by heart. The din inhibits conversation, but we were soon down into the relative peace of the underground railway – not the Metro in this part of town, but the FGC, the Ferrocarrils de la Generalitat de Catalunya – where ace organiser Julie revealed that she had booked us in at a classic Catalan restaurant, Els Quatre Gats ('The Four Cats'), which nowadays markets itself as simply '4Gats'.

This homely looking restaurant on Carrer Montsió, not far from Plaça Catalunya, forms the ground floor of Casa Martí, a striking building designed in 1896 by Puig i Cadafalch of Mataró. In fact, as a turn-of-the-century tavern, Els Quatre Gats was a local meeting place – THE local meeting place, some would say – for many of the modernist artists and architects of the time, including Rusiñol, Utrillo and Picasso, who put on an early one-man exhibition here. The most prominent painting in the bar is a copy of an 1897 work by Ramón Casas, the bar's original financier, showing himself and Pere Romeu, its original host, struggling along on a tandem. (Incidentally, Casas's full surname was Casas i Carbó and he was therefore Mr Houses and Coal.)

It was to seats under this painting that we were shown, to await our table, by a short, slim waitress of about twenty, with large, heavy-rimmed spectacles and a nervous air. This female version of Woody Allen was probably on her first ever shift and took our drinks order with some confusion, only to run into immediate trouble with a senior waiter on the grounds that customers awaiting tables were not to be offered drinks. However, remembering that the customer is always right, Woody still got hold of our two aperitifs and managed to sneak them round to our table at a sort of crouch and then, still crouching, to complete an improvised circle back to the restaurant as though she were not really serving customers at all.

A few minutes later, with a conspiratorial gesture, Woody beckoned us into the dining room and, with two rather over-firm pushes of the chairs, installed us at a table.

'Wait here,' she hissed, as though we might do something else, and scurried off to cause fresh mayhem elsewhere. Having waited until she was out of sight, we pushed our chairs back in order to breathe again, just as a calmer waiter brought our menus.

With its tasteful ceramic decorations, its scurrying waiters and lazy jazz pianist, Els Quatre Gats is a fine place to eat and it's not surprising that all tables were either full or being filled. Julie chose Catalan salad, *chuletas de cerdo* (thin slices of pork you can almost see through) and *tarta de manzana* (cold apple tart) with vanilla ice cream. I chose green salad, which usually includes succulent Catalan olives, veal steak *carbonizado para un inglés* ('burnt for an Englishman', which usually gets it on the plate in an edible form) and *crema Catalana*, a local version of crème brûlée.

For me this was quite adventurous as, where food is concerned – and unlike Julie – I don't venture too far from the known and trusted. Anything that goes in my mouth has to pass a stringent familiarity test. In Costa Rica I ate nothing but tortilla, pizza and fruit; in Cuba nothing but rice, beans and fruit. When I lived in France, I pretended to be vegetarian for the first year until my French was good enough to persuade them to cook their meat properly – a simple task they'd somehow failed to achieve over the previous three thousand years, and still do. In China I almost starved. In Japan I undoubtedly would. Between you and me, I'd quite happily eat beans on toast and Cheddar cheese sandwiches for every meal until the day I die. It's the venue and company that matters.

Shortly after our orders were placed and menus taken away, Woody appeared from nowhere and placed menus in front of us.

'I'm sorry,' said Julie. 'We've just ordered.'

'Oh,' she whispered. 'Who from, señora?'

'From your colleague over there.'

'Hmm. Ah.'

And with that she slunk away once more. Throughout the meal, we watched her big, black spectacles dashing between tables and in and out of doors on a most earnest but apparently random mission. She never returned to us and we were never charged for our aperitifs, but I hope Woody kept her job. Whatever it was.

What puts the 'Catalan' in Catalan salad is a miscellany of cooked meats – mostly sausages of various kinds – and Julie declared hers excellent, if a little on the large side. With the exception of a green salad, most salad dishes in Catalonia are substantial enough to form a main course – and often priced accordingly. Newcomers should be aware as well that salad dressing is virtually unknown here and you're expected to help yourself to the olive oil, wine vinegar, salt and pepper that are usually already on the table. Although it was clear from the waiter's raised eyebrow that my 'burnt' steak did not meet with his approval, it did pass my stringent 'no blood' and 'little fat' tests and was delicious: why can't English restaurants cut their steaks this thin? Had he hung around, the waiter would have been even more appalled when I pulled out of my pocket one of the malt vinegar sachets from England that I carry around for use on chips. Though their chips are fine, Catalonia's wine vinegar just doesn't work on them. To give the locals something to think about, I always leave the empty sachet on the plate.

As we ate, Julie reminded me that, during the 1977 trip to Lloret in the company of her 'film star' friend Jude, they'd had a day out in Barcelona too.

'Did you all come down?'

'No, just the two of us – plus a bunch of English oddballs that filled the coach. Unfortunately.'

'Unfortunately?'

'Well, on the way back I remember that everyone was jabbering about what they'd done in Barcelona. We'd tried to take in the cultural highlights, of course – the Sagrada Família, a few other Gaudí bits and pieces and so on – but behind us were the Terylene Twins.'

'Not the Terrible Twins?'

'They were that too. Two brothers in their early twenties who wore matching Terylene jumpers and trousers – you know, the sort of clothes that used to generate static electricity. Turns out they had matching tastes in women too. They'd spent all day in the red light district...'

'Barri Xino?'

'I think so. And through the whole journey up to Lloret we had to listen to their grubby little exploits. Yerrgh! Makes me shudder just to think about it.'

'Were their electric trousers all charged up?'

'Stop it!'

'And anyway, how did you know they had odd balls?'

'Shut up!'

Outside, the evening was still warm and we decided to walk back to the hotel, rather than take the Metro or a taxi. In fact, armed with an address I'd recently tracked down on the web, I'd already suggested a short diversion. And so we found ourselves standing outside Number 70, Carrer de Muntaner.

It was here on St Valentine's Day, 1912, that Joan Pujol García was born. He quite possibly saved my father's life.

In his twenties, Pujol was forced to fight on the Nationalist side in the civil war, but in 1941, being fervently anti-Franco and anti-Nazi, he volunteered his services as a spy to the British Consulate in Madrid. He was refused. This led to a more audacious plan: after a few lies and half truths, Pujol was accepted as a spy by the Germans and codenamed 'Arabel'. His reports, allegedly from England to Berlin via Portugal, were intercepted by MI5, although Pujol was in fact in Lisbon. It gets even more complicated. Now with some credibility, he hoped, he presented himself once again to the British in Madrid. Refused again. Eventually, in 1942 and with the help of his wife and the US Embassy in Lisbon, Pujol was accepted by the British as a double agent.

In the meantime my father, Corporal Ronald Guise, had been recruited by the British Army's Intelligence Office (he always maintained that he'd mistaken a door bearing the initials IO for room number 10 and had attended the interview by mistake) and joined the planning staff of 185 Brigade HQ, specialising in mapwork during secret preparations in Scotland for the eventual Allied invasion of Continental Europe.

It was in April 1942 that Pujol was eventually taken to London, where he was codenamed 'Garbo' (a reference to his acting abilities), and work began on a vast and intricate operation, involving twenty-seven fictional German agents under the control of 'Arabel' and over 500 fictional, coded wireless messages from London to Madrid and thence to Berlin. Among the various fabricated stories supplied by the 'Garbo Network' was the crucial one that the Allies' chosen location for their cross-Channel assault was the Pas de

Calais. This, therefore, was where the Germans built their main defences.

On the morning of 6 June 1944, D-Day, my father landed on Sword Beach in Normandy, tasked with the distribution of identifying armbands to the Resistance before the bulk of the invasion force landed. Thanks partly to Joan Pujol García, neither he nor the other 175,000 troops who landed that day were expected. Corporal Guise's diary entry for the day reads:

> 'Sea rough. Fair crossing. Glad to be ashore. First stop Hermanville.'

My father survived the war, which is why I'm here.

In 1985, having belatedly received his MBE in London, Pujol eventually visited Normandy and was brought to tears by the number of war graves, explaining that, although he'd been told he'd helped to save thousands of lives, he should have done more. He died in 1988.

Having learnt of Joan Pujol García's existence only recently, from a display at the Bletchley Park Museum in England, I'd never been to his birthplace before. It's now a rather uninspiring postwar apartment block, although the older block next door is a reminder of the gentler world he was born into. There is no plaque. We just stood for a while in silence.

Day 7

Old Friends: Barcelona to El Prat de Llobregat

It's a fine feeling to wake up in one of the world's great cities. Even though I lived here for three years, I still feel the energy of the place oozing in through my pores and know that anything can crop up as soon as you step into the street. Not that visiting Barcelona is quite the same experience as living there. Around the time of this ride, Barcelona was the twelfth most visited city in the world, way ahead of Madrid, which was twenty-sixth. A massive boost to the city's profile had been given by the 1992 Olympic Games and it was in the three years following this that I found my own Barcelona address a big draw for friends.

After a year in the suburbs I moved into a tiny, dark, third-floor apartment on the borders of the Gràcia and Sant Gervasi neighbourhoods of the city. Rental prices were high and among the compromises were a balcony so small it would take only a single, three-legged stool, a street so narrow that I could easily watch TV in the flat across the road and a lack of air conditioning that on midsummer afternoons would turn the living room into Dante's Inferno.

Fortunately most of my days were spent in the air-conditioned luxury of the factory where I worked. Driving home around six or seven always presented the same challenge: the spiralling tour to find an on-street parking space. It was quite early in my stay that I was first alarmed to see an empty car slowly moving along the street. Or rather being moved. If you spotted a space that wasn't quite big enough, but would be if you added in the next space along, then you'd proceed to merge those two spaces by the Spanish Shunt – a slow, to-and-fro movement of bumper on bumper – until the space magically fitted the length of your vehicle. This rapidly taught me two things: 1) To minimise the damage to your own car, leave it parked with the handbrake off and 2) Get an old car. Stashing my precious British Corolla in the factory car park, I bought a pre-dented old Renault specially for driving and parking in Barcelona.

When you're on holiday – at least when you're young – late nights tend to be part of the deal. But when you have to be up and commuting by seven-thirty, getting a good night's sleep is crucial. Getting a good night's sleep in Gràcia was sometimes out of the question. First there was the ordinary traffic: horns, engine revs and radios echo very effectively in narrow, canyon-like streets. Then there were the tradesmen, doing business late into the evening and each with his trademark sound: the metal-clanking of the knife-sharpener, the van horn of the bottled gas man, the indecipherable calls of countless other trades.

And then, of course there were the neighbours: eating, drinking, gossiping and – loudest of all – watching endless TV soaps until the early hours. Did none of them work? Add to these noises the cacophony generated by the frequent – and, to a foreigner, quite unpredictable – fiestas and, in retrospect, I have to wonder why I lived there at all. I expect the question may have crossed your mind too.

Well, one of the biggest attractions was that on days off I was never short of new things to do: top-class football matches, museums, art galleries – all the stuff you expect from a major city. But Barcelona has more: a string of beaches actually in the city, boat trips to float you past the latest cruise ships, an impressive upland (Montjuïc) from which to survey the whole town, another (Collserola) in which, occasionally, to hide from it... and for me in particular, I could indulge two of my own favourite pastimes. The first seems to be a specialisation among certain middle-aged English males. Trains, trams and buses – slow, fast, old, new, steep, bendy – this city has them all, just waiting to be ogled, snapped and experienced. The second is more universal: on a warm summer's evening, what more relaxing way to pass a few idle hours could there be than to sit on the terrace of a street cafe, wine glass to hand and the free entertainment of Barcelona street life before you?

All I can say is that I enjoyed far more than I endured of my time in Barcelona and would recommend the city to anyone under fifty with an inquisitive mind and a positive bank balance. Now that I fail the age qualification, a double-glazed and air-conditioned hotel room seems a slightly better overnight option. At the Via Augusta we both slept well.

'You came to Barcelona even before the trip with the Terylene Twins, didn't you?' I asked Julie over the standard city hotel breakfast of croissant, bread and jam.

'Yes. On another day out, this time from Calella on that sixties school trip.'

'Where did they take you?'

'Well, it's not the sort of thing you'd expect on a school trip today – we went to a bullfight.'

'Blimey, you'd have the PC brigade up in arms nowadays! How old were you?'

'Seventeen.'

'Were you shocked?'

'Not at all. In fact, it was all much quicker than I'd expected. I remember we were in the cheaper seats and had to wear improvised paper hats to keep from baking in the sun. After the bull came out there was a bit of taunting and a lot of posturing and then the matador came in for the kill. I was expecting a long, drawn-out affair, but it seemed to be over in seconds.'

'Doesn't sound very good value for money.'

'Oh, there were half a dozen bulls, one after the other.'

'Which bullring was it?'

'It was on Plaça d'Espanya, I think. Is there another one?'

'I've been to the Monumental on Gran Via.'

'So were you shocked?'

'Well, the bagpipes were a bit gruesome, I suppose.'

'Bagpipes at a bullfight?'

'It was a concert. *Tubular Bells*. Mike Oldfield.'

In July 2010 the Catalan parliament voted to ban bullfighting in Catalonia from 2012. There'd been broad opposition here for some time, ostensibly on the grounds of animal welfare but also because it represents the rather pompous posturing of Castilian culture, embracing not only bullfighting but flamenco too, and from which many Catalans try to distance themselves. You see it on car stickers: while the symbol of Spain is a bull, the symbol of Catalonia is a donkey. Donkey fighting? I don't think so.

After nearly a week on the road, we'd both got a relatively free and easy day ahead, simply agreeing what time to be back at the hotel for an excursion to meet some old friends. While Julie flicked through some leaflets in reception, I mounted up again with two targets in mind. First, though, I pedalled – or rather freewheeled – pretty randomly down through the Eixample towards the warren of streets and alleyways that form the Barri Gòtic ('Gothic District').

The majority of Barcelona's millions are squashed into a remarkably small rectangle of about seven kilometres by five. Its boundaries are the River Besòs, the sea, the dramatic outcrop of Montjuïc and the Collserola hills. The slope of the coastal plain to the sea is very regular hereabouts, a fact worth remembering when wandering around the Eixample district, the city's vast and elegant – but rather monotonous – grid of nineteenth-century blocks. Especially late at night after too much wine. In such circumstances, the simple rules 'Downhill street = towards the sea, uphill street = towards the hills, level street = neither' can get you home hours earlier. Believe me.

The Barri Gòtic couldn't offer a greater contrast. This is one of the four districts of the old town, where the city grew up over a period of 1,800 years, from the Roman town of Barcino, whose foundations can still be seen *in situ* in the Plaça del Rei, through all the phases of Catalan history until the nineteenth century, when the Eixample was first developed.

When I first moved to Barcelona, it was around these streets, and those of the neighbouring district of La Ribera ('the Shore') that I most enjoyed strolling, simply taking in the sights, sounds and smells of what to me felt a very foreign city. (It turns out that what many recognise as 'the smell of Barcelona', and which I always notice on first emerging from the underground onto the city streets, is from the drains.) Pleasanter smells come from the endless bar-restaurants of the Barri Gòtic, most tiny but some much bigger, including not only Els Quatre Gats but also another favourite, Los Caracoles ('The Snails') on Carrer d'Escudellers, whose outdoor spit-roast apparently used to be a favoured spot for prostitutes from across La Rambla to warm themselves up on wintry nights.

Laundry, bird cages and bicycles dangle from the dark walls and iron railings of the Barri Gòtic's narrow balconies. Residents too lean out to chat with those opposite or to pull up the shopping on a well-used rope. Lifts are a rarity around here and the stone-stepped staircases frequently narrow, sharply curved and up to six storeys high. Often enough a small removals van can take up the entire width of a street as it winches furniture up or down, or even makes use of an angled hoist, a little like an external escalator, to reunite owner and chattels.

Every time I return to the Barri Gòtic, I recall two incidents in particular from my time as a resident. One was in my very first free weekend in town.

Calling at a bar in one of these back alleys, my Californian work colleague Ken and I had settled at a table next to a small group of locals who were just ordering their own drinks.

'Beer, Ken?' I asked.

'Sure,' he replied. 'How's your Spanish?'

'Barely exists. What about yours?'

'Nope. Catalan?'

'Zilch. Mind you, those beers look like the ones we want, right? And I know what they're called 'cause I just heard this lot order it.'

'Go for it, Richard.'

The waiter came over.

'*¿Señores?*'

'*Hola.* Er, *dos mismos, por favor.*'

'*¿Señor?*'

Must be hard of hearing.

'*¡DOS MISMOS, POR FAVOR!*'

But once again it was a case of:

'*Es imposible, señor.*'

'Impossible?' I said, resorting to English. 'But why?!'

'Because you have just arrived.'

'So what?'

'*Mismo, señor*, means "the same again".'

The second incident, some time later when I should have known better, involved another friend, known as 'the Wanderer'.

One balmy evening in the 1990s, the Wanderer and I were ambling along Carrer de l'Argenteria in the general direction of a bar when, drifting out from an old stone building on our left, came the sound of a choir. The building wasn't a church and bore no noticeboard. Of course, anyone else would have assumed it to be a private house and walked on by. This anyone else included me. In the Wanderer's mind, however, live music creates a chemical reaction whereby etiquette and reserve are instantly dissolved, so that the man lurched right through the open door and headed straight for the source of the harmonies. In a move I now acknowledge as hopelessly naive, I followed.

In a large room to the left of the entrance hall a group of twenty or so hearty singers, of both sexes and several age groups, stood in front of red plastic chairs, giving their all under the direction of a stern bespectacled man of about fifty who faced them from behind a small table at the front. They were singing in Catalan. For a minute or two the Wanderer beamed at the scene, now and then tapping his foot, while I, the Laurel to his Hardy (or is it the other way round?), smiled wanly while edging steadily back towards the door. At the end of the piece, the Wanderer applauded vigorously, causing most of the singers to cast a rather surprised twitch to their right as they sat down. From the room opposite a short man in a black waistcoat approached.

'¿Senyor?'

The Wanderer: '¿Estupendo, no?'

Waistcoat: 'Ah, sí, molt bé.'

The Wanderer, slipping clumsily into Catalan.

'What's going on?'

'It's a local music society, senyor.'

'Can anyone join?'

(At this, I accelerated my retreating steps.)

'Well, I don't know, senyor. The gentleman at the front is the chairman.'

'Thank you.'

And with this, the Wanderer waved enthusiastically at Spectacles and pointed at two empty chairs, saying:

'¿Podem?'

My Catalan was good enough to recognise the first person plural. PodEM? Two chairs?! My lurch for the street was too slow. The Wanderer had beckoned me to the chairs and, his infectious enthusiasm overpowering all, I found myself sitting with a sheet of Catalan lyrics on my lap, a befuddled grin on my face and a mystified conductor a few feet in front of it, gesturing everyone to their feet.

I think the song translated as 'Manel's Lament for His Lost Love Across the Sea'. I did my best. When Spectacles urged us for more *'pasión'*, I tried to imagine my lost beer across the street. The Wanderer was in his absolute element, his own passionate rendition of Manel's lament compromised only by an irrepressibly broad grin. When Spectacles drew us dramatically to a close, and the Catalan choir once again sat down, the Wanderer stood for a moment, issued another breathless *'¡Estupendo!'*, followed by a *'Merci, merci a tothom'* and then turned to usher me, like a mother hen flapping her chick along, into the street. Every one of the twenty pairs of choral eyes watched us go with the same mystification as when we walked in – though now with the suggestion of a smile on their lips.

Over the delayed beer, I suggested that, in gatecrashing a private music society, we might possibly have overstepped the mark.

'Ah, how Protestant you are, Richard!', denounced the Wanderer. 'In ten years' time you won't remember a single thing you did at work today, but you may just remember singing with a Catalan choir.'

Fifteen years on and he was right twice in one sentence.

Smiling once again at the memory that morning, I turned Tetley down Carrer de la Lleona, passed through the perfectly proportioned arcades of Plaça Reial, which I was sorry to see had fallen even further into inexplicable decay, to emerge in the flow of tourists spilling down Les Rambles. Thus it was that I arrived again where I'd left the coastal route the previous evening, at the Columbus statue. This time I turned right.

My first target was immediately before me: the Zona Franca, where lie the city's modern port installations. Many's the time I'd driven along the Ronda Litoral, the coastal section of the ring road, looking over at the huge freighters, giant cranes and multicoloured containers of the commercial port. Any boy would want to get closer and this seemed the ideal opportunity, on the ideal form of transport.

How wrong I was.

At the first barrier, the *hombre* with the machine gun made it quite clear how wrong: no public access. A quick scuttle up the steps to the Ronda also made it clear that there was no cycle access that way either. Map out, head scratched, shoulders dropped, sigh exhaled. With Montjuïc forming a natural barrier to add to the man-made one, I'd have to go inland.

Oh well, at least this would take me through a few neighbourhoods I'd never visited before, and so I set off up the broad thoroughfare of Avinguda del Paral.lel. (That dot between the two Ls is no mistake. In both Catalan and Spanish, double L is normally pronounced as a Y; indeed in Spanish it's counted as a separate letter. The dot means this isn't LL but simply L followed by another L and therefore pronounced as in English.) Here I experienced a pleasant novelty: a cycle track to protect me from the traffic. Never had I known such a cycle-friendly feature in Barcelona. Of course, cars were parked all over it – you wouldn't expect the city's drivers to pay undue attention to a new law, nor indeed to any law – but still, the thought was there. In fact, the city had recently also initiated a public cycle hire scheme called *'bicing'*, which seemed to be thriving. Good luck to them.

The route around the foot of Montjuïc eventually turned left. This 173-metre hill dominates much of the city and has regularly played important – and infamous – roles in its history. In the nineteenth-century Catalan insurrection Barcelona was shelled from Montjuïc's fortress by a garrison loyal to Madrid and during the civil war many prisoners from both sides were imprisoned in the same fortress, some of them being executed here. The hill has many sporting connections too: its roads hosted the Spanish Grand Prix between 1969 and 1975; its stadium, built for the city's 1929 International Exposition, was to form the 1992 Olympic Stadium; and later this became the home for Barcelona's 'other' first-division football team, Real Club Deportivo Espanyol de Barcelona – or Espanyol for short. (The impact of the city's more illustrious team was to crop up later.)

After half an hour of backstreets, police sirens, shouting matches and general street life, I sneaked into the edges of the Zona Franca via the back door. It may not have been the harbourside activity I'd hoped for, but this strange part of town was still fascinating in its own way. Smells of diesel, burnt rubber and dust wafted past as I picked my way through a land built for giants. Giant silos loomed over giant lorry parks from which giant artics thundered into giant roads, there to be held up by giant traffic lights as a tiny cyclist pedalled across in front of them. I was evidently once again in a *situation irrégulière*, where bicycles had not been in planners' minds but where I believe Tetley and I were not actually illegal. As a new woody smell heralded a giant pallet store, I seemed to be entering a very long, very narrow building site. It was only later that I discovered this to be for the overhead section of the city's new Metro Line 9, serving the commercial port and which the authorities hope may take some of the traffic off these roads.

With grime in my eyes and dust in my throat, I pulled over at a transport cafe for some refreshment. At least part of it had started life as a caravan, but now this cafe, which must have been the oldest structure for miles around, boasted two entrances, two bars and a substantial menu. It was mid afternoon and quite hot. Workers and drivers were knocking back not just beer and wine, but brandy, rum and a kaleidoscopic selection of liqueurs. I restricted myself to a cheese *bocadillo* and an *agua con gas*.

'Are you lost?' asked the friendly barmaid, in Spanish.

'Well, I know where I am,' I stated, 'and I know where I'm going to...'

'... but you can't find the cycle track to get there,' she completed.

'Correct. How did you know?'

'The few cyclists we get in here are all looking for the track to the beach.'

She was spot on.

My second target for the day was something I'd also gazed longingly at many times before, this time from the air. If you're landing at Barcelona Airport from the north, after you've flown over the city and just before the runway, you pass over a bewitching patchwork of rectangular green fields and dead-straight ditches. Between these runs the occasional narrow track, ending at a broad beach, deserted but for a shack with a few tables. A secret beach I'd always wanted to find. The tracks looked too narrow for cars and so, once again, the bike seemed ideal.

Following the barmaid's crystal-clear instructions, I cycled through another giant building site (which subsequent research revealed to be another massive project: the diversion of the River Llobregat to create yet more space for the port) and finally over the muddy brown river itself and officially, therefore, out of Barcelona and into the county of El Baix Llobregat. In fact, I was cycling in the outskirts of the suburb which gives its unfortunate name to Barcelona's airport: El Prat de Llobregat. *'Prat'* is Catalan for meadow. Here Tetley finally found himself in his natural environment again as we left the main roads to follow a signposted cycle route through the Espais Naturals del Riu Llobregat, the 'River Llobregat Nature Area'.

Though the lanes that I'd seen from the air turned out to be wide enough for vehicles after all, there was hardly any traffic. As the urban area receded and I found myself once more passing by fields of vegetables, artichokes this time, the only sounds were the wind in the hedges, the toads in the ditches and the frequent birdsong wafting from places hidden from view. At a small information centre a handwritten board helped me out by identifying in Catalan, English and Latin the latest species observed here: crested coots, Caspian terns, little gulls and slender-billed gulls. The Caspian tern I admit I'd never heard of, but apparently it's the world's largest tern and in Europe is normally only found around the Baltic Sea and Black Sea.

Just past the information centre another noise reminded me why there were so few people around this otherwise enchanting corner of the Catalan coast: roaring low overhead was an easyJet 737, followed closely by what I think was a Bombardier of Iberia Airlines.

Right here, literally a few metres from the end of the runway, a small area had been marked off from the fields and covered in powdery red clay. On this were fixed about a dozen large concrete seats, slung at a low enough angle for their occupants to gaze skywards. And occupants they had, with their cameras, binoculars and notebooks. First bird-spotters and now plane-spotters. Equally earnest and equally valid, I'd say. What a fabulous location for plane-spotters, in fact. Confirming the latest official Catalan obsession, the local council had even put up a couple of noticeboards with information on the airport's construction and how it worked.

As I waited for the next landing, I spoke to a young man who was just propping up his motorbike near one of the seats.

'Is this all new?'

'Oh, yes, from not so long ago. But I used to come here before. I think the council thought our bikes were a nuisance parked on the road.'

'Are there any particular planes you're looking out for?'

'Not me. I just like to be near these big machines.' We both said nothing for the next minute as another airliner thundered at what felt like just a few feet above our heads. Yes, I suppose it was exhilarating – in a deafening sort of way. 'But some of these [he waved at the five or so men and one woman with notebooks], they know when a rare aircraft is coming. I don't know how.'

Naturally I asked one of them if a rare metal bird was due, but not that day, apparently.

Leaving the spotters to their noisy hobby, I pushed off again as I was nearing my goal. Little bicycle signs had now started pointing to 'Platja del Prat', which sounded like the place I was after. Another kilometre or two along the track, now busy with late afternoon joggers, I emerged between scrubby-looking trees at a long, narrow and completely empty beach, onto which the Med was pushing lines of little wavelets, each issuing a tiny 'shoosh'.

Barcelona's secret beach turned out to be less secret than it had seemed from the air. The 'shack' turned out to be a bar (closed), a restaurant (closing) and some sort of equipment store (locked). Together with a car park (empty) and bus stop (queueless), these all attested to the place being anything but secret in the season. Today's users were just two joggers, a police car, Tetley and me.

With the blue sky and, for an Englishman, the sultry temperature, I left Tetley by the wall and sat for a while as Platja del Prat's only occupant, watching a dark-blue container boat inching its way into the port entrance to my left and a couple of now distant, white aircraft lining up to land at the airport's western runway. As I looked up, I imagined that at least some passengers must be looking down at me and wondering about this secret beach and so I gave them a small wave.

Since the short, unshaven policeman leaning on his car was apparently looking for something to do, I plodded up the beach towards him, inventing as I did so a query in Spanish:

'Excuse me, please. Can I get around the south side of the airport on my bike?'

His reply was, I believe, also in Spanish but with a strong Andalusian accent:

'Pueseñol caminobama lejoqualli partegente seguridamergenci tonceyo crequetienuste pasaporlo troladel aeropuerto.'

Since Andalusians tend not only to drop the last letter of each word but also run it into the next, as well as speaking as fast as an angry Glaswegian, his response could have been in Martian for all I understood of it. However, his gloved right hand had flapped in a way that made it quite clear that the words amounted to 'No' and so, thanking him politely, I set off back the way I'd come.

With lazy lanes and sleepy fields gradually falling behind me, I returned to civilisation in the form of El Prat de Llobregat's railway station. Here I had just enough time to read a huge notice revealing the exact cost of the local section of the new high-speed line to be 168,427,641.56 euros, and to wonder what the 56 cents were spent on, before I was lifting Tetley and myself into a tight space at the bottom of the stairs in a double-decked commuter train for the ride back to Barcelona.

The rendezvous Julie and I had got lined up was for after-work drinks and tapas at an old haunt called El Mesón (literally 'the inn') in Sant Cugat, another train ride away beyond the Collserola hills that offer the city of Barcelona some protection from northerly winds. Well, it was no longer 'after work' for us, of course, but was for the others. The date had been arranged out of the blue by an old English friend, Chris, who'd also invited along a former Catalan work colleague, Montse (short for Montserrat). Chris's Spanish partner Isabel made up the party.

In the hi-tech multinational where we'd worked on a nearby industrial estate, Chris, Montse and I had made up half of a department which, in the old days, used to be called 'Documentation', but which the 1990s fad for euphemisms had transformed into 'Learning Products'. Yes, between us we churned out those parts of a computer device which you hope never to need: the user manuals, help screens and all the other mumbo-jumble of advice to users. Chris, the other anglophones and I wrote the stuff in American English (even though we were all from Britain or Ireland), while Montse and her team got it translated into a dozen or so other languages. After many years, Montse, a proud Catalan, finally succeeded in persuading our American bosses to add Catalan to this list, but Chris and I never did manage to add British English. Instead of starting the manual in American:

'Welcome! And congratulations on investing in your plug-and-play WhizzBang X500! It's fun to use – and if you run into trouble, it's fun to fix! Enjoy!'

We might have written in real English:

'So your machine's on the blink, eh? Thought you'd never need to open this book, didn't you? All right, don't panic. You've probably just twiddled the wrong knob. Now, stop blabbering and concentrate.'

In a sea of American earnestness, we were an island of British light-heartedness – though we delivered the goods too, of course. It perhaps shouldn't be a surprise that Montse fitted perfectly into the atmosphere of mickey-taking, since Catalan humour seems to be closely aligned to the British variety: ironic, self-deprecating, occasionally slapstick. Catalans regularly remind me with a grin that their annual national day, *la Diada* on 11 September, celebrates not a victory, but the 1714 defeat of Barcelona by the Bourbons. One Catalan work colleague, who'd spent some time in England, wondered out loud how his countrymen could have been defeated by a biscuit.

Monty Python's Flying Circus and *Blackadder* were very popular here, as was *Fawlty Towers*. The Catalan TV3 channel, however, deftly dubbed waiter Manuel's explanation for his ignorance – 'I from Barcelona' – with 'I from Mexico'. In any case, a pedant may point out that if he'd really been from Barcelona, he would not have been Manuel, but Manel.

Montse's skill with languages demonstrates another positive aspect of Catalonia: as almost all Catalan children are bilingual from infancy, in Catalan and Spanish, their facility to pick up other languages later in life is astonishing. It's something we Brits could learn from.

'So, Richard,' asked Montse, having heard me order food in Spanish. 'How's your Catalan?'

I'd known it was coming. Each morning at the coffee machine, she used to test my progress, limited as it was.

'Ah, well, I've still got the books and tapes.' She gave me a severe look. 'And, um, *parlo solament una mica de català.*'

'You could say that fifteen years ago.'

'Well, you see I spend so little time in Spain, it takes all my effort to stop my *castellano* from going too rusty.'

'Next time we meet I want to hear an improvement.'

'Yes, miss. Er, *més cafè*?'

After catching up on the office gossip, Chris reminded me of the times when we'd both first arrived in Spain, Chris not long after me, and shared a flat right here in Sant Cugat.

'What was it you said to our neighbour?' he asked.

'Ah, yes. Well, I'd only learnt a few simple Spanish phrases by then and two of them were *"Encantado"* and *"Un cortado"'*.

'Very useful. "Pleased to meet you" and "A small white coffee".'

'Yes, and I mixed them up. The first time I saw her on the stairs I offered my hand, saying "Hello. I'm a small white coffee." Never saw her again.'

'She started giving me odd looks too. Didn't we even have problems just getting the right beer at this very bar?' remembered Chris.

'Yes, all we wanted was draught beer, but *"Dos cervezas, por favor"* only brought bottled beer.'

'Till we finally discovered that's not how they ask for it.'

Chris was right. It eventually dawned on us that what the locals actually order is the shape and size of the glass they want their beer in, the default contents being the local draught. So, for example, *un tubo* (literally a tube) is a tall straight glass, *una jarra* (a jar) is a mug and – nowadays my usual – *una caña* or, in Catalan, *una canya* (a stem) is a fluted glass.

With various destinations to head for, we reluctantly drank up and paid up – all with a facility that would have seemed remarkable all those years before to the two linguistically challenged Brits.

Back in the big city, Julie and I opted for a *digestif* or two at another favourite, the Café de l'Òpera, opposite the Liceu near the bottom of the Rambles. The next morning we'd be going our separate ways for a few days and, what with the repacking this necessitated and the trip out to the suburbs, we hadn't had time to compare notes on our respective days until now. Having kept her fascination in check as I regaled her with tales of building sites, transport cafes and undercarriages, she set me the same challenge as I heard all about Mango, Zara and Desigual.

'Buy anything?'

'Well, I was on a mission for some fabric, but in the end I bought a frock from down here on the Rambla. Needs a bit of work though.'

'What kind of work?'

'Well, it's made from a very nice jersey fabric, it's an elegant black and red… but it's got a weird styling feature: its arms reach the floor.'

My puzzlement must have shown.

'I think, because it's jersey, you're supposed to push the sleeves up. But I can't be bothered with all that. I'll just cut 'em off. Anyway, it was a bargain: down from a hundred euros to fourteen!'

'You can't have shopped all day, surely?'

'No, my little legs got tired and I did what I overheard someone at breakfast say they'd do. I took a ride on one of those open-top buses.'

'Now that's something I've always intended to do. Where did it take you?'

'Well, I think you can take other routes, but I picked it up in Plaça Catalunya and it took me to Montjuïc, Plaça d'Espanya – where I saw the bullring I'd visited – past Camp Nou, along Diagonal… then I forget, but eventually back to Catalunya.'

'Were you up on top?'

'Of course. Otherwise, what's the point? Most of the others seemed to be hopping on and off, but I just sat back and enjoyed the ride. Gives you a better idea of the layout of the city than from a car.'

'Or a bike. I got lost a couple of...'

Screech!

Like everyone else in the cafe, we stopped whatever we were doing and turned to see where the noise had come from. From the taxi that had screeched to a halt right outside the door, a woman exited in dramatic fashion. She was perhaps in her forties and dressed like a 'lady' from the nearby neighbourhood of El Raval (aka the Barri Xino), where, at that time of night, business would be starting to boom. Stretching her long legs wide apart, and thereby causing an already short skirt to rise further, she suddenly screamed in a voice that would have been heard over the road at the opera:

'¡Ramón!'

And again:

'¡¡Ramón!!'

All customers and waiters continued to stare. Except one. A rather short, middle-aged waiter near us immediately turned his back and continued earnestly to clear the tables.

'¡¡¡Ramón!!!'

(Lest there actually is a waiter of that name at the Café de l'Òpera, I should make it clear that I've substituted the real name.)

At this point, as the taxi wisely pulled away, fare paid or not, several pairs of eyes turned to the busy but hapless waiter. He shook his head vigorously. Still no hap.

Ramón's lady friend approached the door from the outside, to find that an employee had swiftly bolted it.

And so, still on the pavement, she removed her blouse and twirled it wildly around her head.

'*¡¡¡Ramón!!!*'

The barman looked at Ramón. Ramón looked at the barman. The barman jerked his head to the door. Ramón looked at the floor and then back at the barman, who jerked his head again. Ramón handed his towel and then his apron to the nearest customer and headed slowly towards the door, the woman fixing him with a steely stare above pouted lips.

At this point another screech of tyres heralded the arrival of a police car, which Ramón's friend, still glaring at him, greeted by removing her skirt, casting it to the floor and lying, legs spread wide, on the bonnet. One large policeman and an even larger policewoman quickly removed the almost naked body, thrusting her and her abandoned clothes into the back seat. Before the car left, Ramón, to his eternal credit, unbolted the door and suggested to the police that he accompany them too.

With the third tyre screech of the evening, the police car pulled away – to prolonged applause both from the cafe's customers and from assembled passers-by. I doubt whether the opera itself put on a better, more melodramatic show that night.

When passing through the city in the 1940s, Rose Macaulay had noted that Barcelona rivalled Marseille and Naples in the impression it gave 'of tempestuous, surging, irrepressible life and *brio*'. This little incident confirmed that in the twenty-first century the *brio* is still alive and well.

Day 8

Solo to the South: El Prat de Llobregat to Calafell

Having checked and double-checked that Julie had what she should and I had what I should, I finally pedalled away from the garage, wobbling a little as I turned to wave, not yet used to the weight of the extra luggage packed into the big, blue handlebar bag to last me four solitary days. Solitary in order to give the ride a little variation and Julie a break back at Llançà, where, without me to get under her feet, she planned to do some painting. Artistic painting, that is – I hadn't abandoned her to a house of stepladders and tins of emulsion.

Solitary but not lonely, for I'm one of those fortunate souls equally happy in company or alone. Not deliriously so at carrying all the overnight gear on the bike, I had to admit, but pleased to have the unusual luxury of 200 schedule-free kilometres ahead of me, where much of the territory would be new and where no overnights had been pre-booked.

First stop was the station at Plaça Catalunya to pick up the train back out to El Prat de Llobregat, happily against the flow of the late commuters. Taking a bike by train in Spain seems a much simpler task than in Britain, where such a hoo-ha is made of it: special bicycle tickets, special bicycle carriages, special bicycle restrictions. On most services here in Spain, it seems you just swing your bike onto the train and go. No fuss, no sweat.

And so, after a short train ride, it was with a broad grin on my face and a little song on my lips that I headed out of El Prat, this time pointing Tetley and me at the very southern extremity of Catalonia, just beyond the River Ebre.

Even though it was only mid morning, the temperature must have already been in the high twenties. It promised to be a sticky few days.

The flatlands of the Llobregat Delta, home to Barcelona's seaport and airport, are otherwise largely given over to agriculture. The network of irrigation channels this entails initially forced me inland to the old main road that passes through the straggling settlement of Gavà. Here, just beyond an exuberant fig orchard, a sign pointing to the left announced 'Recommended itinerary for bicycles'. Excellent. Hoping the itinerary might involve the seashore at some point, I dived once more towards the fields and allotments and did eventually pop out onto another beach at Gavà Mar.

Though the beach itself was empty, the beachside cafe was not only open but served a marvellous, freshly squeezed orange juice. Sipping it on the cafe's only chair, I toasted my own good fortune at being alive, fit and all set for another day beside the sea under the protection of Spokey the Cycling God. With no more than a drop of rain so far and, despite a few off-road adventures, still no hint of the P word, this god of mine seemed to be doing a better job than most others and I can certainly recommend Him... no, probably just 'him'. You need no capital letters, no church, no holy book and no priests. Just a decent bike and an optimistic outlook – and you'll be fine.

Gavà Mar's cyclable promenade pointed south, apparently to infinity but at least to Castelldefels, its more substantial neighbour. The last time I'd been here, shortly after moving to Barcelona, I was looking at local property. The town being within easy commuting distance of the city and having a laid-back, vaguely Californian air, property turned out to be far too expensive for my budget. Today, block after block of four-storey apartments looked like second homes still shuttered up for the season.

As the Garraf Massif shouldered its way to the sea, the delta landscape finally fizzled out, along with the promenades, forcing me onto the hectic and narrow coast road, the C-31, whose sharp bends and even sharper gusts of wind frequently had me walking Tetley along the drainage ditch beyond the white line for my own safety. But even here, Spokey was smiling on me today, as he placed on the roadside right in front of me a smart, new Italian straw hat – one which I knew to be unworn since it still bore its 25-euro price label. Smartly it went into my big blue bag and smartly it hangs on the hat rack at Llançà to this day.

The windy and winding C-31 finally disgorged me in Sitges. Pronounced 'Seeches' and meaning 'silos' (as in underground grain stores), this seaside resort is a class apart from any I'd passed through since S'Agaró, back on Day 5. A favourite among that modernist clique, which embraced the Els Quatre Gats characters, Sitges was home to one of its key figures, Santiago Rusiñol, whose studio, Cau Ferrat, still stands prominently on the headland in the centre of town and is now a museum. The Sitges Film Festival, first held in 1967, kept the cultural flame burning, while nowadays it's a renowned destination for the gay tourist. (Funny how that always makes it sound like there's only one.)

Looking as butch as I could manage in my tight padded shorts, I pulled over for a lunch break at a very blue cafe facing San Sebastian beach. Blue walls, blue railings, blue parasols, blue chairs, blue aprons. No blue food, fortunately, and so I ordered *bikini* and *sin*. In Catalonia this is a safe enough option: a *bikini* is a toasted ham and cheese sandwich, while a *sin*... well, let me explain with reference to the tale of a first-time visitor to our Sant Cugat office, a young Irishman.

When he arrived late one morning, his state prompted me to comment at the coffee machine:

'You look a bit rough, Michael.'

'Probably do. Out on the town last night and had too much local beer.'

'What beer were you on?'

'Oh, it was a killer, Richard. I should've known from the name: Damn Sin! And there it was in English as well.'

'Actually, it's Spanish,' I had to reveal.

'And why are you grinnin' like that?'

'Damm is the local Barcelona brewery and *sin* means "without".'

'Without what?'

'Without alcohol.'

Well, my Sitges *sin* went down easily too. Most Spanish alcohol-free beer is streets ahead of the gruesome, tinny equivalent you get in Britain. I could have hung around on that shady terrace for some time but, with legs stiffening, I soon pulled on my kit once more and pushed off into the backstreets of Sitges, the seaside route being closed by building works. It was siesta time and, as I pedalled around the old town, the only sounds to be heard, apart from Tetley's creaks and squeaks, were a Supremes track floating from an upstairs window and a megaphone-assisted German guide listing the delights of Rusiñol's old studio, Cau Ferrat.

Running along the southern beaches of Sitges is an especially elegant promenade, heavy with palms, where older apartment blocks approach the shore. The atmosphere of this stretch of coast, the Costes de Garraf in the county of El Garraf, is quite distinct from El Maresme on the other side of Barcelona: slower, lazier, without the sense of a big city just along the coast. Perhaps part of it is because, without the intrusion of the coastal railway, for many years the settlements have reached right to the shore. From the nineteenth century many Catalan *Americanos* built mansions here to show off their good fortune.

Just after the older blocks petered out, a noise from the beach caught my attention.

'Whoa!' Thud! 'Uurgh! Ha! Hee-hee!'

Peering around a sturdy palm tree, I gazed on a pile (for this is literally what it was) of six or seven children in the sand, laughing, cheering and separating limb from entwined limb. As I pulled over to watch, four of them stood up, arms on hips and then around each other's shoulders, before two of the others started to scramble up their backs. Eventually it dawned on me. A *castell*! I was entering prime *casteller* country.

It started over two hundred years ago, not far from here at the small inland town of Valls. Human towers or *castells*, rather like those of circus acrobats, are built by many participants standing on the shoulders of others, until as many as ten levels have been built, the topmost level comprising a single person – usually a child. Unlike the circus, though, teams of *castellers* form rivals in regular *castell* competitions.

It's a not just a test of human strength and balance but a test of preparation and coordination, as well as an expression of community spirit and Catalan nationalism. Yep, you can just see old Frank Franco seething at the very idea. Banned! But just like the circle dance, the *sardana*, following the dictator's death the *castell* has come back stronger than ever.

Another parallel with the *sardana* – indeed with most folkloric activities around the world, I'd wager – is the wealth of jargon that surrounds the construction of *castells*. The mass of people, sometimes hundreds, forming the ground level is the *pinya* (literally a pine cone, something that sticks together); a part comprising only two per level is a *torre* (tower) and one per level an *agulla* (needle). The person at the top, who must raise one hand with four fingers stretched out (symbolising the stripes of the Catalan flag) before the *castell* is dismantled, is called the *enxaneta*. A *castell* team is called a *colla* (gang).

The tradition is particularly strong in this southern area of Catalonia and top of the rankings at the time of writing, with about 50 per cent more points than any other *colla*, are the Castellers de Vilafranca. The aim is not simply (simply!) to construct the highest *castell*, but to dismantle it steadily and safely, one layer at a time. Injuries do occur. Even deaths – two in the eighteen years prior to the time of writing.

Needless to say, the bigger *colles* sprout a labyrinth of committees, councils and officials almost as numerous as the participants. *Castells* are a big deal round here.

Doubtless the seven young boys on Sitges Beach (now they were disentangled I could count them) were trying to emulate their local *colla*. After this ride I looked it up and, lo and behold, just a few weeks after I'd passed through the town, the Colla Jove de Castellers de Sitges achieved a magnificent 'four-by-eight' (eight levels of four people each), successfully built and successfully dismantled. As I watched, the 'one-by-two' of the Colla de la Platja collapsed in a fit of giggles yet again.

The track that continues to hug the coast being for walkers only, Tetley and I were obliged to push inland once again, where we spent a while penned into the hard shoulder of the main road as it swung between low hills of pine and vine, interspersed with sturdy farmsteads where not a soul moved under the merciless afternoon sun.

Soon, however, I found myself pedalling through the outskirts of another substantial town: Vilanova i la Geltrú – so good they named it twice. In fact, the union of the two towns of La Geltrú and Vilanova de Cubelles is over seven hundred years old and the 'they' was King Jaume I, who granted the joint city its charter during the period of Catalan-Aragonese independence. Nowadays, Vilanova i la Geltrú is a significant industrial centre and local 'county town', administratively looking down on its smaller but more fashionable neighbour, Sitges.

The afternoon having now turned sultry, I was pleased to get in the shade of an awning at a little bar facing the harbour. With its jumble of sheds, cranes and forklift trucks, this was a working port rather than a marina; indeed, the town I'd cycled through was clearly a normal town rather than a resort. Thinking this would make an interesting change for an overnight stay, I asked for advice from the waiter.

'Can you suggest any hotel around here?'

'Your bicycle, señor.'

'Yes, I'm cycling along the coast.'

'No, your bicycle it touches my awning, señor.'

He was right, although only the handlebars and saddle touched.

'Oh, sorry, but it is clean.'

'But it touches.'

Getting up to move it, I tried the hotel question again.

'Ah, señor, you don't want this town. You want Sitges. Tourists stay there.'

'But I'm headed south.'

'South, yes. Tourists go south too. Not here in Vilanova. No, never here.'

Well, whether I would really have been Vilanova's first ever tourist was to remain unknown, since the grumpy waiter's *café con leche* refreshed me sufficiently to take his implied advice and push off. Though I wouldn't know it for another hour, this turned out to be a good move. Most of this hour was spent spinning along what eventually declared itself to be 'The longest *passeig marítim* in Catalonia'.

Level, well surfaced and almost empty, it was an easy ride. There's something especially relaxing about cycling by water. My very first rides beyond my own network of streets as a child were along the banks of the River Trent in

Derbyshire and I remember well shifting my gaze between the switchback of the waterside track and the rolling grey currents of the river itself, as though we were locked together in a narrow, winding world of our own.

Which is all a pretty poor excuse for the semi-dreamlike state into which I'd probably slipped when a screech of brakes snapped me alert. A few metres directly in front of me, another bike wobbled to an unsteady halt against a stone bench. Gripping the brakes tightly, I juddered to my own graceless halt.

'*Hola*, hallo, *salut*,' said the diminutive cyclist, a woman in her early twenties I'd say, slipping off a saddle set at its lowest possible position.

'Hallo will do,' I said in English, 'Sorry, didn't see you.'

'I am single only bike on ze track and you did not see me?'

'No, sorry, must have been hidden by the palm trees,' I said vaguely and then, removing my helmet to wipe a hand across my brow and to change the subject: 'Hot day for a bike ride.'

'More hot in ze sout.' She removed her own helmet, revealing, instead of the tumble of locks I'd expected, a head of dark hair cropped almost as short as mine. Just as sticky too, judging from the energetic scrabbling that followed.

'Where have you come from?' I asked.

'Rotterdam.'

'That's a long way in a day.'

'Oh, not from Rotterdam today,' she said seriously, observing me closely in case she'd accidentally fallen into conversation with the village idiot. 'Today from Amposta. And you?'

Having quickly assessed her day as twice the distance of mine, I considered making something up, but in the end stuck to the truth, or something close to it.

'Barcelona,' I admitted.

'Oh, it's not far,' said the Serious Little Dynamo bluntly, 'but I zink you are a small bit older from me.'

Two blows landed in one sentence. A counteroffensive was the only option.

'Older THAN you, yes. You don't look Dutch, if you don't mind me saying so.'

'Is true. I am possible ze most short woman in Rotterdam, yes? But I aim to be ze most tough also.'

'Well, this is good training for that. Where are you headed?'

Scratching her damp hair again, she looked puzzled.

'My head?'

'What is your destination tonight?'

'Ah, yes, a campsite near Sitges.' She pronounced it Sit-ges. I now noticed her bike was loaded with camping equipment. 'And you?'

'Ah, Calafell probably. Just along here.'

'Is a campsite?'

'Er no, I'm staying in hotels.'

'Of course.'

When could two words have hidden such a damning assessment? Of course, meant Serious Little Dynamo, you are an old man, you cycle pathetically short distances and you don't even make your own camp at night. What hope is there for you? I wondered how she would have reacted had I admitted to a support vehicle for most of the trip.

'How far are you cycling altogether?' I asked, hoping to regain some credibility myself.

'I start in Valencia and I go to Perpignan.'

'Oh, I've come from near Perpignan,' I said, bending the truth. 'How long will it take you?'

'I haff four days after today.' I shouldn't have asked. I knew what was coming next. 'And you? How lonk from Perpignan?'

'Oh, I've stopped off to see some friends...'

'How lonk?'

'Eight days.'

'Well,' she said, glancing at my waistline as she put her helmet back on, 'It will make you fitter, yes?'

'Yes, and maybe your ride will make you taller.'

'Taller? No, I sink I am too old to grow more. OK, bye-bye.'

Waving as she pulled away, Serious Little Dynamo wobbled perilously close to the wall.

'Bye!' I called, adding: 'It's pronounced SEECHES by the way!'

At least I'd had the last word.

The record-breaking Passeig Marítim de Sant Joan de Déu had started in Cunit and, by the time I'd spun into Calafell 6 kilometres later and seen St John of God's endless promenade disappearing over the horizon, the Vilanova caffeine had worn off, leaving me to realise I'd spent long enough on a sticky saddle for one day. Time for a wash and brush up.

Calafell on Sea seemed to be all apartment blocks and no suitable hotels, except for the expensive-looking Miramar, and so it was via a very helpful young man at the tourist office that I turned inland to Calafell on the Hill, where, waiting coolly and cleanly on a tranquil backstreet, was the quite perfect Hotel Antiga.

SOLO TO THE SOUTH

One thing the Spanish in general and Catalans in particular do well is hotels. What the traveller needs is:

- availability
- cleanliness
- value for money

For me, Catalonia rates good, good and good respectively. These high scores are apparently nothing new, for back in the nineteenth century Ford was moved to comment that 'the Catalan takes kindly to the hotel and kitchen'. Again from my own experience only, France rates good-variable-good for example; Italy poor-variable-poor; and Britain variable-variable-poor.

At the Hotel Antiga I was welcomed by a calm and efficient lady who seemed to run the whole place single-handedly. Ignoring my sweaty state, she stored Tetley in a downstairs cupboard and directed its rider to a large and cool first-floor room, complete with balcony and palm tree view. Forty-two euros including breakfast (2009 prices). Can't beat it.

Showered, napped and smartened up, I soon re-emerged in reception feeling pretty good about life and announced to Señora Antiga, who was busy doing the books:

'¡Casi humano ahora!' (Almost human now!)

From her nervous look, I can only imagine this didn't translate the way I'd intended and, smiling sheepishly, quickly exited stage left. Since it turned out that Calafell on the Hill had no restaurants, I found that my 70-kilometre day (the longest so far) required another 4-kilometre round trip on foot, back down to a seafront cafe to eat. No matter. Unlike Serious Little Dynamo, I'd secured a comfy bed for the night, the air was balmy, the ever-present Mediterranean was sparkling and my *botifarra* and beans went down as well as only food after exercise can.

The '*botifarra*' is a tricky chap. It is a large Catalan sausage, usually translated in English as a Cumberland sausage, although that gives you an idea of the size rather than the taste. Usually served with *mongetes*, a mushy kind of bean, it's quite a filling dish that often appears on a Catalan eatery's 'worker's menu' at lunchtime. Naturally, it satisfies hungry cyclists too.

What is tricky about the *botifarra* was brought home to me one evening at a Llançà bar where '*Botifarra* Night' had been advertised. Having been suitably restrained at lunchtime, I presented myself at the bar, licking my lips in anticipation.

'Is it *Botifarra* Night?' I asked.

'Indeed. They've already started,' said the barman, indicating the green tables occupied by men and women playing cards. 'Feel free to join them, señor.'

Freedom I did feel but, feeling hunger a little more acutely, I went next door for a pizza. *Botifarra* is also a card game.

Washing down my sausage and beans with a digestif of cool *rosado*, I turned once again to Rose Macaulay's little book. From Barcelona, where she'd railed forcibly against the 'extravaganza of bad taste' that was (and is) the Sagrada Família, Miss Macaulay had turned inland through Sant Cugat, Martorell and the wine districts of Penedès before returning to the coast right here.

After 'the whole population of Calafell' had helped her extract her car from the sandy track by the shore, she'd put up at the Miramar Inn, which must have been on the site where now stood the six-storey block I'd judged too expensive. Here her landlord took several hours to complete the forms required to register a foreign guest, since, she tells us, she'd been the first such to stay there. After dark she'd bathed in the sea in front of the inn and, impressed by her description, I too walked beyond the lights of Passeig Marítim to the beach, where, slipping off sandals, I crunched down to the water's edge to paddle in the silky waters of the Mediterranean. The arc of lights around the bay might have been brighter than in the 1940s, but the lap-lap-lap of little waves between the cool sand and the black deeps, together with the silver dancing reflections of a crescent moon, reminded me that even after sixty years of development some things never change.

Day 9

The Wrong Shirt: Calafell to Cambrils

From the deep overnight silence of the Hotel Antiga I'd imagined I was its only guest. But as I took a seat at breakfast, so did a couple in late middle age. Having taken one look at me, somewhat to my surprise both started to sing – or rather chant:

'¡Seis a dos, seis a dos, seis a dos!' (Six to two, six to two, six to two!)

I looked vacant.

The gentleman pointed at my shirt.

'Ah,' I said as it eventually dawned. 'El Barça! Yes, yes, six to two.'

Some explanation is needed.

All over Catalonia, FC Barcelona enjoys a level and intensity of support that any football club in the world would envy. Yes, even Manchester United, even

AC Milan, even FC Bayern Munich. Well, not quite any club: no Real Madrid supporter would admit to envying anything to do with their arch-enemies.

And therein lies the explanation of many things, including the reaction in the breakfast room that morning. When, after the civil war, Franco banned the flying of the *Senyera*, the yellow and red striped Catalan flag, the blue and red (*'blaugrana'*) stripes of the football club's flag effectively took its place. While speaking Catalan was officially banned, it was spoken more or less freely at the club's stadium. To many, allegiance to Catalonia took the temporary form of allegiance to 'Barça'. This is the basis of the club's modern-day claim to be *'més que un club'* (more than a club).

It has an incredible 170,000 members (more than any other football club anywhere), an even more unbelievable 1,300 officially recognised supporters' clubs around the world (by way of comparison, Manchester United has about 200) and the biggest football stadium in Europe. Camp Nou holds nearly 100,000 spectators, which is actually 20,000 down on its capacity before 1980s safety regulations came in. Having seen a few games there myself, I have to admit to being impressed by the sheer scale of the stadium. British spectators used to hearing the grunt of a player tackled on the near side of a league ground may be surprised to know that many fans in the back row at Camp Nou bring binoculars as a matter of course. From up there, the ball looks about the size of a marble on a cricket pitch. When a friend's young boys accompanied us to a Barça match one evening, even their boisterous chatter was stilled as they emerged from the long walk up the back of the stand into the arena.

'Who do you think will sco.... oooer... wha!' managed one.

'Could be... eeeargh... ooyer!' gulped his brother.

In sport, in culture and in business, FC Barcelona is big. Too big. This is why I don't support them myself. However, one thing that scores more highly with me than mere football is cycling comfort and I'd recently been given a Barça shirt, whose fabric structure magically kept out much of the heat. With the forecast being hotter still, I'd pulled it on that morning... a morning that fell just a few days after Barça had beaten Real Madrid 6–2 in a league match. In Madrid. To give an idea of the impact of this result on Barça supporters, the local response to the 6–2 drubbing of Madrid exceeded even that after all three of their European Cup/Champions League victories in 1992, 2006 and 2009, for all of which I also happened to be in Catalonia. In Llançà, fans watching on TV burst into restaurants to announce each of the six goals – and no one minded. Fireworks lasted long into the night.

All in all, I felt it undiplomatic to mention that, actually, in terms of La Liga, I follow the fortunes of a Galician club, Deportivo la Coruña. I hadn't got a Deportivo shirt though.

'Yes,' I managed. 'Six to two. Remarkable. Were you at the match?'

'¡Hombre! If only. We watched it on TV, didn't we, Pili?'

This seemed to spark off an hilarious memory in his wife, for now they started giggling like teenagers. Try as they did to explain the joke to me, I couldn't understand a word. Señora Antiga, however, got it immediately and started sniggering as well. Before long, breakfast was overtaken by roars of laughter and such barely controllable snorts that tears began to roll down my face too. To this day I haven't a clue what the joke was, but we were all still smiling when I wheeled Tetley out into the square. It was only just after nine but, sure enough, uncomfortably warm already. My Barça shirt would earn its keep today.

Having coasted back down to Passeig Marítim, I did my stretches on a seafront that was deserted but for two cafe owners noisily pulling up their shutters. As I pedalled away from the centre of Calafell, even these sounds faded, leaving only the riffling of the surf and the rhythmic roll of Tetley's tyres on St John of God's endless promenade. What a fabulous morning to be out in the world again! Not a soul on the beach, either. On the Catalan coast, combine May or October with midweek and early morning and you'll probably have a bewitching few hours with just your own thoughts and the glitter of the rising sun on the lazy Mediterranean.

With no immediate navigation to do and only a few shouts of 'Barça!' to be acknowledged, my own thoughts turned to the map, strapped as always around Tetley's handlebars. Since Castelldefels I'd been using the 1:250,000 sheet, covering the whole of Catalonia, which I kept for stretches where I had none with a larger scale. In all honesty, this is really too small for cycling and navigation had frequently demanded not just that I be stationary but also that I squint through a little magnifier extracted from my bumbag.

The morning's first map session brought two items of news. First, in leaving the county of El Garraf and entering El Baix Penedès, I was now edging along the Costa

Daurada, 200 kilometres of 'golden coast' stretching all the way to the Delta de l'Ebre. Second, I would soon be able to swap my annoyingly small-scale map for a much more suitable 1:100,000 sheet called 'Terres de l'Ebre/Camp de Tarragona'. The place where this would begin to save my squinting eyes was the Arc de Berà, which in any case was a prime objective for the day. I upped my pace to get there for a mid-morning break.

We last encountered the Romans at Empúries on the Gulf of Roses, where they had supplanted the Greeks as the dominant traders around the third century BC. Two centuries later they'd annexed the whole of the Iberian peninsula as the new Roman province of Hispania. Three territorial divisions sufficed: Hispania Baetica in the south, Hispania Lusitania in the west and here in the north-east an enormous region covering about half of Iberia, named Hispania Tarraconensis, after the regional capital, Tarraco (modern-day Tarragona). In Roman times, then, Tarragona was much more important than little Barcelona.

The line of the major Roman road passing from the Pyrenees through Tarragona and on to the rest of Hispania is partly followed hereabouts by today's N-340. As it was under Emperor Augustus that Hispania was finally conquered, the whole route from the Pyrenees to Cádiz was known as the Via Augusta (hence also the name of our hotel in Barcelona). Around 13 BC, during the reign of Augustus himself, a magnificent triumphal arch was built at the point where the Via Augusta entered the territory of Tarraco. It's still there, on a traffic island, with twenty-first-century traffic rumbling past it on the same route as the Roman armies. Nowadays it's called the Arc de Berà.

Pulling Tetley up the kerb and onto the island, I leaned the bike against a handy milestone, marking 75 kilometres from Barcelona, took off my helmet, wiped my brow and sat with legs stretched before me on the cool grass to look up at the arch. On another Tuesday morning in spring, 2,022 years before, a foreman or a slave had doubtless also looked up to assess their progress. Well, I could tell them their work was still in remarkably good condition. The supporting blocks around the two bases may be a bit battered and the two columns a little pockmarked, but the graceful line of the arch itself is as sharp as ever it was. While some classical remains are nowadays fenced off, this one remains quite unprotected and I strode up to feel the rough sides, sharp corners and delicate fluting of this monument dedicated to the triumphs of a long-dead emperor.

Its modern name is actually not so modern, referring to Berà, a representative of another invading force, the Franks, and the first count of Barcelona from AD 802. Berà took part in the Frankish campaigns that pushed the occupying Moors south from Barcelona beyond here to the far bank of the Ebre.

Better though my larger scale map was, it didn't make clear whether, if I returned to the shore, I'd be able to get much further south. Entering a small housing estate, I pulled up next to three walkers – two men and a woman – whose boots suggested they knew what they were about.

'Excuse me. Is there a cycle route to the south that avoids the main road?'

'It would have to avoid the sea as well,' remarked the elder man. I didn't know quite what to say to this. Seeing my confusion, he leaned over my map. 'To the south is the sea.'

He was right. While I'd been describing my general direction as southwards, the orientation of the coast had in fact turned west. Recognising the triumph of a fellow pedant, I smiled and rephrased the question.

'OK, west. Is there a cycle route to the west?'

'Ah,' answered the happy pedant, 'there is indeed.'

Between them the three walkers gave me wonderfully precise directions on how to navigate a shoreside track not only to nearby Creixell but through to Torredembarra, some 5 kilometres away. Thanking them profusely, and waving reluctantly at their parting 'Barça!', I took the first turn they'd indicated. This led me behind a large hotel and across a car park into a small nature reserve… where I was forced to pull up as Tetley's tyres sloshed into the edge of a lake. A lake that barred the only route south. Or west.

Charitably acknowledging that it may be recent flooding, I turned back towards the main road. Now simply following the same signs as the cars, I looked around as I pedalled in the wide zone between white line and ditch. The landscape had become flatter and pretty boring, the large patches of rough ground interspersed with bunches of cranes hoisting into place new developments that looked just like the old developments. As if to confirm that Catalonia was slowly becoming Spain, nation as well as state, more and more of the unofficial signs – shop names, hoardings, graffiti – were in Spanish. Only the signs put up by the local authorities – street names, directions, public offices – were in Catalan.

Dominating Portbou are the railway sidings and station, from which tracks of both gauges enter the tunnel to France. The frontier lies along the top of the far ridge.

A sculpture by Joan Padern at the Art Parc, Colera, just south of the French border. The sculptor was born in the village.

Keep bags, straps and children well under control if you enter Llançà's unnamed 'pot shop'.

Blue, green and white are the colours of Cadaqués. Its seventeenth-century church dominates one of the town's coves.

A windy day on the beach of the Gulf of Roses. The northern Catalan coast is regularly lashed by the *tramuntana*, a north wind from the Pyrenees.

La Cobla, a sculpture by Francesc Anglès i Garcia on L'Escala's seafront, depicts the standard line-up of the band which accompanies Catalonia's traditional *sardana* dance.

The *sardana* was banned by Franco but is now enjoyed at almost every festival, as here in Llançà's Plaça Major.

A stretch of the wild coast that gives the Costa Brava its name. This view is from the road between Sant Feliu de Guíxols and Tossa de Mar, part of the Tour de France route three months after this was taken.

Frank Gehry's sculpture at Barcelona's Port Olímpic is supposed to be a fish, but personally I'm not convinced. Where's its head?

Early morning in spring is the time to avoid the crowds on the Catalan coast. Tetley the Bike ready for the off on Passeig Marítim de Sant Joan de Déu, Calafell.

The Roman amphitheatre at Tarragona.

The little house at the southern end of Catalonia, at the border
with the Comunidad Valenciana.

Tetley the Bike takes a break by an orange grove near Ulldecona.

Public art or graffiti? '*Bici es Vida*' ('Bike is life') says the
pennant on this unusual machine near Sant Esteve d'en Bas on
the Vía Verde del Carrilet I.

Cycling doesn't get much more idyllic. Poppies flank the Vía Verde del Carrilet I near Sant Feliu de Pallerols.

Bike on a stick. One of several near the old station at Llambilles on the Vía Verde del Carrilet II.

On the main road, one sign always mystified me. You pass it every so often all the way from the South of France and hereabouts it turned up yet again. Featuring pictures of lions and giraffes, it advertises the Réserve Africaine de Sigean, guiding the passing motorist – or cyclist – to this outdoor zoo with a handy map. It's in France. It's over 300 kilometres away. Now, I don't know about you, but even if I were driving a car with two bored children on the back seat, I don't think the comment: 'Tell you what, kids – we'll pull over at that zoo for some fresh air, say, tomorrow morning!' would keep them quiet for long. As if to confirm that this attraction's marketing folks have been given a bottomless budget, the sign I passed here was for people travelling south – in the wrong direction.

Yep, after we've been to Morocco, let's go to that French zoo!

As the modern Via Augusta approached ancient Tarraco itself, more Roman remains popped up: an ancient stone quarry, a second-century funeral monument right by the road and finally, near the city centre, the jewel in the local imperial crown – Tarragona's amphitheatre. It may not be the biggest or most complete example, but you'd be hard pressed to better the location.

The coastal hills here run right down to the Mediterranean shore and the city of Tarragona perches high above the sea. Stand in the right position – city behind you, amphitheatre in front – and the last two thousand years melt easily away as you see the structure the way the Romans would have seen it: two tree-lined headlands framing a golden beach with, in the background, the sparkling waters of the 'Middle Earth Sea' and, in the foreground, this stunning statement of Roman engineering and culture glowing a rich yellow-brown. Alas, subsequent citizens of Tarragona have used the theatre as a quarry and less than half of its terracing remains. I was pleased to see, however, that between the amphitheatre and the modern town lay a modern playground – like most in Spain, without any age limit – and so the dramatic site above the shore still echoed to the whoops and shouts of youths letting off steam in the midday sun.

Leaning on the fence to take it all in, I was beginning to steam a little myself and, with Spanish lunchtime well under way, I pushed Tetley inland in search of shade, drink and food – in that order. What I found, a few blocks inside the line of Tarragona's Roman walls, was a cool cafe terrace in the Plaça de la Font, where a thirst-quenching *horchata*, followed by tortilla and *sin*, hit the spot with such precision that I ordered exactly the same again.

Horchata (Catalan: *orxata*) is a strange drink, which I'd never even heard of until I'd lived in Spain for a few years. Originating in Valencia, this weird, grey combination of water, sugar and tiger nuts is served very cool. The strange thing about tiger nuts is they are not nuts at all, but the sweet, nutty tubers of a sedge introduced to Spain by the Arabs. The strange thing about *horchata* is that, while in hot weather it's incredibly refreshing, on a cool day it's quite disgusting.

Of Tarraco, the Roman historian Florus, who taught rhetoric here, wrote: 'Of all cities which are chosen for a rest, if you will believe me who know many, it is the most delightful' (quoted in Macaulay). In the nineteenth century, Ford took up the same theme:

> *Tarragona, as a residence for invalids, is remarkably healthy: the air is mild, but from its great dryness, bracing and rather keen... the walks are excellent, looking down to the sea; while in various directions on the land side are scattered pine woods, heaths, and aromatic wastes, where the wild-lavender and sweet-smelling shrubs perfume the air even in mid winter.*

As I slumped, post-tortilla number two, in the Plaça de la Font, the Tarragona air was having the same effect on me as it had had on both Romans and Victorians who chose this spot for their R&R. I didn't even mind the intrusion of an uninvited accordionist whose repertoire seemed to consist entirely of cheesy tunes from 1960s films. To be honest, I've a soft spot for these tunes – 'Volare', 'Stranger in Paradise' and so on – as they're often the soundtracks from those romantic comedies that had created the image of the Mediterranean that I'd been carrying around in my head for years before I actually came here. They always seemed to star David Niven or Tony Curtis or Anita Ekberg and often involved laid-back conversations in outdoor cafes very like this one. Cafes that were out of doors – gosh! Tarragona had indeed been in my original plan for an overnight – but two o'clock was no time to end a day's cycling.

Both the reason Tarragona had been a planned overnight stop and the reason it had ceased to be so were down to my fellow gatecrasher of the Barcelona choir, the Wanderer. I'd hoped that my passage through Tarragona would prompt a personal appearance, as guide to a city he also admires.

However, in all matters the Wanderer is what an aunt of mine would have called rather 'adjacent', and in the matter of appointments he's even more adjacent than the Spanish. I had, the previous autumn, proposed a specific date in May for a day to be spent together in Tarragona: not with any expectation of commitment of course, for the Wanderer carries no diary, but more to plant the idea in the wandering brain.

My proposal was, I subsequently learnt, received in the Spirit House, a bar in Dundalk, Ireland, there to cause some consternation among the musicians with whom the Wanderer was passing a mellow hour or two.

'May?' asked the fiddle player. 'Would that be the month of May next year? Sure and you might be dead and gone by then.'

'So I might,' admitted the Wanderer.

'Just a minute,' commented the fiddler. 'That wouldn't be that cyclin' friend o' yours that pedalled right the way across Scotland stayin' in those B&B places instead of a hayrick or a lonesome bothy with just a prayer and a lament on the whistle for company, to see if God would look after him till mornin'... would it?'

'It would,' conceded the Wanderer.

'Och, the man mus' be English. No reliance on the Almighty whatsoever.'

The text message I'd received that evening from the Wanderer read: 'Greetings from Dundalk! Have just repeated your proposal of rendezvous in Tarragona one day next year to assembled musicians and other drinkers here and all agree such long-distance planning the work of the Devil! Excellent idea but timescale impossible to conceive. Cheers!'

The fact that the Wanderer no more believes in the Devil than I do does not deter him from classifying people by the religion of their ancestors. There are cultural Protestants such as myself (he would claim), who plan to do things and then, by and large, do them; and there are cultural Catholics such as himself, to whom things are done – things which provide an endless source of grievance, complaint and folk song.

Another message had followed about an hour later: 'Taxi driver firmly against any visit to Spain at all on grounds of widespread presence of p**ftas and absence of cows. Wonders who would want to take holiday in cow-forsaken place?'

So, forsaken as I was in the middle of a city I knew not at all, I decided to turn tourist for an hour – that is unless a long-distance cyclist is already tarnished with that label. To save precious weight, I'd pre-printed a single page off the web for one or two places and Tarragona was among them. The eleven highlights, it said, were five Roman sights, three churches, two convents and an old town hall. I'd got about an hour on a bike. Religious buildings were out – I leave those for people to whom they mean something: Rose Macaulay, for example, who seemed positively obsessed by them. Having already 'done' the amphitheatre, I was left a whistle-stop tour of five sights. First up, the Old Town Hall.

Well, right in front of me on Plaça de la Font stood a fairly old town hall, but the word *'Ajuntament'* ('council' in Catalan) above the door was a clue that this wasn't old enough. A short, steep walk with Tetley up the narrow, cobbled streets, accompanied by the judder of cars and the rattle of shopping trolleys, brought me onto Carrer Major, where another, smaller, humbler town hall stood among the shops, in mustard-yellow and this time with the word

'*Ayuntamiento*' ('council' in Castilian) above the door. It dates from the sixteenth century and nowadays seems to be mostly an art gallery.

As the heavy wooden doors were open, I wheeled Tetley through and was rewarded by one of those classically Spanish courtyards – a small atrium, light and cool at the same time, all narrow columns, lazy archways and potted plants. As I craned my neck upwards, a voice behind made me jump.

'Whuurgh.'

'Sorry.'

'Sorry.'

'I'm sorry, señor, there's nowhere to put your bicycle here,' said the polite young woman with an ID badge around her neck.

'Ah, no problem. I'm just passing through. In fact, I'm looking for the Roman forum.'

'It's out here, right and right again. More cobbles, I'm sorry.' She seemed to be in a permanent state of apology. 'Have you travelled far?'

I gave her the gist of my journey.

'Oh,' she said, disappointment in he eyes. 'But you haven't allowed enough time for Tarragona. I'm sorry.'

'You're right, but it's me that's sorry, señora.'

And so, all apologised out, I followed her directions, past buildings so old that at least five generations of stones and bricks were visible in the same wall. In fact, it's said that a discerning eye can distinguish in the walls of medieval Tarragona certain inscriptions that clearly mark them as having been 'recycled' from Roman remains. Not being discerning enough, I continued until emerging in a sudden burst of colour. Walls of cherry-red, salmon-pink, vermilion, ochre and deep green surrounded a tiny square, in the middle of which stood a busy cafe terrace next to a short length of free-standing, ancient wall. The nameplate said Plaça del Forum. Forum? This? It wasn't what I'd expected. Tarraco may not have been Rome, but after all it was the provincial capital. Bemused, I asked a passing waiter if I was in the right place. This was a mistake.

'Was forum,' he rattled in abbreviated Spanish, 'is square, are buildings, is long ago, is history, there circus, I go.'

And he did, back into the bar. During the nanosecond of the uttered 'there circus', he'd waved towards one corner of the little square and so 'there circus, I went'.

A few streets later and this was more like it. Just inside the city walls the remains of the Roman circus, which was used for chariot racing and the like, lay over quite an extensive area right next to a modern street, Carrer de Sant Oleguer. It dates from the first century AD, probably during the time of Domitian, the eleventh Roman emperor. The track, a tunnel and several lines of walls have been revealed, and what especially impressed me were the remains of a bank of terracing, from which citizens must have cheered and jeered as their favourites hurtled around the track. On a baking day such as this you could almost smell the dust clouds as they billowed over the fans. Ford had been similarly overwhelmed by the strangely evocative nature of Tarragona's Roman remains. 'Even the ruins speak Latin,' he ventured, 'and bear the impress of Caesar; what a sermon in these stones, which preach the fallen pride of imperial Rome!'

Continuing along the street, I found that I'd returned to the spot where I'd entered Tarragona, opposite the amphitheatre. Feeling rather dusty myself, I decided to skip the other two sights and return to cycling. Even without a guide, tourism to order isn't really for me.

Pedalling off in some relief, I crossed the Rambla Nova and shot down through the network of dark, narrow streets that lead towards the shore. Towards but not quite to, for access to the docks is as restricted in Tarragona as in Barcelona. No matter, for this meant a jiggle through the old fisherman's district of El Serrallo, which showed distinct signs of heading upmarket: busy restaurants, gaily painted facades, badly parked BMWs and Audis.

On the bridge over the River Francolí, which drains much of El Camp, the Tarragona hinterland, I was surprised to notice the pleasant but entirely unexpected smell of new-mown grass. As I pulled up and peered over the parapet, what I saw was a tiny sliver of river wandering not between the usual urban debris but, sure enough, between two broad swathes of neatly mowed, bright green grass so rich and smooth that I half expected to see two sets of stumps, eleven men in whites and a pavilion.

Tarragona's western industrial suburbs also match Barcelona's in their vast areas of new cars, closely parked next to the ship that had either brought them or was about to despatch them. There were huge pyramids of a substance that looked remarkably like talcum powder, followed by giant golf balls containing gas or petrol. The goods leaving Tarragona in the past have been even more precious, for it's said that in the eighteenth century, whether by fair means or foul, the British removed shiploads of priceless antiquities from this port.

Having escaped the main southbound dual carriageway, I was pleased to find myself once again by the gentle shores of the Costa Daurada, at La Pineda, to be greeted by a sight that made me laugh out loud. A roadside cafe had done its best to tempt my countrymen with a sign that read, in bold white letters:

'Bugger & Chips'

Not today, thank you. This reminded me of another sign outside a building up in Llançà that announces itself as a *'bugaderia'*. Nothing distasteful goes on there: it's Catalan for laundry. Nor does a *ferreteria* sell ferrets: it's Catalan for ironmonger's. Whether or not they opted for the bugger and chips, there must have been plenty of English-speaking tourists around here, probably drawn by the nearby theme park of PortAventura, as I also passed bars called 'The Dubliner' and 'Bees Knees II' before pushing up and over the neck of Cap Salou to be greeted by as stunning a view as I'd seen in this entire jaunt down the Catalan coast.

The cycle track dropped away across a rolling clifftop of miniature olive trees, pale green against the darker, taller fronds of tamarisk, but both quite outshone by the dazzling magenta and crimson flowers of a thousand Hottentot figs. Beyond this kaleidoscopic show, the cliff edge was marked by spiky, green and yellow clumps of agave, pointing up at a majestic stretch of silver-blue sea that caressed a huge sweep of coastline ending in the low, jagged peaks of what looked like a Caribbean island thrown across the Atlantic and dumped into the Mediterranean just for effect. After standing agape for several minutes, I leaned Tetley against a bench where I pulled my map out of its case and folded it over. This sweep of coastline, the map told me, took in the towns of Salou, Cambrils, L'Hospitalet de l'Infant and

L'Ametlla de Mar before disappearing westwards into the Gulf of Sant Jordi, the great natural harbour at the north of the Delta de l'Ebre. Of the delta itself, so dominant on the map, nothing at all could be seen. On the other hand, what dominated the visible horizon, but seemed absent from the map, was that unexpected island.

A gulp from the water bottle and a severe scratching of the head solved the mystery. That was no island. What appeared to rise from the shimmering Med, but which actually rose from the invisible flatlands of the delta, was the Serra del Montsià, a 764-metre-high massif that looked relatively insignificant on the map but in reality was a huge landmark that would be ever-present over the next two days. The view that I sat and stared at for a few more minutes stretched over 60 kilometres and was, in effect, the end of Catalonia.

Salou turned out to be the start of another long stretch of relentlessly over-developed *costa*, where one town blurred into the next and where, for the most part, the names of the settlements seem to be their only link with the original fishing villages that must once have been scattered along a largely deserted shore. One exception was Cambrils. Not that it was any less developed, just that at its heart, it retained the air and some of the architecture of a real town. It was here that I decided to put up for the night, at another excellent and reasonably priced hotel in the backstreets, the Hostal Can Solé.

(English-speaking visitors to Catalonia should be aware that *'hostal'* does not generally imply a hostel; except at the top end of the market, it seems to be used interchangeably with *'hotel'*. Another linguistic note is that the prevalence in Catalonia of hotels and restaurants named '*Can* something' is because this is an abbreviation for the Catalan *'casa d'en'*, meaning 'house of' – the same as the French *'chez'* – followed by the name of the owner or chef.)

With the luxury of time for an aperitif before eating, I settled in front of a beer (alcoholic this time) on the terrace of a corner bar in the old port quarter of Cambrils. Here I trawled the leaflets I'd picked up in the hotel... and therein found the answer to a question I really should have resolved soon after moving to Catalonia.

For most of the first half of the 1600s Europe was at war with itself. Catholic was fighting Protestant; Bourbon fighting Habsburg; France fighting almost everyone. This was the Thirty Years War. Being Habsburgs, Philip III and IV of Spain had lined up against the French Bourbons. Though part of the Spanish Empire, Catalonia was on the whole unenthusiastic about the war and when Catalan peasants were obliged to accommodate many of the Castilian troops, it was a step too far. In what the Castilians call the Catalan Revolt, a Catalan republic was declared, eventually fighting WITH the French AGAINST the Spanish. From a Catalan perspective, the revolt is referred to as the Reapers' War (*la Guerra dels Segadors*), lasting from 1640 to 1659, when the Catalans were finally defeated.

The local significance of all this to Cámbrils is that, early in the Reapers' War, a three-day siege of the town by Castilian troops ended in particularly bloody fashion when, despite the terms of the Catalans' surrender, the troops murdered many of the townspeople.

Recalling that the annual Catalan national day marks a defeat, you won't be surprised to learn that defeat in the Reapers' War is also regularly commemorated, being the subject of the Catalan national anthem. It is this that I hadn't clearly understood, although the clue is in the anthem's title, 'Els Segadors'. The lyrics leave little to the imagination in their references to the 'villainous' Castilians:

Endarrera aquesta gent
tan ufana i tan superba.
Bon cop de falç,
Bon cop de falç,
Defensors de la terra!
Bon cop de falç!

(Drive them back, those people
So conceited and so arrogant.
A good blow with the sickle,
A good blow with the sickle,
Defenders of the land!
A good blow with the sickle!)

Humming the tune which I'd heard often enough, and now whose message had finally sunk in, I ambled down to the seafront where, from among the many almost empty restaurants, I chose the Taberna del Mar for an excellent Catalan salad and *chuletas de cerdo* (pork chops) with chips, washed down with a carafe of the local red. It's a shame that green vegetables are so rare in Catalan restaurants; most meat or fish comes just with chips – plus, if you're lucky, a sad-looking, grilled red pepper. Julie and I have concluded that Catalans must get so many of their vitamins from salad vegetables – lettuces, courgettes, tomatoes, peppers and so on – that they don't need the extras with their main course. Another theory is that their preserved products (carrots and beans in particular), which incidentally tend to come in jars rather than cans, are so good that the they're often chosen over the fresh version – although a restaurant would never stoop so low, of course. Altogether it's a bit of a mystery.

The view over the marina was a relatively new one, for Cambrils' substantial harbour was built only in the twentieth century. But, harbour or no harbour, the town's maritime tradition goes back a long way for it was from here that Catalan-Aragonese King Jaume I's troops set out to conquer Mallorca during the period when Catalonia itself became an imperial power.

The town, however, owes its origins not to the sea but to its location at the point where the narrow coastal plain from the south opens out into the vast, fertile area of El Camp de Tarragona, which I'd been skirting all day. Tomorrow morning's route would see me entering that corridor to the south, between the sea and the uplands. As I wandered happily back to the hotel, I suspected that it might not be quite as easy a run as today's.

Day 10

To the Delta: Cambrils to Sant Carles de la Ràpita

Brushing off the croissant crumbs, I laid my large-scale map over the breakfast table and examined, through my small magnifying glass, the stretch where the Tivissa-Vandellòs mountains (a name new to me) pushed the main road, the motorway and the railway into a tightly interwoven wiggle close to the shoreline itself. I didn't particularly fancy battling with a line of articulated vehicles again.

'Taking your BTT to the mountains?'

I jumped, dropping the magnifier. You can't help it when you're concentrating so hard that the world outside your head all but disappears. It was a short, wiry man – presumably another guest – who was peering over my shoulder, my jump making him laugh out loud. This seemed to be the Coast of Breakfast Laughter. A 'BTT' is a *bicicleta todo terreno*', a mountain bike.

'Er, no. I'm trying to avoid the mountains. Actually, it's not a BTT anyway. It's a hybrid.'

Not knowing the Spanish for 'hybrid', I'd just pronounced the English word in a Spanish sort of way. Another guffaw from Wiry.

'Bravo! I agree. Bikes and mountains don't mix. I used to cycle up and down this coast until my knees made problems for me. Where are you headed?'

'To the Delta de l'Ebre.'

'Today?'

(At least it wasn't 'Like that?')

'Yes, today. I hope so. But I want to avoid the *carretera* if possible.'

'Ah, the trucks they are nowadays too big, too close. But I think you must use the *carretera* now and then.'

'What about here?' I asked, pointing at the interwoven wiggle.

'Unfortunately, yes.'

'And here?' I pointed at a stretch where the main road looped inland, leaving the coast to the motorway and railway.

'Ah, here there is a beautiful rural road. Between L'Ametlla and L'Ampolla.' He waved a vague finger at the map. 'It's probably too small to see on here. But I propose this road, this track. Here you are truly *en el quinto pino*.'

'*En el quinto pino?*' I asked. Literally it meant 'in the fifth pine tree'.

'Ah, in English you say "in the middle of no place".'

'Nowhere,' I corrected.

'Exactly! I wish I cycle with you today,' he continued in English, 'but my knees... and my work. I must go. Good luck!'

Having thanked him for the advice, I passed the magnifier over the area he'd waved at and, yes, there was a very thin black line there, wandering among the brown contours. A line that could be a road. Of sorts.

Although for cyclists there was no alternative to the main road south from Cambrils, once again there was for walkers.

> Just as with the French Grandes Randonnées, there's an extensive network of long-distance footpaths in Spain, extremely well mapped (unlike most cycle tracks), well signposted (ditto), regularly marked by the same reassuring red and white painted lines as in France and even with the same abbreviation: GR for Gran Recorrido (Spanish) or Gran Recorregut (Catalan). All the way from the French border at Portbou to the border with Valencia at Ulldecona, the mighty GR-92 follows the entire coast of Catalonia rather more closely than I'd been doing. In many places we'd shared the same track, the same promenade, but here where Cambrils petered out was one of the spots where I'd have happily swapped cycle shoes for walking boots, to stride out through the trees and across the fields that hugged the shoreline.

Slinging Tetley over my shoulder was, alas, not an option and so my tubular black friend and I trundled inland to pick up the N-340 once again.

Actually, the traffic wasn't too heavy that morning and for a while I even tagged onto the back of two other cyclists. Smiling cyclists. They may have been smiling at the recent memory of approaching the rear of an English cyclist who, unaware of their presence, was singing 'Blue Suede Shoes' at the top of his voice. (The 2/4 rhythm is perfect for steady pedalling – try it.)

As the morning wore on, the temperature nudged up another couple of notches. There was no breath of breeze. As I looked around, I noticed that the landscape itself had begun to look more like that of a hot, dry country. This was the county of El Baix Camp. With the hills bustling in from the right, low olive groves were interspersed with large tracts of scrub on thin stony soil that looked impossible to cultivate. In the distance, moving clouds of dust followed a truck or a motorbike as it rocked along a dirt road between the fields. Nearer to the road, nothing moved save the occasional darting lizard that scuttled away as I passed. In the built-up areas cars were parked, wherever possible, in the shade of trees, walls or corrugated sheets. This felt more like the southern *costas* than the coast of Catalonia. Too dry for crops, some fields were sprouting bungalows. Vast campsites spread out in the direction of the sea: Els Prats and then Miami Platja. A convoy of four-by-fours bounced out into the road by some neon signs. Maybe more southern California.

At L'Hospitalet de l'Infant (named after the hostel of the monarch's son rather than a children's hospital), I pulled over at the railway station to check some train times for the next day when I expected to be bouncing back off the end of Catalonia by train for a few kilometres. However, just as I'd found at Cambrils station, there seemed to be a local shortage of pocket timetables and so, realising yet another use for the digital camera, I snapped images of the timetables posted on the station wall.

South of L'Hospitalet de l'Infant, the landscape took another dramatic turn, for here first one and then another huge industrial installation hove into view right next to the road. It turns out that they were two nuclear power stations: Vandellòs I and Vandellòs II. At the time, of Spain's seven nuclear power stations, these were the only two in Catalonia and the only two on the Mediterranean coast. Two power stations, two accidents: a fire in 1983 at one and a ruptured pipe in 2004 at the other. The increasing traffic had me scuttling rapidly past, like those roadside lizards. By lunchtime I was more than pleased to leave the noise and dust of the N-340 and drop back down to the coast at the fine little town of L'Ametlla de Mar.

Well, it looked pretty fine to me from my vantage point in the shade cast by a vast blue and white parasol on the terrace of a clean, cool cafe, where I was already on the outside of a long, languid draught of chilled *sin*. Beyond and below a grand, white balustrade, the modest harbour showed a dizzying pattern of rippled and smooth blue water between about a dozen moored vessels. And here's the odd thing: they were all fishing boats. No pleasure craft, no marina. Other than the bar-restaurant where I sat, legs splayed to catch any hint of breeze, the town had revealed nothing for the visitor at all. Excellent. Another working town, like Vilanova i la Geltrú. Except this one had a friendly waiter.

'Where are you going, señor?'

Like Cubans and Scots – but unlike the Welsh – Catalans are by and large interested in cyclists passing through their town. I outlined my itinerary.

'Ah, you have the best time of the year, señor. I wish that I too am on a cycling holiday.'

'When do you take your holiday?'

'In the winter I go to South America. To Brazil this year and to Chile the next.'

'Do you cycle when you're there?'

'Señor, you do not have a wife, I think.'

'Not exactly.' I'd used *'de verdad, no'*, literally 'in truth, no'.

'Ah, with a wife in truth your days are not your own, señor. If you will cycle and she will shop, this means that you both will shop.'

'Perhaps one day you both will cycle,' I suggested, thinking of Julie, who'd already volunteered for a stint at the pedals later in this trip.

'You do not know my wife, señor!'

Indeed, I did not. I wondered if it was the short, plump lady who brought my next *sin*, along with a *tapa* of juicy green olives and a crunchy *bikini*. Best not to ask.

Alternately pedalling and pushing Tetley through the narrow and at times steep streets of L'Ametlla, I couldn't help noticing how jovial and relaxed its citizens seemed to be. Women stopped in the middle of the road to admire a friend's baby while the male drivers of the cars thus delayed simply beamed through their windscreens at the scene. Imagine that in downtown Derby. A final oddity that makes L'Ametlla still stick in my mind among the long series of coastal towns south of Barcelona was that, from loudspeakers tucked up under balconies and strung from lamp posts, a constant barrage of chat – not music, just chat – peppered the streets with information. From what I could understand of the Catalan, it was mostly information on how to claim state benefits, particularly unemployment benefit. Although jolly music is commonly heard wafting from such speakers at fiesta time in Catalonia, this was the first time I'd heard them used for this purpose.

Just beyond a bridge over the motorway I found the start of the thin black line recommended at breakfast by Señor Wiry. On the ground it was a dusty brown road that had certainly been surfaced one day. One day some time ago. With a long haul inland to rejoin the trucks as the only alternative, I threw in my lot with the thin black line, since the map suggested it might re-emerge at the coast near L'Ampolla, a dozen kilometres to the south.

Soon the road surface improved. At first the route ran strictly parallel to the motorway but then began to wander around a little. White-walled, single-storey houses were scattered here and there on either side, some quite old, some large enough for several families and all surrounded by substantial grounds. This was no poor district. As I pedalled further from town, more and more of the properties were hidden behind locked gates and high fences, which – as I discovered when occasionally stopping to peer through – hid the odd swimming pool and shiny black Mercedes. Before the Autopista de la Mediterrània was built in the 1970s these homes would have been just a pleasant walk from the sea, which kept poking its sparkling head above the trees to my left. Now there was no way across the motorway. I saw no eastbound, i.e. sea-bound, track, no tunnel, no bridge for a good 6 kilometres.

Though the occasional dog barked, their masters didn't appear. In fact, no one at all appeared until the tiny hamlet of Racons, where an elderly lady carrying a basket round to her neighbour's house stopped to nod at the passing cyclist – or perhaps at his Barça shirt. Beyond Racons, the landscape became more undulating, the slopes more challenging. At the top of one rise, I pulled into the shade of one of the pine trees that skirted much of the route – perhaps Señor Wiry's mysterious fifth one – to take an eager draught from my water bottle and squirt the rest over my head. A thermometer outside a chemist's in L'Ametlla had said 29 degrees, but it felt much warmer out here in the sticks.

Standing up to stretch my back, I squinted at the views to the west. Dry stream beds wound between small olive groves where the dark-green bushes blotched a regular background of baked red soil. While some of the fields belonged to the roadside smallholdings, I could now see that beyond were a number of larger, white-walled farmhouses. Beyond these, two or three lines of hills shimmered in the haze, the most distant merely a vague line of jagged, dark grey against the light grey of a clear sky that rose into a deep blue above my head.

With the last of the water now dripping down my temples, I set off quickly so that it would still have a cooling effect as I freewheeled down the other side of the hill. I was grateful to Señor Wiry. This isolated, wandering route through the backwoods was what cycle touring is all about: rural, deserted, scenic and, for cyclists of a certain age, challenging.

Seeing a bridge over the motorway at Cap Roig, I took it and, on a rise, was surprised to see land beyond the sea. My angle had changed again and there, forming a grey and golden line between the misty-blue sky and the deep-blue sea, was my first view of the Delta de l'Ebre. From the previous day's vantage point at Cap Salou, the flatlands of the delta itself had been too far away to be visible.

After pedalling through a broad area of allotments, and by now pretty desperate for a drink, I rolled into L'Ampolla. I'd also rolled into another county: El Baix Ebre.

Another harbour, another cafe. Apart from a refreshing *agua con gas*, the main entertainment here was the herds of schoolchildren spilling from a fleet of buses on their way home. 'Herds' is unfair. 'Herds' are what English children run riot in. Catalan children are what English children used to be: boisterous but good-humoured. A boy walking backwards for a lark, as we all did, knocked over one of the cafe's flowerpots, but, with a red face and a hand of apology, he put it back again. Spotting me rolling the cold glass over my sweaty forehead, two girls theatrically wiped their own brows, puffed out their cheeks in mock exhaustion and ran off giggling. Several waved goodbye to the bus drivers, instead of leaving the buses in tatters before setting off to terrorise the town. What's the difference? Sunshine? Families? Discuss.

With the delta now all around, roads and lanes spread out like butter on toast, giving a greater choice of route. With my destination the lowest bridging point at Amposta, I chose the back roads through Camarles and L'Aldea.

In the Cantabrian Mountains of northern Spain, at a point nearly 2,000 metres above sea level but less than 50 kilometres from the Atlantic shore, rises Spain's longest river, the Ebre (or Ebro in Spanish). That is, at 910 kilometres, it's the longest entirely in Spain; the Tagus, while longer, flows into the sea at Lisbon. The Ebre also carries the largest volume of water, from such a huge catchment area of over

80,000 square kilometres that on a map it looks like almost all of north-east Spain. Over the years, sediment deposited by this vast flow has pushed the point at which the river finally enters the Mediterranean further and further eastwards until the delta itself now covers over 300 square kilometres.

My old geography teacher, Mr Plampin, had he not, alas, already joined the earthly sediment himself, would have been pleased to know that after forty-two years I still recalled from O-level days that there are three types of river delta.

'And they are, Guise?' he would have inquired, looking over his spectacles.

'They are, sir, the fan delta, the bird's foot delta and...'

'And?'

'And another one, sir.'

'Indeed. There are many other ones, Guise, but you have hit upon the one we see here at the Ebro. Look at the map, Guise. What does it look like to you?'

'Er, it looks like a dog to me, sir.'

'A dog, Guise?'

'Yes, the face of a dog running very quickly into the sea, with his shiny nose raised high, his ears pressed back and his long chin hairs flapping in the wind, sir.'

'Chin hairs? What are you talking about, boy? The delta of the River Ebro is an example of a bird's foot delta, where the flow of the river dominates the topography rather than – rather than what, Guise?'

'Rather than the waves or the tides dominating, sir.'

'Exactly. And what other example of a bird's foot delta can you name?'

'The delta of the, er... of the Bird's Foot River?'

'See me afterwards, Guise. It is of course the Mississippi Delta.'

'Paul Simon says the Mississippi Delta looks like a guitar, sir.'

'Afterwards, Guise!'
'Sir.'

Mr Plampin would be right. The tiny tides of the Mediterranean have had little effect on the delta's shape. Over the years the Delta de l'Ebre has supported livestock, deer-hunting, fishing (in its many lagoons), citrus fruit, vegetables and, since the seventeenth century, rice cultivation. Nowadays nearly all Catalonia's rice production comes from here. Since 1983 it's been designated a natural park, due to its importance as a habitat for wildlife, especially as a vast wetland and a stopover for migrating birds.

The Ebre has played an important role in the history of Iberia too, not least in lending its name – 'Iber' to the Romans – to the peninsula itself and to its indigenous population, the Iberians. For a while the Ebre formed the southern frontier of Roman Iberia (with Carthaginians beyond); and later the northern frontier of Moorish Iberia, al-Andalus. More recently, the Battle of the Ebre formed a decisive phase of the civil war – and I hoped to learn more of that later on.

For the time being I simply enjoyed the change in landscape and in pace, as I zoomed across the neck of the delta from L'Ampolla to Amposta. (History could have been kinder to a passing cyclist by choosing names more dissimilar than L'Ametlla, L'Ampolla, L'Aldea and Amposta – I admit that in writing these lines I've continually had to check that I hadn't confused one with another.) It felt suddenly like the Fenlands of eastern England. Flanking the road were irrigation ditches and embankments, beyond which sat squat little smallholdings protected by neat lines of low trees. To my left, further out into the delta, rectangular fields of dark soil and, more and more, of shimmering water – the rice fields which reminded me that this wasn't the Fens after all – stretched to a horizon dotted with clumps of darker trees and the occasional large white farm.

The road itself followed the field boundaries and at the corner of one, a field of ripening artichokes, I stopped to take a photograph, only to be waved away by a distant farm worker with what I took to be a volley of abuse. Raising a hand in apology for I know not what indiscretion, I hurriedly pedalled away.

Camarles felt like an abandoned town. Even though the siesta should just have been over, the tourist information office, railway station and only visible bar were all closed. Large warehouses and a food processing factory bore no signs of life. This was in sharp contrast to the delta's main town, Deltebre.

Though not on my cycle route, I'd visited that singular town before and remember feeling suddenly transported to deepest Latin America. Bashed-up cars rattled along rutted streets between single-storey houses, most of whose occupants seemed busy in their gardens, where potatoes and onions struggled for light among rows of giant kale and trees heavy with lemons and oranges. As we passed, they'd all looked up, not at the car with the British registration but at the old van behind, on whose roof were strapped two rusty loudspeakers, excitedly tempting the gardeners to drop their hoes and hurry along to a clothes sale at the local church (not in Catalan but in Spanish, confirming that the delta marks the end of Catalonia).

The approach to Amposta from the north is dramatic. The flat, empty lands of the delta come to an abrupt end at the left bank of the Ebre itself, where a grand suspension bridge leaps the broad, blue-green rippled surface of the river. The jumbled walls, roofs and towers of the town rise from across the water like a medieval enclosure. With the afternoon sun dipping behind it, Amposta's cool, deep shadows welcomed me into town.

Handsome from afar, Amposta is less so from within. In Richard Ford's 1845 book, he called it 'a miserable, aguish, fever- and mosquito-plagued port... with some 1,000 sallow souls'. I wouldn't go so far as that: it just seemed an ordinary sort of town in an extraordinary sort of a place. Tetley and I cruised along tidy shopping streets – albeit with most of the shops still closed, again strangely for post-siesta – and across neat squares, for the most part empty of people. A corner bar attracted me by the simple attributes of being open and having some customers. The two customers in question were both tough-looking males who would have walked easily into jobs as bouncers. One, the elder and rounder, sat on a red plastic chair, placing orders with the younger and less round. I knew the latter wasn't the waiter as the real waiter came outside to take my own order. As Fatty had ordered ice cream and coffee, so did I. He turned to look at me, the chair threatening to collapse beneath him as he did so.

'Hot day,' I said. 'Ice cream's a good idea.'

Fatty grunted. His gofer brought out his ice cream, which Fatty proceeded to consider carefully, half an eye still on me. Feeling I should reassure him that I was just passing through, I chanced a question.

'Is the road to Sant Carles down there?' I asked, pointing down a likely side street.

'You're cycling all the way to Sant Carles?'

'It's not far is it?'

Before he could reply, Gofer interrupted: 'It would be far for my *amigo*, eh?'

Gofer's smile was not matched by any from Fatty, who said something unintelligible to his friend that had him scurrying back inside the bar. Fatty took a mouthful of ice cream, rolled it around his mouth while looking high up the building and then turned once again to me.

'It's down there, then right, then straight-straight until you meet the *carretera*. From there it's about nine kilometres.'

'Thank you.' I thought it was worth my usual follow-up question too. 'Do I have to use the *carretera*? Is there an alternative for a bike?'

While I was asking this, Gofer came out with Fatty's coffee and the waiter with mine and my ice cream. Gofer had heard my question.

'Yes, there is one,' he said. 'At halfway you can cross the channel to a smaller road. It's very tranquil and has no trucks.'

Another few words passed between the two of them.

'For once,' announced Fatty, 'The boy tells the truth. You have this choice.'

Happy with their advice, I ate up, drank up and paid up in pretty short order and was soon back in the saddle, waving my informants goodbye.

Amposta's rather dreary suburbs eventually led to the predicted main road, where a branch of the motorway came in from a new bridge that had recently taken the title of 'lowest crossing point of the Ebre' from the suspension bridge by which I'd arrived. Actually, I'd had my eye on an overnight in Amposta, but something about the atmosphere of the town put me off, something I couldn't put my finger on. This may not have been a good decision, for a stiff south wind had got up from nowhere, making progress difficult. It was by now late in the day, my legs were tired after sixty-plus kilometres and, fool of fools, I'd forgotten to top up my water bottle at the bar. Beyond L'Enclusa I did switch to Gofer's minor road, but the direction, straight into the wind, was still the same. In such a short stretch I must have stopped half a dozen times to take sustenance from a mouthful of Tic Tacs and let out a long sigh of relief as I eventually passed the sign announcing my arrival in Sant Carles de la Ràpita.

Having been here several years before I knew there was no shortage of hotels and soon found one, the Hotel Plaça Vella on another backstreet, where I presented myself, a bedraggled and weary traveller, to the receptionist. In contrast to everywhere else I'd stayed so far, this place was actually busy. Guests swished up and down the stairs, children played on the floor, the receptionist juggled phone calls with other jobs – but he did have a room for me, as well as a suitable slot for Tetley just under the stairs. Result.

Even after a shower I still felt road weary. Although rapid food followed by rapid bed was the plan, this was soon scuppered by the sight in a nearby bar of a sea of radiant faces reflected in the glow from a large TV screen. Must be another Barça game – nothing else in Catalonia draws such crowds out of their apartments and into the nearest bar for two hours of worship. I poked my head into this one.

'Barça playing again?'

'*Sí*. Champions League.'

'How's it going?'

'Nil nil.'

No clues as to whether or not I was destined for a night of mass cheers and fireworks till midnight. Barça supporters have enough sense of humour for occasional mass laughter too. Later that year I was in another bar watching another Barça game when the camera picked out in the VIP seats the Italian prime minister, Silvio Berlusconi, dropping decisively off to sleep. Mass guffaws.

Finding a tapas bar with music instead of the TV (no noise at all not being an option in Spanish bars), I was settling down to some particularly spicy *patatas bravas* (small chunks of fried potato in a hot sauce) when an English couple came in. The following half hour opened my eyes to another side of the Spanish *costas*: the seaward side. Being neither sailor nor swimmer, I'd tended to forget that half the pleasure of the seaside – or for some people, all of it – involves being on or in the water itself. This couple had spent the last five hours sailing up the coast from Dénia, a big resort on the Costa Blanca, about 200 kilometres to the south.

'Was the wind right today?' I asked, hoping this might be a reasonable question to ask a mariner.

'Ha!' replied the skipper. 'You're not a sailor, are you?'

'No, not at all. What did I say wrong?'

'Well, we misled you. When we say "sailed", it doesn't necessarily mean we used sails.'

'Really?'

'No. Ours is a motor launch. It took about five hours in that. Under sail it'd take all day.'

'Or more,' added his wife and first mate. Skip nodded.

'Oh, I see,' I said, smiling. 'Sorry. Are you staying in a hotel in Sant Carles?' I'd hoped to find some safer ground but unfortunately had just dug another hole.

'What?! No, we sleep on board, of course.'

'Oh yes, of course. Sorry.'

'No need to keep apologising, old man. What brings you here?'

So we exchanged a few tales and, from what I learnt about the hazards of boating, my little frissons of navigational uncertainty on the bike were put into perspective. The cost of my rides was also severely humbled by the astronomical expense of just owning a boat, let alone putting to sea in it. For my new sailing friends, who did indeed carry two bikes with them, cycles merely came into the 'pocket money' category.

Happier than ever that my own current leisure activity was the right choice for both health and budget, I retired to a welcoming bed. Though the street noise outside the window kept me unmistakably up to date with the score (one groan to one cheer, Barça winning the tie two-one on the away cheers rule), the fireworks lasted barely half an hour this time, before I fell easily into a sleep punctuated by dreams of fat truck drivers eating exploding ice creams.

Day 11

Accidentally in Paradise: Sant Carles de la Ràpita to Prat de Comte

The last half day of my coastal jaunt dawned cloudy and cooler and for this I was grateful. With only a short day ahead, I took time after breakfast to wander down to the harbour.

Sant Carles de la Ràpita is an unusual port for this coast, in that it doesn't look out to the open sea, but rather into a huge natural lagoon, El Port dels Alfacs, separated from the sea by a 5-kilometre sand bar, La Barra del Trabucador. Now a nudist beach, La Barra has extended over the years from the southern coast of the delta and now ends in a curved spit called La Banya ('the horn'). That cloudy morning La Banya closed in the south-eastern horizon with a thin, grey line.

Sant Carles itself is squashed between the coast and the limestone massif of Montsià, which, as I'd seen for myself from Cap Salou two days before, dominates the landscape for many miles around. In fact, since Amposta I'd been in the county of El Montsià.

Sant Carles was developed by Carlos III as a trading port in the eighteenth century, being at the mouth of a navigation canal from the Ebre at Amposta, but difficulties in dredging the lagoon led to the project falling short of the king's plans. Nowadays Sant Carles is more a fishing port and, at the landward end of the harbour where I sat, boasts a vast pleasure boat marina.

Cycling out of town along a scenic – and, as usual, almost deserted – Passeig Marítim, I found Sant Carles de la Ràpita to have an atmosphere distinct from any of the other coastal towns I'd passed through. Not an unpleasant one at all. Maybe it was the cloudy weather, maybe the lack of beaches in the middle of town, maybe the mix of industry and tourism... or maybe the fact that I'd embarked, albeit briefly, on another *costa* entirely.

The Costa Daurada had ended yesterday as I'd entered the delta region from the north. As I now left it southbound, I'd entered the Costa del Azahar. I freely admit I'd never heard of it, but now I'd learnt that it extends from here all the way to Valencia, or thereabouts, and that it means the Orange Blossom Coast. In fact, as I was still theoretically in Catalonia (just), I should really use its Catalan name, the Costa dels Tarongers (Coast of the Orange Trees), although this is rarely seen on maps.

Whatever its name, this was a jolly, low-key stretch of coast. South of the pretty little seaside town of Les Cases d'Alcanar, a line of low, crumbly red cliffs dropped down to narrow pebble beaches, where the noisy surf kept up a constant background of riffles and swishes to accompany my last hour beside the sea. Seagulls beat their way energetically above, all heading north, and as a bonus I even experienced here that rarity on Mediterranean coasts – 'the smell of the sea', which turns out to be from gases emitted by tiny bacteria feeding on seaweed. And for cyclists in particular there was a bit of a breakthrough.

After 450 kilometres of my whingeing about Catalonia's lack of coastal cycle tracks – or half-hearted attempts at them – here, for the last few hundred metres, was a real one. In smooth grey tarmac, running between the road and the cliff and wide enough for two bikes to pass, was a track marked not for pedestrians or horses or skateboarders or anyone else except, specifically, cyclists. There it was in white paint: a picture of a cycling stick man above the magic word: BICI. Thank you, the Generalitat de Catalunya. A little late, but much appreciated.

The very end of the Catalonian coast is a beach called Platja de Sòl de Riu ('river soil beach'). Here the map marks a river flowing into the Mediterranean, Riu de la Sénia, forming the boundary with the Comunidad Valenciana and mentioned by Ford as dividing Catalonia from the *'tierra caliente'* (hot land). But on that May morning, whatever water may once have flowed in the river had either evaporated or lay in the stinking swamp a few metres behind the beach.

No matter. Leaving Tetley at the top, I skipped down a short flight of steps to the beach, where, after scrambling with some difficulty over the unusually large pebbles, I sat down with a crunch, faced the sea and celebrated my arrival with a draught of still-cold water and a Murray Mint.

Unlike the northern frontier of Catalonia at Portbou, with its heavy traffic and plethora of signs, this was quite solitary and strangely anonymous. Nothing announced it as being the frontier of anywhere.

With the sound of the surf, I didn't notice the man and woman walking across the beach from the Valencia direction until it was too late to ask them to take a photograph – and maybe modestly slip in the news that I'd just cycled the entire Catalan coast. Five hundred kilometres may not constitute any record, but nonetheless I felt an irresistible urge to tell someone. At the top of the steps the couple were talking to an elderly man. I gathered my bits and pieces together and scurried up after them. By the time I got to the top, they'd moved on, but the old chap remained. He was quite short, carried no bag and wore no hat. I smiled at him.

'Good morning, señor. Cooler today.'

He smiled back but made no comment.

'Excuse me, but would you take my photo, please? With my bike?'

This seemed to meet his approval.

'Of course, señor. What would you like in the view?'

'The beach, I think. The end of Catalonia, no?'

'Indeed.'

This was my chance.

'I've just come from the other end.'

He looked confused.

'From Portbou.'

This registered immediately.

'From Portbou by bike! You certainly must have a photo. Stand there, the bike there. No, left a bit. You must have the beach. From Portbou! *Ay, ay, ay.*'

The photo taken by the enthusiastic old man featured not just Tetley and me, but also the metal barriers keeping us both from following the crumbly edge of the cycle track down into the waves: an event that had clearly happened very recently. Feeling that I should now modestly divert attention from myself, I changed the subject.

'Have you walked far yourself this morning?'

This made him toss back his head and laugh.

'Two metres, maybe three!' He nodded at the small house behind him. Having been concentrating on the beach, I'd hardly noticed it, but there beyond the road stood the most perfect, square, white-walled little house you could hope to see, with a burst of dark-green cacti and brightly coloured flowers framing a low-walled drive up to its neat brown gate.

'Ah, you live here – I didn't realise. What a stupendous house you have, señor. In a stupendous location too.'

'Yes, yes. If only it will stay out of the sea.' He nodded at the crumbling cliff.

I couldn't think what to say about this very evident, potentially tragic situation. So I simply nodded and said: 'I hope so. Good luck, señor, and thank you for taking my photo.'

He inclined his head, shook my hand and, having said 'Portbou – *ay, ay, ay*' once again, returned across the road to his house. Thank you, Señor of the Little White House. You made me feel that I might actually have achieved something in these eleven days.

Ten and a half, to be precise. For now all I had to do was to follow the lane inland, along the left bank of the little waterless river, via the small town of Alcanar, to the station at Ulldecona. Here I would catch a train to a reunion with Julie. What I hadn't expected was that these last 10 kilometres would include yet another stint that any touring cyclist would have to file under 'Idyllic'.

Geologically, the Serra de Montsià extends all the way to the river and the run up to Ulldecona crossed the small-scale, undulating foothills of the massif. Little lanes and tracks, most enclosed by low, drystone walls, wander hither and thither across a landscape of olive trees, scrub, cacti, purple patches of convolvulus – and orange groves. Of course, the Orange Blossom Coast! Until then it hadn't quite dawned on me. Poking out from their neat, pointed green leaves over the uneven walls to the lane were hundreds and hundreds of oranges – spherical ones, wobbly ones, smooth ones, pockmarked ones – all of them, from what I could tell, just on the edge of ripeness. Some of the rows seemed to have been picked already, their wide walkways littered with dropped fruit. It was like pedalling through a painting. For a lad from the chilly English Midlands, it was as though I'd found myself accidentally in paradise.

To add to the deeply rural atmosphere, at one blind junction a woman carrying on her head a basket of black vegetables stepped in front of me so unexpectedly that I did well to avoid her. They were, to be more precise, the black stems of vegetables, for not only did I recognise them but I knew why they were black. What I didn't know is why, so long after Easter, she was only now taking them to the compost heap, which is where, as I glanced back, I saw her dumping them.

In my sixteen years in Catalonia, I'd had two experiences with *calçots* (which is two too many), one beginning with a misunderstanding, the other ending with one. One morning, at the factory in the Barcelona suburbs where I earned my living, our secretary Mireia poked her head over the partition and stared at me.

'Ri-chard,' she said. 'We're going to a *calçotada* at lunchtime. Would you like to come?'

'What is it?'

'Why, we barbecue *calçots* and eat them of course.'

'You eat shoes?'

Looking up at the light-fittings before again fixing my gaze, Mireia replied: 'Shoes are *calçats*, Ri-chard. These are *calçots*. Onions. It is the time of the year. It is the *calçotada*.'

Well, two hours later, after a long lunch, followed by an extended period in the company washroom, I saw Mireia's smiling face rise once more above the partition.

'So, what did you think of your first *calçotada*?'

'Interesting. Are the *calçots* always that big?' (Some you could only just get in your mouth whole.)

'Some are even bigger.'

'Why do you eat them in that strange way?'

'You mean like this?'

Tossing her head back, she mimed lowering a large spring onion (for this is in effect what they are), into her mouth.

'Yes.'

'How else could you eat them?'

'With a knife and fork?'

'Ah, Ri-chard, you are so English. Anyway, your shirt is nearly clean now, I think.'

'May I keep the bib?'

'You may.' Indeed I did, but without expecting to use it again as protection against the invasive black embers of a giant, burnt spring onion. I was wrong. Not long before the start of this ride, at Easter – the traditional time for *calçots* – our Llançà neighbours invited Julie and me round for their own *calçotada*. It would have been impolite to decline.

After the same strange and messy eating ritual as before, Rosa asked if we had any particular Easter traditions in England.

'Well,' said Julie, in Spanish, 'we eat what we call "hot cross buns".'

The phrase meaning nothing to our Catalan friends, Julie proceeded to explain. (I should mention that we'd both been drinking for long enough that our confidence in Spanish had begun to exceed our ability.) Rosa was confused.

'This cake, it has what on the top of it?'

'A cross,' repeated Julie.

'Surely not,' said Rosa.

'Yes, yes,' insisted Julie. 'You know, like the cross that Jesus died on.'

More furrowed brows. Rosa explained their consternation: '¿Murió Jesús en un crucero?' ('Jesus died on a cruise ship?')

'Ah, no,' admitted Julie, realising her error before the Spanish translation of the New Testament had to be rewritten. 'Not *un crucero*. I mean *un cruz*.'

Many of the junctions were unsignposted, but Tetley and I happily picked a route by instinct and the countryside eventually delivered us to Ulldecona, where a giant roadside poster, featuring five pigs with their trotters on a fence, announced the *'Cirque Fantasía'*, at *'Precio Crisis €5'*. The crisis, I assume, was the recession.

Despite the best efforts of the Generalitat de Catalunya, this far south the lingua franca seemed to be Spanish. The friendly corner bar where I sank a quick beer (alcoholic now, for cycling was virtually over for the day) was called 'La Pollera' (the hen coop) and the hens cooped up in there with me were all speaking Spanish, even before I'd asked for directions to the station.

At Ulldecona station itself a final character to grace this jaunt along the Catalan coast made a sudden and dramatic appearance. As the southbound train prior to my northbound arrival pulled away, it left on the opposite platform a small man in a jacket two sizes too large and a hat that I imagine must have been a fedora before he'd pulled it tightly into the shape of his head. As the passengers around him made for the exit, he turned and faced the three of us across the tracks. His arms immediately started to make the kind of gestures I'd seen karate masters use before dealing the telling blow. Then, while he fixed us each in turn, some urgent message was conveyed with his fingers before he clearly indicated himself and then the disappearing train. Not a sound did he make. I looked at my two fellow passengers, but one read a newspaper and the other tapped a foot in tune to his headphones, both clearly dismissing the man as one or two carriages short of the full train set. It seemed to me, however, that these weren't random gestures but something with an urgent meaning.

As it happens I know a little British Sign Language and, leaning Tetley against my body, I signed: 'I'm confused. What do you mean?' At least I hope I did.

In response, he simply lowered his arms by his sides, raised both eyebrows and stood thus frozen until our train arrived a minute or two later. As it pulled out with Tetley and me on board, I looked out of the window, but the Silent Gesticulator of Ulldecona had disappeared. I'm pretty sure I didn't imagine him.

Inland from the Serra de Montsià, more massifs loom up from the west side of the Ebre valley. Snaking between two of these, the Serra dels Ports and the Serra de Pàndols, is a narrow but immaculately surfaced road, heading for a village called Bot. It was two-thirds of the way there, at Prat de Comte ('Meadow of the Count'), that Julie and I were staying that night, in what appeared to be the social hub of this tiny mountain village, an inn called Ca l'Àngels.

Soon after we took our seats for dinner in the room that served not only as restaurant, but also as reception, bar and waiting room for the local bus stop, our hostess approached. We were keen to tell her our news.

'We've just seen some wild goats on the hillside,' I announced.

She held her excitement in check.

'Like the ones on our room key,' added Julie, rattling the illustrated metal fob.

Smiling as an indulgent mother to playful offspring, the hostess-cum-waitress changed the subject to the matter in hand. Waving a small piece of paper above her head, she started listing the meal options.

'*Hay ensalada, hay embotits, hay...*'

'May we see the options written down while you read them?' I asked, pointing at the piece of paper.

'*¿Qué?* Oh, this is not the menu, señor. This is, *oy, un secreto.*' She smiled, but offered no further explanation.

So we listened to the verbal menu and after an elaborate description of what *berenjena* was (it turned out to be aubergine), Julie opted for *gazpacho*, pork and ice cream and I for salad, sausages and *flam* (crème caramel). The unique feature of both main courses was the sauce, comprising wild mushrooms, green beans and shrimps – an unexpected combination, to say the least. The house wine, which our hostess decanted from a giant bottle into an unmarked one of normal size, was black. Literally, in this case...

Catalan wines have their own classification, similar to those of other regions, and include nine DOs (*Denominació d'Origen*, as they are styled here). Of these, the area of the Penedès DO – famous especially for its cava – is the biggest. The wines Julie and I are most familiar with, however, are those of the Empordà DO, from the vineyards nearest to Llançà, especially the *rosados*.

Overfamiliar, perhaps...

The best way to get an idea of a range of local wines is to seek out an organised *degustació* (tasting). These take place at least once a year in almost every village in Catalonia's wine-producing areas and typically comprise a series of stalls, each offering a choice of wines from a particular vineyard.

First present yourself at the kiosk selling vouchers and glasses. For, say, 6 euros you might buy six vouchers and the loan of a glass. It's up to you at which stalls you choose to exchange your vouchers for wine. Often enough, there's a parallel market in vouchers for some foodstuff: cheese, olives or, as Julie and I found one afternoon at the village of Garriguella, doughnuts. A food supplement is always a good way of soaking up some of the wine.

Once or twice we've attempted to take notes but, judging from the scribble still pinned to our noticeboard after the annual '*Mostra*', a local *degustació* at Figueres, this may be a hopeless task. Devoid of punctuation and with handwriting deteriorating rapidly by the end, it reads:

- Cellers Trobat cava ooh fizzy but nice
- Pere Guardiola plays for Barcelona Floresta best *rosat* ever
- Castell de Panissars surely not Monty's vineyard *blanca* taste diff from smell orange peel Emma Peel never smelt her
- what's wrapped round this olive
- more red oh first *negre* Garriguella Gary who? strong and fruity ha froooty Gary Lineker
- one left some Muscat no that's Per that's Persian Gulf ah Muscat dessert from Martí Fabra aah wrote Round the Horne
- yes train at 1530 back to seaside same tie no time next year in dairy no diary *Mostraaaa...*

Some wodges of cheese might have helped.

One wodge of knowledge that may help new arrivals in Catalonia, or indeed Spain: while *blanc/blanco* (Catalan/Spanish) for white, and *rosat/rosado* for rosé are obvious, *negre/tinto* for red are less so. Yes, Catalans call red wine 'black' wine and the example at Ca l'Àngels was well named, though very unlikely to have been a DO. It was perfectly palatable, but an old man at the bar looked taken aback when he saw Julie and me sticking our tongues out at each other: black as pitch.

With no prices for food, wine – nor indeed accommodation – having been mentioned, what it all came to was to remain *un secreto* until breakfast when we got the tiny, tiny bill. Highly recommended, the House of the Angels at the Meadow of the Count.

It won't have escaped your notice that my progress from Ulldecona to Prat de Comte had been distinctly unbicyclelike. There's a reason for this.

In Limbworld, my left knee is King of Knees. It bends, it supports, it walks, it cycles – all with regal indifference. My right knee, on the other hand, is Knasty Knee. It creaks, it gives way, it swells, it stings. By Ulldecona, it had for several days been sending a single message up the nerve routes to the brain and that message was 'Stop'. Or more recently: 'Stop!!'

Back at the hotel in Barcelona I'd rescued from the depths of my bag the map given to me by Grumpy Old Cyclist in Sant Feliu. Flattening it out on the table, I'd had my Damascene moment. The road to Damascus turned out to be an old railway track and Grumpy's map my burning bush... or rather a bush primed for combustion should it be needed. It was needed. My declared – but vague – intent 'to sample the Catalan interior' after the coastal stint had crystallised into a relatively conservative itinerary, one for which Julie and Dave the Kangoo had collected Tetley and me from L'Aldea station and whisked us up to Prat de Comte for the start. The sample of inland rides would be a systematic one: a selection of Catalonia's Vías Verdes.

As elsewhere in Europe, the railway network of Spain has for a number of years been living a Jekyll and Hyde existence. In one personality, new high-speed lines have been opening with much razzmatazz; in another, with rather less fanfare, smaller lines have been closing.

However, just as other countries have also discovered, if a little belatedly, there is an obvious new use for the routes of these old byways of a forgotten age. With the honourable exception of those cyclists for whom lung-busting ascents and headlong descents are actually an attraction, both cyclists and trains abhor a gradient. The conversion to cycle routes of those abandoned trackbeds that have not been built on has therefore been a notable success, albeit a low-key one.

In Spain's case, the plaudits go to the Fundación de los Ferrocarriles Españoles (FFE, Spanish Railway Foundation), a trust set up in 1985 both to promote the use of surviving railways and to protect and use the country's railway heritage. Since 1993, one of the FFE's major projects has been the wonderful network of Vías Verdes – literally 'Green Ways' – covering 1,700 kilometres over seventy-seven routes at the time of writing. Their popularity was boosted by a 2005 series on Spanish TV which demonstrated the joys of pedalling these picturesque pathways and coaxed many Spaniards out of their cars and onto their bikes.

(Although all the Vías Verdes I rode were in Catalonia, I call them 'Vías Verdes' in Spanish rather than 'Víes Verdes' in Catalan, as it's a Spain-wide project.)

So a new phase of the journey was to begin the next day. With the exception of one that was temporarily inaccessible, I would cycle each of Catalonia's Vías Verdes, getting from one to the other by car. Why not by train? Well, like London for England and Paris for France, Barcelona forms a hub for the modern railway network in Catalonia. One familiar consequence of this is that cross-country travel by train is often difficult – or even, as in the case of this journey, impossible. Pretty soon after pinpointing the location of the Vías Verdes I'd realised not only that cycling between them was out of the question for knee reasons but also that taking the bike to them all by train was impractical. (For details of railway access to the rides in this book, see the section of that name near the end.) That left the car. More 'Two Plus Four Wheels Over Catalonia' from this point, then.

Never mind. After taking in the basic gen from that crumpled little leaflet, I'd got hold of more detailed information – it turns out there are reams of it available from tourist offices – and the Vía Verdes routes looked sensational. As the project's own slogan says, *Vive la Vía!*

Day 12

Vive la Vía! Prat de Comte to Tortosa

As I pushed the bike uphill out of Prat de Comte, to the nine o'clock chimes of 'Ode to Joy' from the village church, an unexpected sight slowly emerged ahead of me: a valley. The reason it was unexpected was that my map-reading skills, in which I'd always taken great pride, had failed to take in the fact that the tight contours to the north-east of Prat de Comte signified not a steep *ascent*, but a steep *descent*. After a closer look, it belatedly dawned on me that perhaps the River Canaletes was more likely to be flowing at the bottom of a valley than along the top of a ridge. Prat de Map.

It was an enormous valley too, with a road snaking from my feet down towards the bottom of it. I shrugged, mounted and freewheeled... until, about halfway down, I pulled up sharply – a movement that seemed to spook a strangely chocolate-coloured squirrel that shot back up the tree he'd just come down. What had caused me to pause was the view.

'Looming' would be too gentle a word. Dominating and towering come some way towards the effect of the mountain to my left. Even 'mountain' seems a bit weak. A glance at the map told me this was L'Agulla de Bot: 'the Needle of Bot'. As good a name as any for the start of a bike ride, but surely 'needle' is too spindly a word for this monster. I stared, I considered. Giant, rugged, brown, threatening, thrusting thing. Sorry, that's the best I can do. In Cornwall it would probably have been called The Devil's Todger. Keeping my head down, I scooted on.

Of Spain's seventy-seven Vías Verdes, Catalonia has seven. Today I'd be cycling one and a half of them: Vía Verde de la Terra Alta ('High Land') and Vía Verde del Baix Ebre ('Lower Ebre'). At least the sequence of the names suggested I might have got the general gradient right.

I joined the Vía Verde de la Terra Alta at the former Prat de Comte station, now a ruin. To name a station after a village that must have been a few hours' donkey ride up the hill certainly showed some chutzpah. However, the railway itself, which closed in 1973, had a very short life – indeed, in a sense it was 'the railway that never was'.

The concept was initially a military one and dates from the mid eighteenth century, when it was thought that invasion from the north, over the Pyrenees, was a perennial possibility. To any invading army, the next obvious barrier would have been the River Ebre, which, thought the Spanish military, could well become a front line – a front line needing supplies on the right (southern/western) bank of the river. (References to the right or left bank are always from the point of view of the river's flow; here, as the Ebre meanders towards the sea, its right bank lies to the south and west.) The plan was a railway from La Puebla de Híjar, near Zaragoza (Saragossa) in Aragon, all the way to the coast at Sant Carles de la Ràpita. The first section, at the inland end, was finally opened in 1895, the next (this one) not until 1942 and the final section... well, never actually.

You can apparently cycle all the way from La Puebla de Híjar to here, but the Vía Verde de la Terra Alta had started just 17 kilometres east of the point where I'd joined, as it enters Catalonia.

I was pleased to be starting a series of rides that would evidently have a different flavour from the previous eleven days along the coast: the all-enveloping hills rather than the big skies of the seaside, the rustle of the trees rather than the riffle of the surf, the heavy scent of pine rather than the fresh smells of the shore. A different bike as well for, having looked at some of the Vías Verdes online, I wasn't too confident about Tetley's performance on their surfaces and so Julie had kindly brought along Benny too, complete with his sturdier tyres. It was immediately obvious that this morning's was going to be an extra special ride, for the scenery was quite breathtaking.

Dropping Benny by the deserted cycle track, I just wandered around gawping for a few minutes. Snaking between the pine trees on the steep slopes above the River Canaletes, the old railway route gave tantalising glimpses both up to the red-rock heights above, where broad-winged birds of prey swooped and swished just as they're supposed to, and down to the shadowy ravine, where the busy, black river bounced over its white-stone bed. A glance to the opposite slopes caught diagonal morning sunbeams bathing the tops in a dazzling mist before picking out glistening, rough rock faces that had been hiding behind the deep-green pines that clung to even the sheerest of cliffs. Travellers on the short-lived railway line must have looked on these same views with the same open-mouthed stares, but today it was as though the show had been put on solely for my benefit, for the biggest contrast with the coast was that, since leaving the inn, I'd seen not a soul.

With some reluctance, I eventually pulled Benny into position, pointed him southwards and set off.

It turned out that the track's surface wasn't what I should have been concerned about – being hereabouts a kind of half-sealed gravel – but rather another, very obvious feature of the route. Mountain railways pass through tunnels; so cycle tracks on old mountain railways pass through tunnels too. Trains have powerful headlights; bikes have, well, bike lights... and the little thing clamped to Benny's handlebars was weaker than most. Those tunnels where I could see from one end to the other were fine, if demanding a little optimism at the state of the unseen track. It was those tunnels with no apparent end that caused some consternation.

Not fear: while many things may frighten me, darkness is not among them. But when pedalling very slowly into a tiny pool of weak, yellow light, strange things start to happen. The rough-hewn walls wander hither and thither. Every speck of white seems like a distant opening. Oddest of all, in the longest, darkest tunnel, I eventually began to wonder if I was making any progress at all. As I pulled up for a break, it occurred to me that, were I to shift Benny from his orientation parallel to the walls, I'd have no idea which way I was heading: the two walls were identical, the two destinations equally pitch black. Moreover, on emerging, I probably wouldn't have a clue whether I'd turned round or not – for, spectacular though the scenery was, it was likely to be similarly spectacular at both ends.

I concentrated, I pedalled, I stared at the floor. I even appealed to Spokey the Cycling God to keep me pointing in the right direction. Finally, one of the white specks above the light pool grew and grew to become first a pinpoint of separate light, then a distant golf ball, then a football... until the sunlight of the tunnel exit eventually bathed me within it. I'd no idea at the time how long that longest tunnel was, but it turns out it was nearly a kilometre, bending first one way then the other as I wrestled Benny's handlebars between its walls.

Soon after emerging two miracles happened simultaneously. I was busy taking photos near the entrance to my next encounter with the forces of darkness when a swish, a crunch and a flash of yellow made me turn swiftly around. Another cyclist – the first human I'd seen in about two hours – had emerged from the tunnel mouth.

'*Hola,*' I said.

'*Adiós,*' she said, pedalling off.

Spain is the only country I know (for I believe it's not solely a Catalan phenomenon) where, as their paths cross, strangers greet each other with a hearty 'Goodbye!'. I wonder if Paul McCartney was holidaying on the Costa Brava when he wrote 'Hello, Goodbye'?

The second miracle was that, from the roof of the tunnel that had regurgitated the yellow-clad cyclist, diagonal strip lights illuminated the entrance... and then didn't. In a state of wonder I stepped into the tunnel. The lights came on. I stepped back out. The lights went off. Closer inspection revealed little movement-sensitive devices at the base of each cable. A little light had also just come on inside my befuddled little head. A sign at the entrance to this tunnel read *'Benvinguts a la comarca del Baix Ebre'* (Welcome to the county of El Baix Ebre). Here, then, are three facts useful to any cyclist taking on for the first time the Vía Verde de la Terra Alta and Vía Verde del Baix Ebre:

- These are not two separate Vías Verdes. They form a single route that happens to cross a county boundary.
- There seem to be no lights at all in the tunnels of La Terra Alta, while the tunnels of El Baix Ebre are all lit where necessary.
- If venturing across La Terra Alta, you'll need a strong flashlight rather than just a bike light.

My confidence restored, I resumed the steady descent, entering each tunnel with an echoey call of 'Lights... on!' It wasn't long before the landscape opened up and the cycle track popped out at a viewing point above the right bank of the Ebre, reminding me that the territory I'd just crossed was the scene of the bloodiest battle of the civil war, the Battle of the Ebre.

By July 1938, the Nationalists were by far the stronger, holding this right/western bank of the Ebre and threatening Republican-held Valencia to the south. A surprise advance by Republican forces across the Ebre from the opposite bank was effectively their last big throw of the dice. Despite initial gains, the combination of the Nationalists holding superior air power and the Republicans being too lightly armed eventually contributed to a catastrophic defeat for the Republic. Over 36,000 died overall and, within five months of the battle's end, Franco had declared victory.

Seventy-odd years later, the feature dominating this stretch of the Ebre is a giant weir, L'Assut de Xerta, with its cluster of waterworks, but you'd be mistaken in taking this for a modern construction. It was the Arabs who first manipulated the river hereabouts, with the idea of controlling the vital water supply downstream. Their work was restored in the twelfth century by one of the Ramons and it seems that successive improvements have been undertaken ever since. Downstream from this point, two channels flow parallel to the river, one on each bank, whose main purpose is irrigation of the rich farmlands of the lower Ebre and its delta. (Though the informative literature insists on translating the Spanish *canal* as 'canal' in English, I'm pretty sure they're nowadays simply 'channels' – the same word in Spanish – unless navigation is by vessels less than 30 centimetres high! The channels are crossed by low, nonadjustable bridges.)

As for the Vía Verde, it too parallels the river all the way to Tortosa, with a character quite different from the mountain section. The tunnels gave way to cuttings through former river gravel, for the river itself used to flow up here, as evidenced by the frequent beds in the cuttings' walls formed of pebbles worn smooth by its flow. The track then cut across the vast orchards in the floodplain itself, winding between orange groves and lemon groves, peach trees, fig trees and cacti. The centuries-old irrigation system was clearly still doing the business.

Finally, the old railway route approached a few small towns. In the mountains, every station had been some distance from the settlement it purportedly served – surely a big factor in its demise. In fact, this stretch had been in full operation for just thirty-one years, such a small return for such a great engineering effort. Here in the valley, I stopped for a coffee in the town square of Xerta, where the thermometer attached to the pharmacy showed 22 degrees, though it felt far hotter to the sweaty cyclist. (Quite why so many Continental pharmacies sport giant thermometers, no one has been able to tell me. Can customers plug themselves in to see if they have a fever?)

After hurrying through Aldover, which smelled strangely of chicken droppings, I lost sight of the Vía Verde in a small town called Jesús. One minute I was pedalling my solitary way along the familiar asphalt track; the next I was surrounded by ambulances in a hospital car park. Confident I hadn't passed out, I pulled up and examined the map – only to come across another mystery. No town called Jesús was marked; everything between Aldover and Tortosa was called Roquetes. Baffled by this sudden bout of radical secularism on the part of the Institut Cartogràfic de Catalunya, I quickly escaped from Jesús, but never again found the Vía Verde.

Tortosa should be a great place. It sits astride a great river, amid impressive massifs and beneath an ancient castle... and yet somehow manages to grab mediocrity from the jaws of splendour.

To an English-speaking cyclist the approach from the west bank is particularly disconcerting. You first pass a building marked 'Bombers' (fire brigade) and then another marked 'Simply Hiper' (a supermarket), before breathing in a heady mix of Chinese food and exhaust fumes as you battle with the continuous line of traffic leading up to and over the river bridge, itself thronged with all manner of road users.

One advantage of cycling is that, when the traffic becomes too much, you can just quit. Anywhere, anytime. As soon as I was over the bridge, I quickly hoicked Benny onto the pavement and down some steps to the river bank, where I leaned on the embankment wall, eagerly gulping some water and taking in the view. Dominating the opposite embankment, graffiti so large and so precisely executed that you suspected official involvement declared '*EL RIU ES LA VIDA. NO AL TRANSVASAMENT.*' ('The river is life. No to decanting.')

It turns out that this was part of a well-organised campaign against plans to syphon off huge volumes of water from the Ebre's flow for use in areas of Spain far removed from here. A month after our visit to Tortosa, demonstrators in Madrid and Barcelona urged the various authorities to resist alleged vested interests and adhere to EU environmental laws in order to protect the Ebre and especially its fragile delta region. Latest news is available at www.ebre.net.

Though the pale beaches stretching out from the far bank suggested the river level was low, it was still over 100 metres across. Two or three fishermen in white beanie hats and green waders stood between the bank and the giant midstream memorial, built to commemorate those killed in the Battle of the Ebre. Alas, even before 1938 the Tortosa area already had a reputation as a battleground.

In spring 215 BC, on the plain beyond the right bank of the Ebre, the Scipio brothers (plus 33,000 other Romans) took on Hasdrubal Barca (and 29,000 other Carthaginians, plus twenty elephants). This was part of the Second Punic War, so called because the Roman name for the Carthaginians was *Punici*. The Roman victory was significant even beyond those heavy Carthaginian losses suffered here, for it kept Hasdrubal Barca's troops from supporting their colleague Hannibal over the sea in Italy, where he in turn was eventually defeated – with Rome gaining complete domination in the western Mediterranean, including Iberia.

Over a millennium later, Tortosa had been under Muslim rule for four hundred years when, in 1148, the town was besieged by a multinational army of crusaders under the count of Barcelona (one of the many Ramons). Once more the consequences of victory had implications further than the immediate overthrow of Muslim rule, for the count's offer of land to the victors extended to those from beyond Iberia, leading to descendents with North European ancestry living in the area to this day.

Having regained both breath and composure, I saddled up again for a brief tour around town. Though the old fish market and the current market buildings are both impressive, it was difficult to find much of interest. I wasn't the first: 150 years before, Ford had judged Tortosa 'a dull town, with narrow streets, and houses marked with the local character of solidity'. In my case, I offer three mitigating circumstances. One is that a great deal of old Tortosa was destroyed in the civil war; in fact, inside the old fish market, now a cafe, you can see photographs of the ruins, including that very building, which has been lovingly restored.

A second is that I'd arrived mid siesta. As already mentioned in the context of museum opening hours, when any North European moves to Spain, it can take some time to adjust to their daily rhythm. In my case, I regularly set off to do some shopping at some obvious time – Saturday afternoon, say – only to find everywhere shuttered and bolted as though a cloud of poisonous gas was on its way. On the other hand, I'd fall into bed around ten o'clock on a summer evening, with the windows open to create a welcome draught – only to be up again within the hour, as half the population stepped noisily onto their balconies to set about the paella.

The third reason for the mediocrity of Tortosa town at the time was that, in the streets below the castle, the JCB ruled. This entire district was, it seemed, being wiped out. Even the Prince's Gardens were temporarily occupied by the Prince's Concrete Mixer. And so it was around cones and through barriers that I pushed Benny up the hill to our hotel.

Alphonso XIII, King of Spain from 1886 to 1931, had a varied impact on his kingdom. In 1914 his family connections with both belligerent sides of World War One was one reason for Spain's neutrality. In 1918, when he contracted influenza, the global media coverage devoted to his illness (doubtless a welcome relief from war news) gave the impression that the pandemic was at its worst in Spain, leading to its subsequent tag of 'Spanish flu'. In the 1920s he granted the appendage 'Royal' to his local football club, Madrid FC, which therefore became Real Madrid. And in 1928, of more relevance to Tortosa, his enthusiasm for promoting tourism in Spain resulted in the concept of the *paradores*, a chain of state-run hotels usually housed in historic buildings of some kind. Nowadays they're all over Spain and here in Tortosa, the *parador* dominates the old town, for its home is the tenth-century Castillo de la Zuda (in Catalan, Castell de la Suda).

Originally built by the Moors, various rebuilds and additions to the Castillo de la Zuda over the centuries have culminated in an impressive restoration by the *parador* team. In fact, it was only after standing back to take in the entire building that I realised the wing with the guests' rooms was a twentieth-century extension, so well did it blend in. But despite the grand building, it was evidently the view that made the place. From various raised positions on the outer wall you can look back along the wandering Ebre valley, gaze up at the jagged El Port massif opposite or stare down to the colourful roofs of the town and the delta beyond, picking out the grey outline of the Montsià massif. Gawping hither and thither from the car park, I felt a little out of place in my cycling kit among the well-dressed guests doing likewise; judging from the registration plates, they'd come from Andorra, France, Italy, Germany, the UK and even Norway. For Julie and me, it was the first time in a *parador*.

As Julie had already texted me our room number – a rare benefit of that devil's tool, the mobile phone – I decided to try to get there without contact between perspiring English cyclist and posh *parador* staff. However, while sneaking through the wood-panelled reception area as inconspicuously as is possible for a short, red-faced man in padded shorts and whose hair positively sparkled with sweat, I failed.

'Ah, Señor Guee-say! How was the bicycle ride?'

'Oh, pretty good, you know.'

'Welcome to the *parador* of Tortosa, señor! Your partner has already checked in. Please wait here while I fill in a form for you to sign. Oh, señor, it must be hot out there today...'

As a place to recover from a cold or from a day in the saddle – Julie and I respectively – it's hard to imagine anywhere more amenable than the *parador* of Tortosa.

'Well, you look a lot better,' I said to her as I finally stumbled through the door of our room.

'And you look a lot worse,' commented Julie, holding up her hand as she let me in. 'No further until you've had a shower. You can phone me from the bathroom.'

And indeed there was a phone from the bathroom to the bedroom. This was luxury I could get used to.

Day 13

Antonio and Xavi: Tortosa to Ripoll

The next day started with a squash as we eased into Dave the Kangoo for the 300-kilometre drive north-eastwards into the Pyrenean foothills and an encounter with the next Vía Verde near Berga. The reason for the squash was of course that we were in the company of three bikes: not only Benny and Tetley but also Buttercup – Julie's own machine, which she'd dragged from its dusty corner of the garage, along with its little bell, its handy basket and its strangely low saddle. Whether the girl herself was up to a ride yet was still up in the air.

So often do you read of a holiday destination being described as 'a land of contrasts' that it's difficult to utter this cliché without a Pythonesque, mid-Atlantic drawl. So with this phrase banned, Catalonia is, shall we say, characterised by a diversity of landscapes. The five-hour drive took us up out of the broad Ebre valley through narrow, dry gullies, lined with steep terraces of olives clinging below dark-green woodland. Occasionally the woods reached all the way down from the hilltops to embrace us in shadow.

Once up onto the *meseta,* the plateau that dominates much of Spain's interior, the landscape changed to one of small neat farmsteads surrounded by row after row of fruit trees and yet more olive groves. Rising from the gently undulating terrain were old silos and taller, newer wind turbines. Spain now gets 13 per cent of its electricity from wind farms, vastly more than most other countries.

After skirting the remarkable pink conglomerate outcrop of Montserrat, whose name alone, 'serrated mountain', paints its own picture, we started crossing some of the many ranges that extend their bony fingers south from the Pyrenees: heavily forested foothills separated by lively, youthful streams that eventually end their days as sluggish old rivers emptying into the Mediterranean – the very same rivers I'd crossed on my southward journey along the coast. Our target that day was the valley of the Llobregat, whose muddy-brown lower reaches I'd crossed on Day 7 after leaving the transport cafe in Barcelona's Zona Franca.

With less to divert my attention while driving than while cycling, my mind wandered again to the early days of my time in Catalonia, the days when a newcomer turns the simplest task into a path strewn with obstacles. The Catalan (and occasionally Spanish) officials involved always did their best to direct me to the end of the path... even though for a short while I appeared to have no name and for a longer while I believe I didn't even exist.

To get by in England, you really need an appropriate accent. In France, it's an education. In Spain, you need a NIF.

However independent Catalans may feel – and may one day be – the heavy hand of the Spanish state still loomed large back in the early 1990s when I endeavoured to become an official resident. I still keep a vital, dog-eared hangover from this former period in my wallet at all times. Illegally, I suspect.

Your NIF is your *Número de Identidad Fiscal*. It's your Spanish identity number. Of course, even before the ill-fated attempts of the last few years, there's long been an identity number system in Britain too. The difference is that that the British have several, not all of which are compulsory. For example, if you never venture abroad, you don't need a passport and therefore never get a passport number, nor need one: seeing a human being in front of them, most British officials would give them the benefit of the doubt and accept that they exist. Not so in Spain. On every official form in Spain, and most unofficial forms too, a little box exists for your NIF. It's usually right there just below the two boxes for your surnames. If you leave it blank, the computer is unhappy.

Of course, the sharp-as-mustard Spanish bureaucrats have noticed that, ever since Christopher Columbus persuaded Queen Isabella to finance his holidays in the Caribbean, more and more alien life forms have been arriving in Spain, and not only entering the country, but getting jobs here, buying houses, having children and generally filling in forms like there's no tomorrow. The question of the empty NIF boxes was bound to come up sooner or later. One young official suggested giving all alien residents a NIF. He was last seen grading sand in the Spanish Sahara. Another suggested using the aliens' own national ID numbers.

Unfortunately, some of them didn't begin with a letter, have lots of numbers in the middle and end with another letter. Last seen measuring cowpats in Extremadura. No, what was needed was a compromise. And that's how the NIE was born. The E stands for *extranjero*, foreigner. As an acronym, it may not have the catchy sound of the 'NIF' – 'I don't have a NIF, but I have a NIE' – but it gives you a fighting chance of proving that you exist.

Soon after I arrived in Spain in 1992, I received my little maroon resident's permit, complete with Spanish address, mug shot, fingerprint (just the one, strangely enough) and NIE. Notice that you had to have an address in Spain before you could get permission to live there, a little logical loop which didn't seem to cause the system any worries. So, armed with my NIE, I merrily filled in lots of forms to order telephones, water, electricity and so on – if not exactly without incident, then at least without NRIs (NIF-related Incidents).

After a few months I couldn't help noticing that my bank balance was steadily diving. I couldn't help noticing it because 90 per cent of my post came from the bank. Spanish banks automatically send you a little chit every time something happens in your account. Hey, you paid your rent! Your phone bill! Your electricity! Gosh, your rent again!! This is in addition to the regular statements repeating the same hot news. (Here lay another instance of the Spanish Problem With Time: until recently, some utilities used to be paid two-monthly, some three-monthly. That handy concept, the month – first formalised 5,000 years ago – was another that just seemed to have passed the Spanish by.)

Since nobody in Spain seemed to accept personal cheques even then, the standing orders and direct debits could often be all there was on a statement. Well, you may expect some salary payments too, of course; indeed, I had more or less expected to get paid myself, and traced my plummeting balance to the fact that I hadn't. Lots of OUTs but a suspicious lack of INs.

My company having confirmed that they'd remembered to pay me, I went round to the local bank, where the cashier spoke the English he'd learnt on a summer course in Brighton. He'd also picked up a certain English affability.

'Carlos, I've got a problem with my account.'

'Please tell me all about it, Mr Guise. And you can call me Charles.'

'Ahem, well, Charles, it seems that although my company's been paying me, none of the money has appeared in my account since I arrived here three months ago.'

'Oh dear, oh dear, oh dear.' The Brighton course was excellent on sympathetic phrases. 'That's very serious. I will investigate immediately. Tut, tut.'

With that Carlos disappeared into a back office, where I heard him raise his voice a few times on the telephone, his angry Spanish being quite out of character with his sympathetic English. After a few minutes, he came back a little flustered.

'I have dealt with Bilbao,' he said, as though he'd taken on the whole city. 'It's a question of NIFs. It's all a terrible mistake, I'm afraid, Mr Guise.' Casting his eyes down, it seemed that Carlos was taking this as a personal failure.

'What's the problem?' I asked.

'Well, in a nutshell,' he said, 'most of the employees around here are Spanish.' A perceptive observation. 'And we Spanish all have NIFs – it's a kind of, well, identification number.' He drew closer to the glass between us. 'We don't mind really, you know,' he added, obviously versed in the typical British reaction to IDs. 'Well, of course, you don't have a NIF – why should you? It makes no difference to me, but I'm afraid it makes a big difference to the computer in Bilbao. It thinks you're a...' and here he looked either side of him and lowered his voice, 'a foreigner!'

'God forbid!' I cried.

'Absolutely, God forbid,' hissed Carlos. 'Of course, I know you're British! But here in Spain, you see, you're a foreigner!' And with that bombshell, he sat back and was silent.

'Um, about my salary,' I ventured.

'Ah yes.' In his admonishment of his fellow countrymen's inexplicable failure to realise that they, not the British, were the foreigners, Carlos seemed to have forgotten the matter in hand.

'Since I opened the account here,' I said, 'I've been given a NIE. It's here on my resident's permit.' I pushed it through the hatch to him.

'Ah yes,' he repeated. 'Excellent. A NIE. Yes, yes, the computer in Bilbao will like this. Turning to his screen, he tapped in my NIE. 'Yes, very good. You now exist. Excellent, excellent.'

Returning my precious permit and congratulating me once again on my new-found existence, Carlos bid me good day, and soon after, three months' salary duly arrived.

In the following two years, I slipped in and out of existence three times in as many minutes as an official at an office called 'El Tráfico' juggled with my NIE, my lack of NIF and yet another number – one till then unknown to me – my special personal NIT (*Número de Identidad del Tráfico*), which for a Spaniard is naturally the same number as their NIF, but for an alien, is a unique non-NIF, non-NIE number. CAM? (Clear as Mud?)

Also, in the intervening two years the Maastricht Treaty had come into effect, making the Spaniards and me – and even, heaven forbid, the French – all European citizens, and giving me the right to vote for my local (i.e. Spanish/Catalan) MEP.

Now, since the man at the Sant Cugat police station had plonked my lone fingerprint next to my NIE and issued me with my resident's permit, I had moved to the seaside at Llançà. Suspecting that there must be some kind of electoral registration system; suspecting further that – true to Spanish tradition – it would involve me showing up personally at some local office between the hours of 9 a.m. and 2 p.m.; and suspecting finally that my presentation at such a meeting of a resident's permit with an address in Sant Cugat would not go down very well, I set about getting the address changed.

Were such a document to exist in England (and maybe it does for a Catalan), such a transaction would have been done by post. (This was before the Internet added another non-contact option.) When I told a Catalan friend that driving licences, passports and all those kinds of things were not only updated by post but actually issued by post in Britain, and that, during the best part of four decades as a British resident, I'd never to my recollection set foot in any government office, she gave me a disbelieving look. Having experienced the Spanish postal system, I can understand that look.

In Spain, in this case, you have to go to the local police station.

In Llançà, the police station was then a shady room just behind one of the cafes in the Plaça Major. As I entered, a barmaid was bringing out a tray of empty beer glasses. The local constabulary was resting against the wall.

'*Buenas días,*' I said, 'I'd like to change the address on my resident's permit.'

The constable pulled himself to attention and asked me to repeat myself. This usually happened with my accent at the time. I did.

'Ah, you want *La Policía*, señor.'

'Isn't this *La Policía*?'

'Certainly not, señor. This is *La Guardia Civil*.' He spoke the last phrase with a Flamenco-like toss of the head. '*La Policía*' – the words seemed to cause an unpleasant smell just under his nose – 'is on Carrer de la Selva.'

I reported to *La Policía* on Carrer de la Selva. They told me I needed to go to *la policía* in Figueres. 'Open weekdays nine till two, señor.'

Clearly there was no crime in Figueres after two and at weekends. However, as I worked office hours a hundred miles away in Sant Cugat, getting there when the police station was open was easier said than done. Two weeks passed and the European elections were getting closer. Having taken half a day off work in the name of democracy, at nine o'clock on a Monday morning, I turned up at the Figueres address they'd given me in Llançà.

'*Buenas días,*' I said, 'I'd like to change the address on my resident's permit.'

Having asked me to repeat it as usual, he said, 'You need to go to the administrative office of *La Policía*. This is the criminal office.'

If he tells me the administrative office is in Girona and open afternoons only, I thought, I'll probably kill him – and then I will be in the right place.

'Where's the administrative office?' I asked.

'Next door. It's just opened,' he said, saving his life.

I went next door. A woman was at the desk.

'*Buenas días*,' I said, 'I'd like to change the address on my resident's permit,' adding to save time: 'I'd like to change the address on my resident's permit.'

The two identical questions seemed to cause her some consternation and so I held up my resident's permit, pointing at the Sant Cugat address.

'I've moved,' I said. 'I now live in Llançà. I must change my card.'

'You cannot change your card, señor.'

This was not the reaction I had expected. 'Why not?'

'Because this card is no longer a legal card.'

'Not legal?! Why not?'

'It is a resident's permit, señor. You are English, no?'

'I am English, yes. I mean yes, I'm English.'

'Then you no longer need a permit to reside in Spain.'

'But...' I didn't know what to say. This card contained my NIE. Without my NIE I didn't exist. I must have stared vacantly for a while.

'Is there anything else, señor?'

'But this card contains my NIE. Without my NIE I don't exist.'

'You could exist with your passport, señor. It has a number, no?'

'It has a number, yes. But it doesn't have an address, no. I mean, it has no address.'

'Impossible, señor.' I showed her my British passport. Unlike a Spanish passport, it had no address. Unlike Spaniards, British people don't live with their parents for ever and therefore we keep changing our address and therefore British passports don't have addresses. 'It's very strange, señor.'

'Strange but true. What can I do?'

'I've no idea, señor. Is there anything else?'

And thus I was dismissed. I could have pursued the mythical electoral registration, but, having already visited five offices only to discover that my only Spanish identity card was illegal, I lost heart. The European elections passed without my vote and the European Parliament seemed to survive the blow.

To this day, my identification documents comprise a passport which is legal but doesn't say where I live, and a dog-eared resident's permit, which says only where I used to live and is in any case illegal, since I'm now no longer a resident. My retention of the permit followed the advice of an official I shall not name.

'If I leave Spain,' I asked, 'should I hand in my resident's permit?'

'You should, señor, but my advice is that you will not.'

'Why not?'

'It is the box on the form, señor. Without the NIE the box is empty. With an empty box you do not exist.'

He was right. Whenever I have to show my NIE, it's usually along with other documents which show my real address; and so I have to admit that the address on the NIE document is false. I'm constantly regarded with suspicion. In the eyes of the Spanish bureaucrat, I think I half exist. I think I half exist, therefore I half am. Or is that 'I am half'?

My English is falling apart as well.

Being non-existent is bad enough, but the incident in which I did exist but had no name is, in a sense, more significant, for the sense of humour of my Catalan friends is revealed in that it's the story they most often ask me to repeat. All I wanted was a telephone line.

Having recently arrived from a three-year stint in France, my little brain cell devoted to foreign languages was naturally full of French, where *'nombre'* means number. This explains why, when asked by the receptionist at the local Telefónica office, where I'd gone to order my phone line, *'¿Su nombre, por favor, señor?'* (Your name, please, sir?), I automatically replied:

'No tengo un nombre.' (I have no name). My reply, however, was clearly not what she was expecting. She looked doubtful:

'¿No tiene un nombre?'

'No. Acabo de llegar en España y no tengo un nombre.' (I've just arrived in Spain and have no name.)

After an uncomfortable delay, she saw an ingenious way around this unexpected problem.

'¿Pues, cual es el nombre de su padre?' (What's your father's name?)

Not seeing the relevance, but keen to help, I told her: '973 3332.'

This was too much. With a lengthening queue behind me, the receptionist pointed to an isolated chair in the corner of the room and instructed me sternly:

'¡Espere allí, por favor, señor!'

For the next hour, all the customers before me in the queue, and then all those after me, were duly called by name and ushered to a desk, there doubtless to be granted their new phone lines. During this time, I imagine, worried committees had been meeting out of public view in an effort to figure out how to enter in their directories a subscriber with no name. Eventually, when the rest of the room had been empty for a long five minutes, and I was still sitting patiently on my little chair in the corner, the Telefónica representative who'd drawn the short straw approached me with a hesitant step.

'¿Er, el hombre sin nombre?' (The man with no name?)

Recalling this embarrassing incident always brings a smile to my lips, but nevertheless at Cal Rosal, the small village on the River Llobregat just south of Berga that was our destination, it was a rather weary carload that spilled out in front of the Bar del Estació del Carrilet after five hours on the road.

During the previous day's ride, I'd had a vision. Not of the Virgin Mary, but of Antonio and Xavi, two imaginary employees of the organisation behind the Vías Verdes. Antonio is a bit of a whizz-kid. He does all the maps and the marketing, putting a wealth of information in loving detail onto websites, leaflets and signposts. His unhealthy pallor tells us he doesn't get out much. Little Xavi, on the other hand, spends all day outdoors, chugging from Vía Verde to Vía Verde in a battered old van, packed high with equipment. Though steady and reliable, leather-skinned Xavi rarely contacts the office.

Having issued Xavi with a big bundle of strip lights for the Vía Verde de la Terra Alta and the Vía Verde del Baix Ebre, Antonio gaily wrote an item assuring users that there was lighting in the tunnels. Unfortunately, it was only after hammering in signs at thirty-five of the tunnels that Xavi found the lights hidden under his rather large lunch box. Bafflement was his normal state of mind. At one point just north of Tortosa, where the route crosses a main road by way of an underpass, I'd imagined Xavi standing back and scratching his head as he tried to match Antonio's signs with the track before his eyes. In the end, he hammered in the sign that I'd puzzled over myself: a finger-post pointing left, featuring a white arrow pointing straight ahead – and a track that actually went right.

Here at Cal Rosal, Xavi wasn't at all sure he'd even got the right place for the start of the 6-kilometre Vía Verde del Llobregat up to the reservoir. For one thing, Antonio had told him that it started at La Colònia Rosal, but Xavi couldn't find any such place on the map. Nor could we. Cal Rosal was in the right spot and sounded so similar that it might be right. What's more, the name of the bar was something of a clue: L'Estació del Carrilet ('Narrow-Gauge Railway Station'). I don't know who Xavi asked, but I asked an old chap sitting outside the bar on a bench with his bike.

'Yes, that's it,' he said, 'that dirt track over there. It's the old railway, but it goes straight up the valley to nowhere nowadays, son.' He looked at me as if I was a bit daft. Julie had been listening to the conversation.

'Did he say it's not surfaced?' she asked.

'Yes, but it's not far. Are you coming?'

'Did he say it goes UPHILL?'

'Yes, but it comes downhill on the way back. Obviously.'

'Well, my cold's still lurking in the odd corner...'

'Don't feel under any pressure.'

'... and these tables outside the cafe are in the sun.'

So, alone once more, Benny and I headed for the track beyond the roundabout, as indicated by the old man. Still no red and green Vía Verde signs, so Xavi obviously hadn't got this far yet. Well, seventy-seven Vías Verdes all over Spain are a lot to cover for one man. Then, just as I was leaving an area of desolation left by some roadworks, out of the corner of my eye I caught sight of a post emerging from a small hillock of weeds. Scrambling over chunks of rubble, I managed to get within squinting distance of it. 'Vía Verde del Llobregat, La Baells' plus an arrow pointing up the valley. Xavi was here! Let's hope he's not still buried under the rubble.

After rising in the Serra de Montgrony, about 30 kilometres north-east of here, the Llobregat first flows west before striking almost due south all the way to Barcelona. The old railway of which this route forms a small part opened in 1881 and ran from Guardiola de Berguedà, at the point where the valley makes its sharp left turn, to Manresa, about halfway down to Barcelona.

For its first kilometre or two, the cycle track hugged the east bank of the noisily rushing Llobregat opposite a few rundown old houses on the west bank, the outskirts of Berga, a sizeable town and an important source of business for the railway. The name Berga is another rare reminder of the region's Celtiberian days, when a tribe called the Bergistani dominated these parts. A myth from those days survives to this day in the form of Guita Xica, a green dragon that allegedly acts as a guardian the people of Catalonia and still forms the focus of Berga's annual festival.

Trusting to my personal guardian Spokey, I rattled along the rutted track inches from the drop to the river, avoiding puddles that must have been from an overnight shower up here in the cooler hills and recalling when, like all boys and girls, I used to head straight for the puddles, not carefully pedal around them. Gradually the valley narrowed, its pine-covered slopes steepened and the track's curves tightened before the familiar black, gaping mouth of a tunnel hove into view. I didn't recall Antonio mentioning these – there were only three this time – but, just as the previous day's, they were the tall, narrow tunnels of a single-track line and, once again, completely unlit – though thankfully shorter.

In any other context, the Vía Verde del Llobregat would be regarded as an idyllic, rural bike ride – a rough but level track surrounded by the smells and sounds of the pine forest, leaping across ravines, curving above a bubbling stream – but, to be frank, after the spectacular scenery of the previous day, it was just a bit, well, small scale. In fact, it was smaller scale than Antonio had thought, for while the the website talked of it reaching the dam at La Baells, which holds back a reservoir of the same name, the cyclable track actually ended by an ancient, cobblestone bridge whose pointed arch spanned the pebble-strewn river, and where a number of four-by-fours had come down from Berga for the fishing.

It was barely an hour after I'd left that I wheeled back into Cal Rosal, waving at the old chap, still sitting next to his bike and again giving me the 'Are you completely mad?' stare, and plonked my sweaty self next to Julie on the cafe terrace.

'Good ride?'

'OK. Bit short.'

'Other cyclists?'

'None at all. Hardly a surprise, as the Vía Verde folks seem to be keeping it a secret. Do I need to change before we drive up to Ripoll?'

Her raised eyebrow having spoken more than words, I hastily made use of the cafe's facilities. Being the site of the old station, the bar displayed several evocative black and white photographs of the line in its heyday: four railwaymen sitting proudly in front of a heavily riveted loco; day trippers wandering across a weedy track to a rake of wooden carriages that would take them, so it seemed from their attire, to a distant beach; and one spectacular shot of a sturdy little locomotive hauling a single carriage through heavy, virgin snow.

'Do you know where this one's taken?' I asked the young barmaid.

'Right here,' she said. 'That row of buildings is where you're standing.'

A closer look showed me she was right. I asked if I might take photos of the photos.

'Please do,' she said enthusiastically. 'Not many of our customers take any interest.'

The hop over the next range of hills to the valley of the River Ter looked short enough on the map, but by the time Dave popped out again on the main road up from Vic, we were both a bit dizzy with the bends. However, wiggly as the cross-country road through Borredà and Les Llosses was, it was evidently popular with the well-to-do, as the wooded slopes to either side were sprinkled with plenty of expensively renovated *masíes*.

Arguably the first bourgeoisie in what was to become Catalonia developed under the Romans, when the relative security achieved by the invaders tempted the rich to build *villae*, large houses with gardens, on the outskirts of towns. It was a trend that, in later years, produced that isolated cluster of sturdy, white-walled buildings that is nowadays virtually an icon for rural Catalonia: the *mas* or *masia*. It is traditionally a low, two-storey affair, with thick stone walls and a gently pitched roof, the ground floor originally housing a kitchen, farm tools and farm animals, the floor above containing bedrooms and a formal reception room, occasionally extending into an elegantly arcaded balcony.

Nowadays, many a *masia* has become a restaurant (hence their common prefix 'Mas'), much frequented for traditional Catalan Sunday lunches, or an expensive renovation project or the ultimate second home and weekend retreat for an entire family. One reason why this has become a practical option for many is the Catalan tradition for extended families buying and owning a property together rather than as individuals or couples.

Our destination on the River Ter was Ripoll and we instantly took to it.

The view of the *Senyera* (the red and yellow Catalan flag) fluttering from the tower of Ripoll's Abbey Church of Santa Maria, set deep in dark-green mountains, is one often seen on the cover of guidebooks and on many a calendar – a picture that gives an instant flavour of the Catalan Pyrenees. It could also symbolise the birth of the Catalan nation, for it was here that the counts of Barcelona were traditionally buried, in a monastery founded by Guifré el Pilós, Wilfred the Hairy, also founder of the House of Barcelona itself.

Pulling aside the curtains in our room at La Trobada Hotel (the 'encounter' hotel), we were greeted by this very view, the setting sun lighting up the flag from behind so that it blazed like a great fire about to set light to the forest backdrop.

'Not much cycling for you today,' said Julie.

'No, but the old knee's benefitted from the rest. And anyway, we've got almost all the driving out of the way in one day. A longer bike ride tomorrow and two even longer ones after that.'

'And another benefit of a short day: time to explore the town?'

'Yes, sure. You know, we're nearer Llançà than Tortosa now, but up here in the mountains it feels a world away from them both, doesn't it?'

By the time the sun had set, we'd dived into the tight network of streets that forms Ripoll's compact town centre. Despite the town's role in the traditional self-image of Catalonia, it didn't feel like a tourist destination, at least on that chilly spring evening. People and water rushed everywhere. The River Freser flows into the Ter here and, with five or six bridges, a mountain torrent seemed to be at every turn. Short ladies with heavy baskets scuttled along the narrow alleys between shopfronts in surprising colours: a lilac *farmàcia*, a chocolate-brown *xarcuteria*, a faded pink shop marked *'Confeccions'*, which turned out to sell clothes rather than sweets. One rather fierce-looking woman bustled through a narrow doorway above which an elaborate metal sign dated 1890 declared *'Cuchilleria'*, below a symbol of crossed knives – in case you had any doubt as to what the word meant. (Why isn't there an English word 'knifery'?) The older shop names were in Spanish, the newer in Catalan.

One word sprung to my mind to describe the atmosphere of this small Pyrenean town: Alpine. At this, I could imagine my old geography teacher Mr Plampin removing his glasses before pinching the top of his nose, eyes closed.

'Where are the Alps, boy?'

'Somewhere round Switzerland, sir.'

'And where are we?'

'Spain.'

'And yet, Guise, in that confused head of yours is the germ of a not-unreasonable idea.'

'Sir?'

'What is it that makes Ripoll's town centre feel Alpine?'

'The mountains at the end of the street?'

'And...?'

'And the sound of a river flowing?'

'Even nearer to you, boy.'

'Um. The overhanging roofs, sir.'

'Good. And why do they overhang?'

'Because they're bigger than the buildings, sir.'

More nose pinching.

'Ah, got it, sir! To let the snow fall off away from the walls.'

'We may make a geographer of you yet, Guise.'

Back at La Trobada, having been tempted by the *'Buffet Lliure'* ('Free Buffet') sign, we presented ourselves in the hotel's small restaurant. A jolly woman with dark hair the shape of a motorcycle helmet approached.

'Buffet's off. Crisis.'

'What crisis?'

'The financial crisis.'

'Ah.'

'But we have a crisis menu.'

Well, the fact that the small place was rapidly filling up suggested a certain local fondness for the crisis menu and so we settled in. It was a menu where – taking one step up from the House of the Angels – we were actually allowed to see the scribbled notes on the little scrap of paper from which the helmet-haired waitress read. To be honest, we could understand neither her writing nor most of what she said, but one thing was clear: at least four courses were on their way and the choices within them were minimal.

First up was a huge basket of *embotits* (cooked meats), from which we were invited to hack off as much as we could manage. Ham, salami, chorizo, *sobrassada* (sausage with paprika), *fuet* (another kind of spiced sausage)... there seemed to be no end to the varieties in the basket left on our table. Just as we thought we'd covered our plates with as much as were dared, another basket landed before us, this time filled with cheeses. Some of the labels were still legible: Serrat, Garrotxa, Alt Urgell – these are local districts and in fact most of the cheese seemed to be Manchego (sheep's cheese) in one form or another, which was fine by me, for Manchego is just hard enough to fall within my definition of 'real' cheese, i.e. not the sloppy stuff the French eat.

When the vegetable soup arrived, we were allowed to retain our starter plates, heaving as they still were, but when Helmet-Hair arrived soon after with the chicken and chips, only I had finished the soup (being a rather fast eater) and Julie's half-full soup dish was unceremoniously whipped away with a rattle of the spoon. Looking around, we noticed that everyone else – three working men, two middle-aged couples and a businessman – was eating away furiously. Conversation was out of the question. Evidently they all knew the drill: eat it or lose it.

After the rapid-fire delivery of the ice creams and its instant follow-up of coffee and small biscuit, we sat back and reviewed the meal. Crisis or no crisis, not only had the food been delicious, but also the service had in fact been outstandingly efficient and executed with a smile. It has to be said that this is more usually the case in Spain as a whole than in, say, Britain. To be a waiter or waitress here is to choose not your summer job but your profession – and it shows. The typical Catalan waiter greets you as you arrive, keeps an eye on you throughout and, knowing you'll beckon him over if anything's wrong, will leave you to enjoy the meal in peace without that artificially scripted 'Is everything all right here?' which has wormed its way into British eateries. There are exceptions, of course, as with the case of the restaurant I shall not name in Portbou, where to draw the waiter's attention you'd need to dance naked on the table juggling two courgettes and singing 'I'm a matador and I'm all right', which I put down to its proximity to France.

Just as at the House of the Angels, any prices at the excellent Encounter Hotel were kept *un secreto* until the morning, when an equally tiny bill was presented.

Day 14

Defying the Laws of Physics:
Ripoll to Olot

'This way. It must start at the station.'

Those corners in which Julie's cold had still lurked were deemed clear enough the following morning for both her and Buttercup the Bike to be dusted down, oiled up and presented to the byways of Catalonia as finely tuned machines. Having examined yet more Vía Verde leaflets which the kindly waitress had dug out for me, I led us off to the south.

Ten minutes later we were heading back north, past the hotel, to a huge sign announcing 'Vía Verde del Ferro i del Carbó'.

'We could see this sign from our window,' complained Julie.

'It's not very clear on the map.'

'I've only got so many miles in these legs.'

'Sorry.'

'And the fact that all these cyclists are hovering around does suggest some kind of cycle route, doesn't it?'

'You've made your point. Should we get on?'

Ferro means iron and *carbó* coal. The main purpose of this nineteenth-century railway had been to transport coal from the mines up at Ogassa down to the Ripoll ironworking area and beyond. But even then metalworking was by no means new to the region, which had seen settlements from as far back as the Bronze Age. In medieval times Ripoll itself had had a thriving trade in nails, crossbows and other iron products. Partly for this reason the town had frequently been attacked and indeed was completely destroyed in 1839 during the Carlist Wars, a struggle between, on the one hand, liberals and republicans and, on the other, Catholics and other royalists loyal to Prince Carlos.

The little line followed the valley of the River Ter and used to connect at Ripoll station with the main line from Barcelona up to Puigcerdà and France – which had been the rationale for my conviction that the Vía Verde would start at the station. Judging from its initial route out of town, some metalworking still survives, though no longer supported by the railway, since this section of the line closed in 1980. The section from the Ogassa coal mines themselves had already bitten the dust thirteen years before.

The cycle track itself dipped under the main road by way of a subway where some of the worst graffiti anywhere on this journey disfigured the walls. Planners the world over still seem not to have realised that any blank, hidden wall just cannot be left white. Although my Catalan is poor, even I had gathered that Catalonia's graffiti vandals must be a pretty humourless bunch – and over obsessed with just one subject to boot. No, not sex, not football, but politics. The politics of the gleefully oppressed. It's a shame the movement for Catalan independence finds its stance most often expressed to visitors through the limited medium of spray paint on concrete and via the limited thoughts of the sprayers: 'Free Catalonia', 'Whore Spain' or even, as here in Ripoll, a personal attack on the royal House of Bourbon. A shame because, whether you agree with the objective or not, it's a perfectly valid movement, led by perfectly eloquent people.

Even the brief skim through the centuries on Day 3 showed that the idea of a Catalonia independent from Spain is by no means new. However, in terms of political parties, the movement got going in the 1920s, when the Estat Català ('Catalan State') party was founded by Francesc Macià. This evolved into the Esquerra Republicana de Catalunya (ERC) (Republican Left of Catalonia), which declared the short-lived independent Catalan Republic of the early 1930s, with Macià as president.

The civil war and the Franco years, of course, boosted the groundswell of support for independence, which was finally able to find legitimate expression and begin to flourish after the dictator's death. Independent polls in the last twenty years have regularly shown about a third of Catalonia's residents to be for independence and about a half against – but, as always, it depends on how you phrase the question.

While we were in Llançà in 2010, the town held a popular vote on the subject, as part of a wider poll across Catalonia, though held in different places on different dates. My understanding is that in Llançà a whopping 90 per cent voted for independence – but two caveats are worth reporting. First, the turnout was remarkably low and second, to reach the building, those that did vote had to duck Catalan flags (no Spanish ones), pass a table covered in leaflets promoting independence (no leaflets against) and listen to council loudspeakers playing traditional Catalan music. Free and fair? I don't think so.

The symbol for Catalan independence is the *Estelada*, a regular *Senyera* but with, to the flagpole side, a white star on a blue triangle (as in the star of the US Confederate flag). In the reductionism of graffiti, this becomes a few horizontal lines next to a roughly drawn star – and you see it everywhere in Catalonia.

Just as ubiquitous, as already mentioned, is the Catalan donkey, representing nationalism rather than independence as such, most often as a car sticker (too difficult to spray?). Far more effective than crude and ugly graffiti.

Ripoll's industrial outskirts soon gave way to unsprayable countryside: rolling green meadows and the clonking of cowbells. No, on closer inspection, these were actually horse-bells. While the horses themselves were no surprise, horse-riding being one of the well-publicised attractions of a summer holiday in the Catalan Pyrenees, this was the first time I'd ever seen bells used on grazing horses and back at the hotel later on I asked the receptionist about them.

'Were there fences around the field, señor?'

'No. Now I think about it, there were none.'

She gave me the look of a mother explaining the realities of the big, wide world to her child.

'Horses, cows, sheep... they all wander into the mountains. And in the mountains is the danger, señor. Perhaps some people they need also the bell on the neck.'

Below the safely clonking horses gurgled the Ter, which I'd last seen as a wide, imposing river when I crossed it on emerging from the market at Torroella on Day 4. Above the meadows of horses and their foals rose the steep sides of the Serra Cavallera – appropriately enough, 'Horse-Mane Mountains' – at over 2,000 metres high, the start of the serious Pyrenees. One of the many information boards beside the track asked itself this question:

'Is there oil in the Eastern Pyrenees?'

After a graphic description of how, about fifty million years ago, the sediments that now rose behind that very board were deposited on the sea floor, bent into shapes convenient for trapping dead organic material and how these sediments were then lifted up and the organic material could then have been turned into oil, the writer concluded... well, concluded nothing actually. So maybe there is oil here and maybe there isn't.

Never mind. This plethora of information boards – so typical of twenty-first-century Catalonia – on subjects including geology, history and the railway itself gave me a regular excuse to stop and wait for Julie to catch up. Even though my own cycling pace may nowadays be described as stately, I still find it physically impossible to cycle at Julie's speed. She seems to defy the basic laws of physics. While a great deal of energy goes in – as evidenced by pumping legs, swaying handlebars and rapid intakes of breath – very little energy seems to come out. Perched aboard Buttercup, she progresses at the approximate pace of a pedestrian pope wandering through his flock, bestowing blessings left and right. I'd thought that the gradient of this cycle track – a modest 1 per cent – would present no problems even to her, but by the time we stopped for a snack at the little old station of Sant Joan de les Abadesses, she'd had enough.

'I'll sit here and contemplate the mountains,' she panted. 'You finish the rest on your own.'

The rest was just a pleasant 3-kilometre round trip up to the old coal trans-shipment depot at Toralles, where the track came to a sudden stop among the wild flowers of the mountains, the remaining short section up to Ogassa being still under construction. Luckily for Julie, this was also true of another 22-kilometre stretch of Vía Verde, between Sant Joan de les Abadesses and Olot, although this has since been opened.

Back at Sant Joan, while Julie summoned up strength for the descent, I wandered into the cafe occupying the old station building to get a beer and there was perusing more old, black and white railway photos when the barmaid approached.

'This railway must have been a vital link to the outside world,' I commented.

'Or a vital link from them to us?' she suggested, reminding me of the alleged newspaper headline in Britain: 'Fog in Channel. Rest of world cut off.'

I laughed. 'Everyone in these photos seems either proud to work for the railways or happy to travel on them.'

'You're right, señor. And who looks happy to travel nowadays on our roads?'

'No one probably.'

'Certainly not me,' she said. 'I'm very happy to be here in the quiet all day...'

As she spoke, three young men – probably workers from a nearby building site – bundled in, singing some raucous song about FC Barcelona.

'Well,' grinned the philosophical barmaid, 'not every day is quiet of course.'

Just before we set off on our return, a strange thing happened. Well, it was strange to me because I'd never seen one in real life. Out of the corner of my eye, I saw something red dart through the bushes at the end of the track. Turning towards the red flash, I caught it just disappearing as it bounced up and down along the lane I'd taken to Torralles. It was on the head of a short, middle-aged man who seemed to be late for something and it was most definitely a *barretina*.

A *barretina* is a baggy woollen hat, usually red and traditionally worn by Catalan men in times gone by. Its exact origins seem to be lost in history, although one suggestion is that it was originally the standard cap for Catalan sailors. Nowadays, however, they are regularly worn at folk events or elsewhere specifically to underline the wearer's Catalan identity. Banned by Franco? In this instance, it seems not. Maybe a Baggy Red Hat Prevention Force would have been one step too far, even for the dotty dictator. Two other places where you may regularly see a mini-*barretina* in modern-day Catalonia are atop the cork of a bottle of locally produced olive oil – or on a small crapping boy. Excuse my French, but it's true.

The *caganer* (crapper) is a traditional character in the Christian nativity scene, not only in Catalonia but also elsewhere in southern Europe. He's usually in a corner, well away from Jesus, Mary and the crew, wears a *barretina*, squats and, well, defecates. Whatever the significance of the character (fertilisation, equality, recycling... there have been many suggestions), he seems to be very popular. When, in 2005, the Barcelona authorities, in one of their more sensitive moments, commissioned an official nativity scene without a *caganer*, there was uproar. Questions in the House. In 2006 the crapper was back.

I'm not suggesting that the runner of Sant Joan de les Abadesses was off for a quick one, but the unexpected appearance of yet another symbol of Catalan identity, here in the middle of the day, did suggest we might finally be 'in the fifth pine tree'.

On the gentle downhill gradient, Julie found another principle of physics to challenge: gravitational attraction. While the strong attraction of planet earth easily overcame the little frictional resistance offered by the wheels of my own bike, sending me on a luxurious pedal-free descent, something weird was happening in Julie's machine, something which required her to pedal downhill almost as much as uphill. We inverted Buttercup to check the wheels: no problem. I observed the brakes while she rode: no problem. We could only assume that its resistance to freewheeling was in some way related to the singularly low position in which she prefers to maintain her saddle and the singularly vertical posture in which she prefers to sit. I confess I'm no physicist.

By now the path was positively bristling with walkers, joggers and cyclists of all ages, shapes and sizes. In fact, this distinguished the Vía Verde del Ferro i del Carbó from the other five I cycled on this trip. Judging from the users' relative lack of luggage and from the Catalan they spoke, it's a fair guess that many of them were locals. Some were very local indeed, since we saw four or five youths burst out of a nearby house to use a set of exercise equipment installed next to the track. This seems to be a relatively recent idea that I've noticed in several parts of Spain – and a very worthwhile one too: public exercise equipment (ropes, climbing frames, parallel bars and so on) designed not for children but for adults, complete with instructions on how to use them to best effect.

Squashed back into the car, we took the old main road east over the Coll de Canes into the county of La Garrotxa. This high route, which poked in and out of clouds that we hadn't seen from Ripoll, featured an astonishing number of green signs pointing off the road.

'These hills must be littered with footpaths,' I said.

'I'm not sure they are footpath signs,' said Julie, who was navigating. 'Slow down a bit. Can Abisme. Can Abella. No, they're pointing at buildings up in the trees and down in the valley.'

'They can't all be farms.'

'Must be holiday homes, weekend retreats.'

'Hardly a retreat if you're surrounded by hundreds of others. They're squashed in like... like...'

'A Can Abeans?'

Julie soon had too much navigating to do to come up with any more puns. The short valley of the River Riudaura had led us into La Garrotxa's county town, Olot, where it flowed into the Fluvià. Not that we could see the river, nor any other feature to help us orientate ourselves, for Olot was very quickly added to the list of places that neither of us could get our heads around. Everyone knows them. From the moment you enter town, nothing seems to slot into place. North seems south, up seems down, in seems out. Julie and I call them 'a bit of a Rouen', after the Normandy town, a successful transit of which proved beyond our combined abilities for about a decade. Some may blame bad 'vibes', unfortunate ley lines or the Devil himself. In the case of Olot, I blame Antonio, the Vía Verde information supremo.

Antonio's little booklet had provided us with a small street map of Olot, with the Vía Verde clearly marked. Unfortunately, nothing else he'd chosen to include – the River Fluvià, a few random street names, some unexplained wiggly lines – could we find at all. I'd marked the location of our hotel with an X from an Internet map. After an unplanned half-hour tour of what seemed at first sight a rather charmless little town, we pulled up in a car park, emerging into what had become a baking hot, airless afternoon.

'Look at this map!' demanded Julie, waving it as a teacher waves a poor piece of homework. 'And tell me which way's north!'

'Um. Ah. No idea.'

'No arrow pointing north. No scale. No "This way to Figueres". No... no...'

'November?'

'Hm,' said Julie, filing Antonio's little map on the floor. 'And the citizens of Olot don't seem to bother with street names half the time. And when they do, the letters are grey on grey and about half an inch high, and I haven't had a shower since the bike ride and...'

'I'll ask someone, should I?'

No directions were required, actually, for the nice old lady I stopped simply pointed at a building about 50 metres away: the Hotel Borrell.

Ramon Borrell was the count of Barcelona from 992 to 1017 and has the unusual distinction of lying in a lost grave: despite his having been buried in Barcelona Cathedral, of which he was the founder, his descendants have apparently misplaced the site. The hotel named after him in Olot, however, is a very modern one, which meant that thankfully the bathroom met with Julie's approval and had us both re-emerging bright-eyed and shiny-haired onto the streets of Olot. We now had, moreover, a proper map supplied not by Antonio but by the very efficient hotel receptionist and were therefore finally able to orientate ourselves in this confusing town. The hotel lay near the foot of a steep hill on the edge of a newly developed area to the south-west of the centre. Well, newly *re*-developed, for the presence of an old factory chimney in the square where we sat surrounded by coffee and leaflets suggested an earlier industrial district. Julie had switched into organisational mode.

'There are two things we should do before we dine,' she said.

'I've got at least two days' cycling to get in before I die.'

'DINE, not die. Didn't you dry your ears properly?'

'Sorry. What are they?'

'A house of volcanoes and an actual volcano.'

'Ah yes. La Garrotxa. We're in a famous volcanic area. Been meaning to come here for ages. Can't say I've seen one yet, though. Some of them are supposed to be not quite extinct, that's to say...'

'OK, save the lecture till later,' said Julie, pointing upwards. 'Those clouds seem to have followed us from the hills.'

Sure enough, it had gone quite dark and the heavy atmosphere hinted at thunder. So with some haste we set off on foot down a wide boulevard of plane trees to the Parc Nou, in the middle of which sat a splendid old house, where you could easily imagine a few murders might once have been solved by Hercule Poirot and which now had been smartly painted in cream and maroon to form the Casal dels Volcans, the 'Mansion of the Volcanoes'.

I can't praise this museum highly enough. Compact but not crowded, informative but not boring, it told us all we wanted to know not only about local volcanic activity but also, surprisingly, about local earthquakes.

When I'd first moved to Spain and began reading up on Catalonia, it came as a surprise to learn that the Iberian Peninsula had any volcanoes at all. It turns out that the most important area is right here in the Garrotxa Volcanic Zone, a nature reserve comprising no less than forty volcanic cones. According to the museum's maps, they seemed to be everywhere, but... wait a minute... looking at one of the aerial photos, I finally twigged. What I'd been looking for was the wrong scale – by a factor of about ten. La Garrotxa's volcanoes are not Etnas or Vesuviases, huge steaming mountains that take a day to circumnavigate; they're little conical hills a few hundred metres high: baby volcanoes. It turns out that technically La Garrotxa is a 'monogenetic' volcanic field, which is one where the magma supply was relatively restricted and, rather than creating a single giant volcano that might erupt repeatedly, it generated many small eruptions, each leaving a small volcanic cone of the ejected material. My idea that some of the volcanoes are not quite extinct was only half right. It's the volcanic *field* that's apparently not quite extinct, having last erupted about 11,000 years ago. If another eruption were to take place it wouldn't be within an existing cone but would form a new one.

Nowadays most of the cones are forested but some are actually built on. Indeed, some are within Olot – including, for heaven's sake, the one just outside our hotel window. Naturally, Julie had already latched onto this and had selected the cone of Montascopa, over on the north side of town, for an early evening walk. Fair enough: if you happened to be nervous of new eruptions, it turns out that an existing cone would be the safest place to be.

Before leaving the museum, however, on the advice of its attentive curator, we took in the ten-minute video which he'd configured in English for us. If you ever go to Olot's Casal dels Volcans, I strongly recommend that you watch this video – and that you skip the rest of this paragraph. With no chairs to be seen in the little, raised auditorium, we leaned against the back wall just as all went dark. Filling almost an entire wall, the screen gradually came to life and began to tell the story of a day many years ago when farmers were farming, wives were cooking, children were playing... well, you get the idea. It was all very relaxing – until I suddenly felt the floor judder beneath my feet. Had a juggernaut rammed the building? Surely an earthquake couldn't be starting here and now. Even more oddly, the on-screen actors seemed to feel something too.... Well, Julie had latched on straight away, or so she said, but I admit it had me going for those few weird seconds. The reason the floor was raised was that, on cue to coincide with the earthquake in the film, a mechanism underneath had vibrated it. Hence the blackout, so that we didn't see that it was only the floor, and hence the lack of furniture, so that we didn't injure ourselves. Bravo, Casal dels Volcans!

So, for all the destructive potential of its volcanoes, what destroyed the medieval town of Olot was an earthquake. It was the morning of 2 February 1428. With a magnitude inferred from historical evidence as eight or nine on the Richter scale, the shocks were strong enough to cause panic 125 kilometres away in Barcelona; the bell tower of the monastery at Sant Joan de les Abadesses was destroyed; and the village of Queralbs, way up in the Pyrenees and nearest to the epicentre, was completely wiped out. If the inferred magnitude is correct, the only similar known event on the Iberian Peninsula was the Great Lisbon Earthquake of 1755.

Though its layout is confusing, Olot town centre is pretty compact and within half an hour we were sitting on a bench with a view, catching our breath after panting up the streets that form the lower slopes of Montascopa.

'See,' said Julie. 'They're all around. They look pretty extinct to me, though.'

'But, as it said at the museum, the whole area's technically just on the dormant side of extinct.'

'And you can still see the effect of that earthquake. In the middle of Olot there aren't any really old buildings, I mean medieval buildings, are there? It makes you wonder why they bothered building a town in the same place again.'

'Nowt as rum as folk, I suppose.'

As if to demonstrate the veracity of the old saying, the calm of our little viewing bench was suddenly disrupted by an argument at a house across the street. At least it sounded like an argument, but comprised just a single voice, that of the woman who eventually emerged with two small dogs. Quite short and somewhere in her fifties or sixties, the woman's appearance was normal but her behaviour was not. She immediately turned to me and, while issuing a volley of unintelligible Catalan, waved her stick in an agitated fashion at the trees just up the street.

'I'm sorry,' I said in Spanish. 'I don't understand. In Castilian?'

Looking at me as if I might just have landed from a neighbouring galaxy, she then launched into an equally unintelligible volley of what I imagine was Spanish. In the meantime, Julie had scurried over some waste ground to try to protect three tiny kittens from her two dogs, who, in an un-doglike form of behaviour as odd as their mistress's, had been sneaking up quietly on their victims. A flash of lightning lit up the scene.

Ignoring both her dogs and the lightning, the Agitated Lady of Olot tried again, this time more slowly – and more loudly.

'PUSHED ME, SHE DID. RIGHT THERE. MADE ME HOLD ONTO THE RAILINGS FOR DEAR LIFE!' With this, she prodded me – in an attempt, I imagined, to make me understand the seriousness of the situation.

'It's all right. They've shot through the pipe,' called Julie, as a rumble of thunder rolled across the hilltops.

'What?' I asked, thinking this might be some kind of daydream from which I would shortly awake.

'The kittens, they've escaped.'

'DO YOU UNDERSTAND?' demanded the Agitated One.

'Oh yes. Blimey,' I said, realising that the attack she'd described might explain her excited state. 'When did this happen?'

'LAST SUNDAY.'

At this, it eventually dawned on me that her agitation might be slightly more than temporary. As usual, Julie had realised this rather more promptly than I and was by now waving me away.

'Ah, well,' I said to the Agitated One, pointing downhill. 'I'm sorry about the attack, but we must be going now.'

'*¡AIE! ¡GUIRIS!*' (Bah! Foreigners!), she shouted. And with a wave of her stick she called over her cat-like dogs and set off up the volcano. As she did so – and I swear I'm not making this up – the Agitated Lady of Olot executed exactly the same double-skip with which Morecambe and Wise used to end their TV shows while singing 'Bring Me Sunshine'.

'Maybe there are still some dodgy fumes seeping out of the volcano,' I said.

'I've told you before not to get into long conversations with suspicious people,' Julie reminded me.

'I thought she might have been in trouble.'

'Anyway, here's the rain. I think we really will have to go back to town.'

Back at the hotel, after drying out, we turned our thoughts to food.

'Did you see those posters advertising "Volcanic Cuisine"?' asked Julie.

'An eruption too far, I think. But we know that the Olotians... can I say that?'

'You just did.'

'... that the Olotians are a bit fussy about their food, don't we?'

'You're one to speak. Why's that anyway?'

'Don't you remember when we said we'd be calling here, someone told us that Olot has the rare distinction of forcing a McDonald's to close down through lack of business?'

'I can see the placards now: "Burgers No, *Botifarras* Yes". Anyway, I think the decision may have been made for us.'

'Why's that?'

'Look outside.'

The rain was now coming down in jugs, as the Spanish say. Opening the window a crack brought in a volley of raindrops and the sound of thunder rolling around the hills. The Catalan word for rain, *pluja* – pronounced 'plooja' – is much more onomatopoeic than the Spanish, *lluvia*, or indeed the English. It was *plujing* it down.

'Nearest restaurant?' I suggested.

'My vote too.'

As it turned out, the thunderstorm was a stroke of luck.

La Veranda ticked boxes for both of us. Clearly a former grand house, its separate high-ceilinged rooms, with their big mirrors and comfortable suede banquettes, appealed to Julie's sense of style, while its escape from the Catalan obsession with fish appealed to my own sense of taste. Its remarkably reasonable prices appealed to both of us. While she followed her asparagus soup with prawns (the menu's only piscatorial concession), I followed mine with cannelloni. By coffee time, the wine had made me overly expansive and I remembered a tip from one of our Llançà neighbours.

'Do you do *ratafia*?' I asked the waitress.

'Of course, señor. *Chupitos*?'

'No. *Ratafias*.'

She and Julie exchanged a glance that told me I might have got the wrong end of the stick.

'*Chupito*,' explained the patient waitress in hesitant English, 'is – how you say – the size. In English is, I think, the shot.'

Well, how was I supposed to know?

'Yes, two shots of *ratafia*, thank you.'

The local Olot version of this liqueur tasted like *anis à la Marmite* – which was fine by me – and went down like... well, like a shot. After a dodgy start, Olot was turning out to be all right after all and we both agreed that we now actually liked it. Quite Olot.

Day 15

740 Steps Before Breakfast: Olot to Girona

Our failure to get to the top of Montascopa had bugged me into the early hours and so I awoke at about seven with a plan.

'I'm going to take the bike to the base of the volcano, lock it up and walk up to the top. I'll be back for breakfast by half eight, I reckon.'

My remarks had been addressed to a motionless form. The form grunted: 'OK.'

The rain had left the air tangy-sharp and, as I pedalled through the deserted streets, Olot reminded me of those childhood walks into town with my mother, where every sight, every sound and especially every smell seemed exotic and new. Glistening grass in a front garden, echoing ripples from a hidden stream, freshly baked bread from a narrow alley.

Wary of another encounter with the Agitated Lady of Olot, I'd opted this time for the path up the western slope of

Montascopa and my route took me past the town's bullring, touted as the second oldest in Spain and now securely locked up. Having done the same with Benny in a nearby car park, I set off on foot along the rough track that clung to the side of Montascopa. Unlike on its eastern side, you didn't need to be told here that this was a volcano, for dark black cinders and other dark debris, like pieces of charcoal, were strewn all around, grass growing out of most of it. In fact, the treads of the flight of steps that formed most of the path were made of this loose material, or had been until yesterday's storm had washed half of it away. This transformed each step into a rather awkward balancing act – and there were 370 of them. I counted.

The view from the top made the ascent worth it, though. While the sun must have been above the horizon for a good hour, it was hidden behind low clouds that still brushed the tops of the conical peaks, some of whose dark-green woods reached right into the suburban streets where Olot's residents were just making their first morning coffees. With its red roofs broken here and there by a soaring church tower or a flat-roofed office block, the town seemed to roll between the hills like a heavy sea in a narrow channel, hurling unwary vessels against the shore.

The slopes of Montascopa itself were barer than those of most of the other cones, its rim occupied by a sparse plantation of silver birch. Walking a few metres in from the rim brought me to the crater itself – and here was a surprise, for it was filled almost entirely by a shallow cup of bright green grass – no doubt the *copa* after which the hill was named. The literature says that the crater is 120 metres wide and 12 metres deep, and seeing an early dog walker on the far side helped me translate this into an area of, let's say, five or six football pitches. You'd be pretty mad to play football on such slopes, but a picnic wouldn't be out of the question. Completing the scene on the far rim of the crater was the nineteenth-century Chapel of Sant Francesc, now closed but still giving the hill of Montascopa a tranquil air that belied its violent origin.

Knees throbbing after another 370 steps on the way down, I whizzed Benny back across town, where cafes and shops were now selling the bread baked earlier. Having breakfasted ourselves, Julie and I made rapid arrangements for an evening rendezvous in Girona before I pedalled the hundred metres or so to pick up the Vía Verde as it used the backstreets to head out of town.

While Antonio had short-changed us with his impractical map, it seemed that Xavi had also been off form in Olot, forgetting task number one in his job description: signs. However, he had remembered two pots of paint, for the only reason I knew I was on the right streets was the green and blue bike and pedestrian logo painted on the ground. I just wasn't 100 per cent sure I was going in the right direction.

It was just short of Sant Esteve d'en Bas, a good 6 kilometres out of Olot and after the street route had turned into the narrow track more typical of a Vía Verde, that a sign to Girona finally appeared – thankfully pointing in the same direction as Benny. Girona, it said, lay '53,000 m' away. A strange way of describing it. This sounded like the other side of the moon.

At least and at last, I told myself, I was on the right route. Bit by bit I was heading back to the coast, in a sort of clockwise spiral. So was the River Fluvià, flowing steadfastly on my right but in the opposite direction, heading north through Olot before lurching east towards Sant Pere Pescador, where I'd encountered the three *amigos*. Today's bike route, however, would initially take me south, back into the valley of the River Ter, as it trundled east to Girona.

An old railway going from one river valley to the next? Yes, but this narrow-gauge railway, El Carrilet, which had connected Olot to the national rail network in 1911, achieved the feat by means of a tunnel – a tunnel now widened and occupied by the C-152 main road. As for the harassed, wind-blown Vía Verde enthusiast – well, he has to pedal round the hairpins up to Coll d'en Bas through an area known locally (and unsurprisingly) as 'the Switzerland of Catalonia': not the sort of phrase that appeals to this cyclist at least.

However, my efforts were soon rewarded by the views. Sitting on a small tussock and eagerly gulping in large draughts of water, I surveyed the scene. Nowhere was flat. Below a deep-blue sky, dark-green forests of pine and (unusually) of beech rolled, tumbled and peaked all around, barely camouflaging yet more volcanic cones lurking beneath. The heavy morning silence was broken by a metallic hammering coming from the ramshackle shed of a ramshackle farm in the shadow of the valley below.

Refreshed and re-energised, I moved on at some pace, as the track curved between the woods, occasionally cutting through outcrops of different coloured rock. A series of information boards, under the title 'The secrets of the Vías Verdes', identified the reddish rocks as river sediment from fifty million years ago and the bluish ones as fine-grained clay deposited by the sea some twenty million years later, both confirming that I'd now moved out of the volcanic area. Away from towns, every one of these boards was blissfully free from graffiti.

On the steep descent the only brake on my speed was the poor surface, which, compared with the other Vías Verdes, presented a few hazards of its own: not only the sudden changes in surface – from dirt to concrete to slabs and back again – but also the deep cross-gulleys caused by yesterday's storm, which must have passed through here too. Benny's thick tyres did their job in negotiating the worst of the bumps.

Though the bends of the track revealed occasional glimpses of snow to the north, in the distant higher Pyrenees, down here in the foothills it was once again pretty sultry. Banks of bright red poppies still flanked the cycle track as it finally levelled out among the fields and farms around the southern borders of La Garrotxa. After a while the odd *masia* was surrounded by scaffolding or occupied by JCBs – a tell-tale sign that country was turning into suburb.

The town I was approaching was Sant Feliu de Pallerols and it arrived suddenly, around a blind bend, in the form of its old railway station: now, predictably and happily, a cafe.

For a change, it was awash with cycles – propped on kerbs, perched in racks, leaning on walls – their owners occupying almost all the tables set out on the old platform. Having plonked my helmet on the only free one, I went inside to order. With my miscellaneous snacks being too numerous to carry in one go, I asked the barmaid to bring some outside. Unfortunately, in my haste, I confused *'fuera'* (outside) with *'fuego'* (fire).

'Could you help me please? I'm on fire.'

Having looked me up and down with ill-disguised suspicion, she did as bid, before beating a hasty retreat. While I'd been inside, two of the four seats around my table had been occupied by two men rather younger than me. Rather younger, rather wider, rather balder and rather keener on tight-fitting, lime-green Lycra. As they began to chat to me (or worryingly, to chat me up), I couldn't get out of my head the image of Tweedledum and Tweedledee.

'You are goink oophill or downhill on your leetle black bicycle?' asked Tweedledum. They were probably German, possibly Dutch.

'Oh, downhill, of course.'

'So are we,' smiled Tweedledee, disproportionately pleased with my answer. 'You are goink all the way?'

'To Girona?'

'Yes.'

'Yes,' I admitted.

After a brief but rather disconcerting discussion on how uncomfortable it can get while pedalling under a hot sun – a subject which had raised a few eyebrows among those other cyclists nearby whose English was up to it – the Tweedles suddenly decided their time was up and waddled over to a pair of heavily packed bikes. With two limp waves and two unnecessarily broad grins, they were off.

'Haff fun! Maybe see you on ze route!' called Tweedledum, his shiny pate now encased in a white helmet which, like all his gear, matched that of his friend.

Maybe not, I thought, raising a polite hand and burying my head in a map. Over the course of a few minutes, my day had assumed a new purpose: how to travel 36 kilometres along a narrow corridor without encountering two others travelling the same route. Perhaps they were simply being friendly, of course, but something about them had roused my suspicions as to what exactly they might have in mind, should our paths cross again. Phase One of my strategy was to stay right where I was for as long as my schedule permitted.

Taking more time than I'd planned to read through the various local leaflets I was carrying, I found that one piece of information was missing from all. Here I was at Sant Feliu de Pallerols, heading ultimately, the next day, to Sant Feliu de Guíxols and I'd no idea who Saint Feliu was. Evidently in the same state of ignorance were an English couple who had arrived, puffing and groaning, from the Girona direction and moved onto the table next to mine.

'Can you feel yer gushels?' asked the young man of his partner, revealing a schoolboy humour unfortunately similar to my own.

'I'll feel yours if you don't grow up!' she retorted.

'Anyway, I've never even heard the name Feliu, have you?'

'Can't say I have. Maybe it's Catalan for Philip.'

'Is there a Saint Philip?'

'I think Philip's "Felip" in Catalan,' I said. 'Only because I know a Bar Felip.'

'Sounds more likely,' admitted the woman. 'Maybe Feliu's Felix.'

'Is there a Saint Felix?'

Well, the shared ignorance of us non-Catholics didn't get us any further that hot day on the old railway platform, but subsequent research in a cool, dark room has revealed that, yes, Feliu is indeed Felix.

Born in the third century AD into a well-to-do family near Carthage, North Africa, Felix studied in Caesarea (in modern-day Israel), where he converted to Christianity. Persecution of Christians within the Roman Empire was patchy at this time and, along with Cucufate, a fellow traveller, Felix elected to devote himself to missionary work in one of the regions where it was at its most severe, here in Hispania Tarraconensis. He duly landed on the coast of Ampurias (now Empordà) and travelled inland to Girona, where, under the cover of being merely a foreign trader, he began converting many pagans to Christianity. Too many.

Felix was brought before the local Roman praetor, who condemned him to a series of ghastly tortures, involving (so says the Biblioteca Electrónica Cristiana (BEC) at www.multimedios.org) iron hooks, millstones and horses, from which he eventually died in the year 304. At one point, according to the BEC, Felix was saved by 'the intercession of an evangelical spirit' and placed gently on the beach at what is now called Sant Feliu de Guíxols.

A few years later his erstwhile companion Cucufate suffered a similarly gruesome death at a Roman fort inland from Barcelona. In Catalan, Cucufate becomes Cugat and the site of the fort is now occupied by the monastery at Sant Cugat, in the same square of that town where we'd enjoyed a lunch with my old work companions several cycling days before. What a lucky life we all live.

Felix is not the only religious link to the route of El Carrilet. With the encouragement of the Church, Christian pilgrimages had begun soon after Felix's time and by the Middle Ages one of the most important was El Camino de Santiago, from various points in Europe to Santiago de Compostela in Galicia, where the remains of St James (Sant Iago) are reputedly buried. One of these routes was – and is – from the monastery of Sant Pere de Rodes, near Llançà, westwards via the Benedictine abbey at Montserrat, near Barcelona. This stretch of Vía Verde coincides more or less with that very pilgrimage route – alas for the pilgrims, an uphill stint from Girona to Sant Esteve, in the opposite direction to mine.

Enough history. Enough delay, I hoped. I asked the English couple the vital question.

'Did you see two fat cyclists in lime-green kit on your way?'

They smirked a each other.

'Couldn't really miss them!' said the man.

'How far away?'

'Oh, about ten minutes before we got here.'

'Speed?'

'Slow.'

Not the answer I wanted. Declining their invitation to explain my disappointed look, I wished them well, warned them of the hills to come and packed myself up. With a rueful wave, I pushed off from Saint Felix of the Pallerols, my mind abuzz with tactics of Tweedle avoidance.

Logical thinking required. I needed to be in Girona by a time agreed for the rendezvous with Julie. The Tweedles were between me and Girona. At their slow speed, I couldn't afford simply to keep pace behind them. Ergo, I had to overtake them. So far so good.

The rest of Sant Feliu de Pallerols passed in a blur of bridges, over and under. Overtaking while cycling was out of the question: I'd be for it... even if I didn't know what 'it' may be. Ergo (funny how Latin helps logical thinking, even though I never studied it), I'd have to overtake them while they were stationary. And when would the Tweedles be stationary? At a cafe. So the dream scenario would be spotting them at a cafe ahead and then sweeping on by, smile on my lips and wind in my sails.

With the track continuing for several kilometres on a steady descent, it was indeed as though the wind were with me for once as I swooped towards the River Ter. The relative flatness of the terrain had allowed the railway engineers the luxury of several long straights and it was as I swung into one of the these that I looked up to see, barely 200 metres ahead, in the shade of a plane tree, two lime-green jerseys. Stationary.

Can't stop here. They've seen me. Can't avoid them. No detours. Can I swish past? How impolite, how... wait... I don't believe it! Oh thank you, Spokey. One's on the phone! Tweedledee, I think. Dum's listening. Would now be impolite to stop!

'¡Hola!' whispered Tweedledum, as I crunched past.

'¡Adéu!' I hissed, with a smile. And for once I meant it.

Wind. Sails. Outboard engine. Full steam ahead! Aye aye, Cap'n.

No backward glances as I dipped out of sight at the end of the straight. No dawdling at information boards. No photo stops, not even at Amer, a place I'd driven through by car and thought unremarkable, but which, from the old railway that curved around the town at the height of its church clock, looked especially photogenic. Amer station used to be the logistical centre of the line, with workshops, sidings and all the paraphernalia of a small-scale Crewe or Derby, until it closed in 1969. All now removed, abandoned or, as with the ubiquitous station cafe, converted.

No time for coffees, just distance to be put between me and the enemy. It was 'doublethink' of course. I was by now fairly certain the jeopardy was as false as in reality TV, but knew equally well that it felt like an adventure – an exhilaration rarely experienced since I was a teenager. I was Hannay in *The 39 Steps*, Kimble in *The Fugitive*. An innocent on the run from the bad guys. My old legs seemed to have lost forty years. I even disobeyed my doctor's advice and pedalled my way up a few slopes, out of the saddle.

Eventually, however, the adrenalin drained away as quickly as it had rushed in and I needed to stop. Keeping my mind in schoolboy adventure mode, though, I hatched the next tactic. Wanting a place where the Tweedles were unlikely to call, but where I could spot them if necessary before they spotted me, I pulled off the track at the village of La Cellera de Ter. Craftily ignoring the first obvious bar, I came across a second, on a backstreet, its single outside table sitting in a half-hidden alleyway. Perfect.

Almost perfect. It wasn't until the barman brought my coffee and alcohol-free beer (a tad out of character for Hannay and Kimble perhaps) that I noticed my table's alarming deviation from the horizontal. Keeping careful hold of the drinks until I grasped them, the barman fixed me with an inquisitive stare.

'This table, señor, has a severe slope. That is why we have thrown it out here with this old chair.' I believe he thought I was blind.

Daft would have been nearer the mark. And so your all-action hero took his manly swigs while leaning uncomfortably on a collapsing plastic chair, between times holding tightly onto the two mugs of barely controllable liquid. That would make three mugs in all.

It was a short run to Anglès. Seeing the names of these Catalan towns, an English speaker can't help but wonder if the Place Name Committee of Catalonia hadn't picked them short-sightedly from an English dictionary. Anglès, Els Àngels, Bar, Cellers, Clot, Colera, Coma, Far, Figueres, Flix, Hospitalet, Limits, Millars, Parets, Pi, Planes, Olives, Quart, Riumors, Roses, Saga, Salt, Sucs, Tossa, Vic – and of course a handful of Prats.

The day I passed through Anglès, it was being dug up. Virtually the whole town. It's not an uncommon practice around here. Unlike in Britain, the local authorities still seem to have retained some common sense and arrange for almost all the utilities – water, gas, roads – to renew their infrastructure at the same time. The streets of Llançà had recently been a sea of mud for about twelve months, but since then we'd had barely any roadworks at all. Seems obvious, doesn't it? The only mystery is the one utility notable by its absence from the list: the electricity company. Just as in the rest of Spain, Catalonia still seems strangely attached to the ugly practice of stringing electric cables along, around and between its buildings like so much burnt spaghetti.

Anyway, not only was Anglès a no-go zone, so was the local route of the Vía Verde, occupied as it was by an army of diggers. Xavi the sign-man, however, had also been busy and diverted me into the undergrowth. Then he diverted me through farmyards, across fields, up improbable slopes, across fords... until, finally, at a meeting of tracks in the woods, he diverted me simultaneously left, right and straight on. Enough, Xavi.

Taking the first real lane I came across, I found my own way back to the main road and stuck to it. The afternoon had become sticky – a chemist's thermometer said 29 degrees – and I was soon leaning by a shady wall licking an ice sucker, green and oddly shaped like a hand pointing upwards. Observing the works in the parallel Vía Verde, I stroked my forehead with the icy green finger but still couldn't figure out what they were doing. The cycle track was pitted with large holes, inside which stood small men in fluorescent jackets and wraparound shades, their hard hats removed while they scratched tangled black hair in evident puzzlement at I know not what. This was not a new Vía Verde, but as to how a simple cycle track could have gone so badly wrong I'm afraid I'm as ignorant now as I was then.

I like Girona. Everyone seems to. However, it's a good example of how different approaches to a town can give you quite different impressions. Arriving from any direction by car, you'd be forgiven for feeling transported to the USA or to France, countries equally blighted by huge hoardings along strips of gruesome car showrooms, furniture stores and builders' yards. Arriving by train, you glide by terracotta rooftops and above squares elegantly laid out with plane trees before rumbling across a viaduct that reveals an enchanting view of the lazy River Onyar washing the timeless walls of the ancient town. A Catalan version of Venice.

A cyclist from the west sees yet another town. After finally rejoining the cycle track in a large area of woodland, Benny and I bounced beside the rushing Ter across carpets of white, wind-blown seeds that tingled the back of my throat, until the trees gave way to arable farmland. Here, black African workers, who seem to appear from nowhere at busy periods for the local farmers, toiled and smiled, stretched and waved while, at each junction in the dusty track, their womenfolk chatted among themselves, sleeping babies wrapped in colourful fabric on their backs.

African savannah soon morphed into shady woodland again, before opening up once more to reveal a long stretch of productive allotments, beyond which rose the distinctive, sand-coloured tower on the corner of Girona's eleventh-century cathedral. It seemed to stand just a few hundred metres from this tongue of countryside that gives a cyclist the best of all approaches to the city of nearly 100,000 souls: ancient Gerunda, Spanish Gerona and now one of the provincial capitals of Catalonia, modern Girona.

I'd had a strange text message from Julie:

'At hotel. Do not ask how to get here. J.'

And so, after crossing into the old town and asking directions from an old man, I found myself using that rare mode of transport, an outdoor public lift, which disgorged Benny and me even higher up the steep hillside that forms the Onyar's east bank. Having rattled along a few more cobbled streets, we finally pulled up outside the Pensión Bellmirall, within chiming range of the cathedral itself. Before I could press the bell, Julie herself unlocked the door. I was a little breathless.

'How did [puff] you know [puff] I was here?'

'Through the window. Keys to Dave,' she said, tossing them to me. 'Plaça de Sant Domènec.' Another toss – of the head to the right – and she was gone.

Oddly brusque, I thought. What happened to 'Oh, you do look tired'?

It was about an hour before the story came out, on the terrace of a nearby bar, but only after I'd regaled Julie with the tale of my flight from the Tweedles and eventually noticed in that slow, dull manner we males are prone to, that my fascinating stories and amusingly imitated accents weren't producing the titters they deserved.

'Is anything the matter?' asked the thick-skinned, insensitive cyclist.

'Only the worst drive I've ever had,' mumbled the unappreciated, hard-working support team. (You may guess that, before you read these words, Julie reviews them.)

'Oh, sorry. You didn't say.' (Glare received and taken on board.) 'Tell me now.'

'All you gave me was the address of the Bellmirall and a street map.'

'Wasn't that enough?'

'It was a pedestrian map.'

'Oh.'

'Yes, oh. No one-ways marked, no widths of the streets, no distinction between streets and alleyways. Plenty of beeps from other drivers, though. Oh yes. Lots of gestures from pedestrians too. Which reminds me: what does this mean?'

She made a gesture. I explained it.

'Thought so. Anyway, I've got some tips you can put in that book of yours for anyone mad enough to take their car into the Old Town of Girona.'

And so I reproduce them verbatim:

You have already gone wrong if any of the following occurs:

- There are no longer any cars following within an inch of your back bumper.
- In order to enter a street, you need to pull in both wing mirrors. (Incidentally, before reaching to pull in the passenger's wing mirror, it's advisable to apply the handbrake.)
- The only way out of your vehicle is through the hatchback.
- Your only exit from the street is via a flight of steps and you don't happen to be driving a 1960s Mini.
- You pass a sign that says 'Access to next street via pedestrian lift'.

She eventually softened after half a bottle of *rosado* and set off for a trawl around the shops by the river bank while I took in the city museum on Carrer de la Força. After a false start in another building also confusingly called the city museum but actually an art gallery (like the French, the Catalans seem to use *musée/museu* for both), I set about the five floors of the real museum. It's well laid out and has a roller coaster of a story to tell.

Girona's site is the key to its history.

I'd known that two rivers converge here: the Ter, whose valley I'd followed that afternoon, and the Onyar. What the museum's displays told me was that at least two more streams, the Galligants and the Güell, join them around here, though nowadays they flow almost entirely out of sight. Where the combined waters burst through a narrow gap in the hills about 3 kilometres north of the city stand the remains of both an Iberian site and a Roman fort, the latter having recently been restored and reopened to the public. We paid a visit a few months after the ride and can recommend it.

The turn off the east side of the N-11a near Sant Julià de Ramis is tricky to spot, but once you're off the main road all you have to do is follow the brown signs to 'Conjunt Patrimonial' until the road ends. Though the site is small, it's worth the visit just for the spectacular views not only of modern-day Girona but also right up the line of the old Via Augusta to the Coll del Pertús, where it breaches the Pyrenees, and across to the Gulf of Roses, where the Romans had first landed, like the Greeks before them. It's easy to imagine a soldier of 2,000 years ago holding a sunburnt hand to a sunburnt forehead and peering into the same hazy sunshine for signs of any threat to the empire. For centuries afterwards this strategically valuable site was still the focus of any north-south routes. As Ford very aptly put it, Girona has been 'placed by its military position in the very jaws of every invader'.

The town itself developed on the small, steep hill on the right bank of the Onyar which Julie and Dave the Kangoo had struggled around earlier in the day. One of the many problems they encountered was the vast city walls, first built by the Romans, enlarged in medieval times and mostly still standing today. A walk along the top of them takes an hour or more and rewards you with the best view of the city – and a set of well-exercised calf muscles.

Before the civil war, Girona's most disastrous period came during the Napoleonic Wars. In 1808 French attempts to take Girona had failed, but in December 1809, after an eight-month campaign against the besieged town, Girona finally fell. Five thousand Catalans died, but not before taking 13,000 French with them. It was little more than thirty years later that Ford undertook his travels in Spain and he tells us that he found Girona still 'much dilapidated from the French siege and bombarding'. These events are commemorated in Plaça de la Independència, a square on the edge of the 'new' town whose elegant arcades lend a definite air of Italy to it. Betraying rather more of the heroic than customary in Catalan monuments, the statue in the square's centre comprises three men – one commanding, one fighting, one slain – above an inscription that reads, in Spanish, 'A los Defensores de Gerona en 1808 y 1809.'

Back in the museum, a brief respite from wars is offered by a room devoted to the *sardana* and revealing rather more detail of the dance's key steps than the display in Torroella. Positioned in front of the diagrams and completely oblivious to my presence, a young German couple slowly lifted and crossed their feet, brows furrowed, upper teeth biting lower lips. Let's hope they'd enjoy the dance more in execution than practice.

The rooms devoted to the Girona of the 1930s were sombre and made no attempt at objectivity (and why should they?). Being largely ignorant of the events leading up to Franco's invasion, I eagerly read every caption and was particularly taken by a dramatic photograph taken not far from here in 1931, with Francesc Macià, soon to become president of Catalonia within the short-lived Spanish Republic, addressing a vast and enthusiastic crowd, almost all sporting flat caps. The following room, devoted to the effect on Girona of the civil war itself, left little doubt that many of those captured in such optimistic mood would not have seen out the decade.

After meeting Julie as arranged on Gustave Eiffel's pedestrian bridge across the Onyar, and taking in the sunset colours on the old tenements whose reflections in the greeny-brown waters grace a thousand holiday photographs, we wandered off to get something to eat. Back on Carrer de la Força we managed to give a waiter a laugh by pondering the relative merits of two menu displays before discovering that they actually related to the same restaurant. It'll be this one, then.

'How were the shops?' I asked Julie. 'Buy anything?'

Now this was, I concede, a stupid question – and not just because she was carrying two bags she hadn't had before. While I can quite easily – and morosely – waste an hour wandering through shops blank in thought, in expression and in achievement, even if a gift deadline is upon me, Julie invariably emerges from any shopping trip with presents for years to come for people I've barely heard of. That display of products which means nothing at all to me would shout out to her 'Betty's birthday' or 'Nigel for Christmas'. It's a gift, in both senses. Just as well some people are capable shoppers, I suppose, or the world economy would be even further down the pan.

'Yes, one or two things,' she said. 'None of which would interest you in the slightest, so don't pretend. But Girona is a good place for ideas.'

After an excellent meal comprising, for Julie, *habas a la Catalana* (beans in a chorizo sauce) followed by *botifarra* and, for me, *patatas d'Olot* (a kind of fried meat and potato pie that I'd forgotten to sample in that town) followed by lasagne, we plodded back to the Bellmirall. The day that had started, for me, with 740 steps ended with another hundred or so for good measure. I could hear my bed calling.

Day 16

Down to the Sea Again: Girona to Sant Feliu de Guíxols

One day I'll introduce the priest-in-charge at Girona Cathedral to the priest-in-charge at the nearby church of Saint Feliu. Maybe they'll agree whose bells are going to chime. At least, I assume the ringings every fifteen minutes and twice every hour, all night long, came from two different belfries. At 2.15 I considered venturing into the street to trace the source of the second set of chimes, two minutes after the first. Or maybe it was at 2.17. But then I might have got involved in the heated debate from across the road about someone's sister-in-law's obsession with blueberries – well, it started as a debate but after an hour or so had degenerated into an endless monologue directed at an evidently unmoved audience. I might also have been mowed down by the continuous line of vehicles from the *autopista*, each with a mysterious clutch problem, which appeared to have been diverted through the narrow, cobbled streets of Girona's Old Town from midnight on. I suppose I could have gatecrashed the party which some insomniac student thought would be a good idea to start around one o'clock; after all, it featured, unless I was mistaken, the unforgettable sounds of Raucous Rafa and his Cacophonous Combo. I wonder if the croissant delivery van sold any to the partygoers as he echoed through the cavernous alleyways about six? Perhaps he didn't even hear them over the hysterical Catalan news summary on his radio. He really should get that volume knob fixed. On reflection, I think I may have been wrong about the blueberries.

So it was a bleary-eyed cyclist that leaned on a lamp post in Plaça Catalunya the next morning. Apart from the lost sleep, it was a particular shame about the noise, since the Pensión Bellmirall was in all other respects an excellent place: a fourteenth-century building modernised to perfectly adequate standards, retaining countless old features and delivering an outstanding breakfast, all at a very reasonable price. As the Dutch lady with whom we shared a breakfast table had slept 'like a pot' (well, maybe that's what they say in Holland), the tip is clear: ask for a room at the back.

Surprised at first to see so many other touring cyclists out and about so early, I then remembered the Lance Armstrong connection. For five years, the seven-times Tour de France champion used Girona as a base for himself and his team after having become disillusioned with Nice. Almost single-handedly, Armstrong turned Girona into a Mecca for cyclists, so that at the time of this ride about seventy professional riders lived in the city.

Well, while they were doubtless setting off for a muscle-testing assault on the hills, I had only 40 kilometres or so ahead of me for my final day's cycling. Being in no particular hurry, I pedalled out of the other side of the square and over to Girona's railway station to view progress on the new parallel station for the high-speed trains from France. Or lack of it. For the project was running a hefty three years late. High-speed lines were waiting patiently – and expensively – at either end of this gap (at the tunnel through the Pyrenees in the north and at Barcelona in the south), but geological problems in the 4-kilometre tunnel under Girona had held up this vital link between Spain's growing high-speed lines and the rest of Europe.

The best view of the building site was from up on the platforms, where I stood with one hand holding Benny and the other shading my eyes. Well, at least the new station roof seemed to be in place. Giant orange cranes poked around among the equipment strewn over the vast concrete expanse like abandoned pieces of Meccano. There's no doubt that the engineers who, over a hundred years ago, built the small lines I'd been following would be stunned at the scale of it all. And perhaps, I like to think, rather appalled at the delay. A railway worker, his flag lowered by his side, was passing on the platform.

'Why is everything so late?' I asked, nodding at the site.

'Ah, señor,' he said, giving me a wink. 'What we have here is a cat in a cage.'

Unsure of my interpretation of his Spanish, I asked a simpler question. 'And when will it finally open?'

'When, señor, will the setting sun bring flames to the sea?'

Not in the next few weeks, then.

Leaving the philosophical railwayman to his duties, I negotiated the lift and cycled back into the streets of Girona. There's something life-enhancing about being on city streets as the town awakes. Shutters rattle up, shopkeepers sweep their portion of the pavement, mothers hurry their prams to the nursery, men in corner bars knock back brandies to steel them for whatever the day may bring.

What the day brought to the banks of the Onyar that day was a busload of red-uniformed schoolchildren, carrying identical clipboards and being shepherded away from the traffic and over the bridge towards the Old Town, where they would doubtless be shown the city's treasures and, more importantly, given the valuable answers to the questions on their boards. As I pushed Benny along Passeig de José Canalejas, they jostled past, chatting and smiling, one or two already snaffling their packed lunches. You often see school groups out and about in Catalonia and rarely – if ever – see the moody animosity prevalent in England. Maybe it's the climate.

The day was already muggy again as I pedalled south to Plaça dels Països Catalans, from where the Vía Verde leaves the city. Because the local road network had been particularly poor when this 39-kilometre rail route opened in 1892, it fast became astoundingly popular with passengers all along the line but especially with the residents of Girona, who finally gained access to the sea at Sant Feliu de Guíxols. They'd even given this *carrilet* their own nickname: El Feliuet.

Another group of people pleased to see it were the local cork manufacturers. Now, here's a nice confession of ignorance. It wasn't until I moved to Spain in my forties that I even realised cork was a natural substance; I thought it was just an artificial thingumajig that you stuck in the top of bottles, probably named after the corkscrew that got the damned thing out. My lamentable lack of cork knowledge, which I'd hoped to correct earlier on this ride at the closed

Museum of the Cork in Palafrugell, was now addressed by another handy en-route information board.

> Cork, as I'm sure everyone else already knows, comes from the cork oak, a tree native to south-west Europe. Round here, in the Gavarres hills that stretch from Girona to the coast, there are thousands of them. The Greeks certainly knew about this springy, watertight material and, with vines and olives all around here too, the rest is cork-stopper history. The main factories to take advantage of El Feliuet in transporting the finished article to the coast were at Cassà de la Selva and Llagostera, both on today's route, and yet more were produced on the other side of the hills in Palafrugell. Spain still produces a large proportion of the world's cork stoppers. Among the cork oak's other uses, of which you may share my erstwhile ignorance, are in the production of baseballs, woodwind instruments, the heat shields of spacecraft and, rather unbelievably, postage stamps.

The Vía Verde del Carrilet II is the cycle route that the Grumpy Old Cyclist of the Sant Feliu cafe had just taken when he gave me his precious, crumpled map. It is nicely engineered, with smooth surfaces, gentle gradients and a series of small-scale, almost toy-like green bridges to carry the cycle track over the streams that tumble down from the Gavarres hills. Crops seem to be harvested almost all year round in Catalonia and, near Quart, the track cut through a long, lazy swell of green-gold maize, speckled with the bright red sails of poppies flapping in the wind.

Quite a few other cyclists were out and about, one thunder-thighed woman overtaking me easily on a rare uphill section, another smartly kitted man berating me as he passed for not wearing my helmet. In Llambilles, cyclists seemed to be everywhere, heading in every direction. This was partly because some of them were stuck about 3 metres off the ground, painted black and made out of metal, in a sculpture designed around a number of abandoned bicycles. Catalonia's penchant for daft sculptures doesn't normally endear itself to me. On the N-11 just south of the French frontier stands what seems to be a giant concrete version of that childhood game where you have to move a ring over a wire without touching it. Drivers on the Figueres ring road are distracted by a huge multicoloured zip, half undone. Next to Barcelona's Port Olímpic stands an enormous bent sheet of metal with holes in, not far from an oversized paper clip. To me they all pose the same basic question: what's the point? Answers are hard to come by, but the metal sheet apparently represents the victory of David over Goliath. Can't see it myself. Maybe the giant paper clip represents the triumph of stationery over humans. Who knows? Not me, but then I'm no artist. I do admit, however, to being a cyclist and these recycled cycles on sticks certainly had something appealing about them.

The disorientated human cyclists, blocked by yet another hole in the track, were heading hither and thither like pedalling headless chickens until they (and I) found our way to the road and back again.

Cassà proved to be bigger than expected and a tip to anyone taking this route would be once again to take the main road through town, rather than the signposted Vía Verde route which took me through enough *polígonos*, you would have thought, to tell me why the Spanish (and Catalan) word for an industrial estate is the same as for a many-sided figure. After miles and miles of them I can report that I still haven't the faintest idea.

Leaving Cassà, its well-kept station, its station toilets and its rather unique milk-dispensing machine, the route abruptly changes character. Dropping down from the edge of the hills, it heads in a straight line across the joint flood plain of various *rieras* (streams) – Verneda, Cagarella, Gotarra – before following the angular field boundaries, as the railway must surely not have done.

By the time I washed up in Llagostera, I felt as baked and scorched as some of the fields I'd been crossing and gratefully pulled into the shade of the terrace at the Hostal el Carril, the 'Track Hotel'.

One characteristic that many Catalan women share with many other Spanish women – indeed, with many other Hispanic women worldwide – is the ability to combine in their conversational speech such breathtaking speed with such an unfeasibly high pitch that the resulting sound is actually painful to endure. Torture would not be too strong a word.

Shortly after I'd towelled myself down on the terrace and just as I was settling down to my *agua con gas*, two such ladies appeared, both already at full throttle.

'And-Nùria-told-him-what-to-do-but-would-he-do-it-you-bet-he-wouldn't-he-went-back-to-that-slut-Dolores.'

(My translations, I should say, are rather loose and based on the odd word whose sense I captured as it shot past my ear with the speed – and whining scream – of a bullet.)

'Does-that-surprise-me-not-a-bit-his-father-was-just-the-same-he'd-drop-a-woman-as-fast-as-look-at-her.'

'Well-I-blame-his-mother-God-rest-her-soul-she-doted-on-that-boy-since-he-was-wee-and-we-all-knew-how-he'd-turn-out-didn't-we?'

'Doesn't-know-what-side-his-bread-is-buttered-that-one-well-Dolores-has-got-him-now-and-Dolores-can-keep-him.'

Accompanying these noises was a battery of swift hand gestures which, if recorded, catalogued and taught, could constitute a new martial art. Nor were the two exponents standing still. While one walked backwards to the bar, the other shifted sideways to a seat, the two now moving towards each other, now moving away, as if enacting the kind of courtship ritual that wildlife photographers travel deep into the Amazon jungle to capture.

After some five minutes of aural punishment, during which I'd occasionally raised my eyebrows at the pair in an attempt to communicate their effect on anyone within a mile's radius – and failed – I packed up and left. The one other customer, a young girl reading a magazine, hadn't raised her head at all. Perhaps she was Dolores.

Not far to go now. At 'Km 29', after a woodland section of eucalyptus and cork oak, Antonio's online notes had alerted me to look out for a 'beautiful place'. I came across it at 'Km 10'. This is because, while Antonio had been counting from Girona, Xavi's kilometre posts started at the other end, Sant Feliu. It's tempting to think that they too were nearing the end of a long journey, here at the eastern extremity of Spain's Vías Verdes, and both getting a little demob-happy. The 'beautiful place' turned out to be the station of 'Bell Lloc', a fair enough description for what looked like a rather swish restaurant occupying the old station building. Other station conversions I'd seen over the past few days, apart from the regular cafes, had been a kindergarten, an ordinary school, a dance school, one house and several information offices.

By now, signs of 'civilisation' were sprouting up all around the track: mown verges, clean four-by-fours, Andorran number plates – yes, Catalonia's thin strip of developed coastline couldn't be far away. It appeared bearing something of a surprise.

Cresting the brow of a low hill, I caught a distant glimpse of a familiar building on the shore of a hazy-blue sea. It was the elegant Hostal de la Gavina, temporary home to the rich and famous on the headland at S'Agaró, which I'd passed on Day 5. It turned out that the route of the old railway almost hit the sea some way north of Sant Feliu, before swinging right to head into town high up on the slopes that must have supported farmland when the railway was running.

Despite its popularity, the private company that owned the line had run into financial difficulties by 1963, when Renfe (the Spanish nationalised railway) took over. To no avail: they closed it in 1969. No longer would rail passengers from Girona whoop at this view of the Mediterranean, which for many must have been their very first sight of the sea.

As for me, it may have been only five days since I'd seen it, but the short spin through the streets of Sant Feliu back to the seaside meant that, despite those disparaging choruses of 'Like that?!' over two weeks before – or perhaps because of them – I'd achieved my goal and finished my little tour of Catalonia. A wiggle through the seafront car park, a jolt up the kerb of the promenade and... bang! Benny lurched against the sea wall, my feet hit the deck, my fists punched the air and I let out my own whoop: 'Whooo-ha!'

The shout brought over Julie, who'd been waiting on a nearby bench.

'Well done that man! How's the knee?'

'Not bad. Couldn't have done it without you.'

'I managed twelve of the four hundred miles myself, remember.'

'Actually four hundred's not much, but the point is: it's mostly four hundred miles of Catalonia neither of us had seen before.'

I was feeling two emotions at once: one expected, the other not. I was sorry the adventure was over but I also felt a strange elation at being back by the sea. Strange, because I'm neither a sailor nor a fisherman nor even a swimmer. When I've mentioned to our Llançà neighbours that neither Julie nor I can swim (or, as they say in Catalan, 'we don't know how to swim'), they've been astounded. Our oldest neighbour had been swimming off the town's most dangerous beach for about seventy-five years. Well, perhaps she's never tried it at Skegness. As a child my only experiences of immersion in water beyond the bathtub were either at that bracing resort on the North Sea (or, as it should be called, the southern arm of the Arctic Ocean) or at a local, unheated outdoor pool in Derbyshire. In either case, I'd go in white and come out blue. Moving my frozen, stick-like limbs in any way at all was painful, moving them to stay afloat out of the question. Julie reports similar experiences at Weston-super-Mare. Fear of drowning set in at a young age and has never left me. A bit like Miss World, the sea is there to be looked at rather than get involved with.

Nevertheless, I feel at home beside the sea and, although I was grateful to the Grumpy Old Cyclist who, at the cafe just along this very promenade, had given me the idea of touring the Vías Verdes, the essence of this journey – and to some extent the essence of Catalonia itself – is the sea.

Julie seemed to be reading my mind. 'Is your next ride going to be another coastal one?' she asked.

'Coastal maybe,' I said, rubbing my knee. 'Ride maybe not. After all, there are more ways to get around than by pushbike.'

I can't finish without a final, grateful comment on Catalonia and the Catalans themselves.

On the Catalonia of the mid nineteenth century, Richard Ford wrote: 'This is the district of... the most ferocious of ancient Spaniards: nor are they much changed,' adding that he found the Catalans to be 'frugal, industrious and honest rough diamonds', but that 'Catalonia is no particular place for the man of pleasure, taste or literature'.

In the mid twentieth century, Rose Macaulay found them strangely ambivalent: 'If their curiosity is sometimes partly hostile, their helpfulness to foreigners in difficulty [is] delightful and admirable.' She agreed, however, with Ford in finding the Catalans distinct from the other residents of Spain, being 'more European, more French... perhaps more Greek, by heritage, certainly greatly less African, than the rest of Spain.'

What does another visitor from England think of the Catalans at the beginning of the twenty-first century? Well, the short – and diplomatic – answer is that the days of lassoing an entire nation inside one set of characteristics are surely gone. No longer do we derive our attributes – good or bad – solely from family and neighbourhood; and even if we did, they'd as likely include influences from 3,000 miles away as from three. No, people are people and all are individuals, the same types of which you'll find the world over.

Catalonia itself, though, is different from the rest of Spain, being one of those nations within a nation. For some, it's a would-be state outside Spain – and, who knows, perhaps this is the century they achieve it. A land of high mountains, rolling hills and broad plateaux, ending in a coastline of thrumming resorts, deserted beaches and cosy coves; of streets full to creaking point when the calendar says it's fiesta and empty as a crater on the moon when the clock says it's siesta.

After spending a large part of the last twenty years here, I now realise how lucky I've been to have chosen – or had chosen for me – a corner of the world that seems to offer everything. And actually, there's one aspect that has been consistent. Almost everywhere and by almost everyone I've been made welcome... even when my own shortcomings have made it difficult for them to know why I was there.

Notes on Catalan
Street Names

Just as a foreigner may be baffled by the number of Wellington Streets in England or Rues Jean-Jaurès in France, I was so ignorant on arriving in Catalonia that I thought Carrer Navas de Tolosa may commemorate some long-forgotten sea captain or ice cream dessert – or anything. The results of some research offered here may shed a little light.

Many of those street names referring to Catalan themes were banned during the Franco years and resumed their original names only after the fall of the Franco regime in 1975. Notice that Spanish references, however, have not been completely wiped out by the recent wave of Catalan nationalism.

11 de Setembre
Catalan national day, *la Diada*, commemorating the end of the 1714 Siege of Barcelona, a defeat for the Catalans and a victory for the Bourbons.

Anselm Clavé
Josep Anselm Clavé, musician and choir master (1824–1874), responsible for reviving many Catalan folk songs. Born in Barcelona.

Aragó
Aragon. Now, like Catalonia, it is one of the 'autonomous communities' of Spain, but in the Middle Ages it was a kingdom that became part of the powerful 'Crown of Aragon', which included Catalonia.

Colom
Either 'pigeon', 'dove' or the surname Colom, e.g. Cristòfol Colom, aka Christopher Columbus.

Consell de Cent
'Council of a Hundred', an organ of government in Barcelona from the thirteenth to the eighteenth century.

Corts Catalanes
Legislative assembly of Catalan government from the thirteenth to the eighteenth century.

Francesc Macià
Soldier and politician (1859–1933), president of Catalonia 1932–1933. Born in Vilanova i la Geltrú, El Garraf.

Garbí
South-west wind. Also called the *llebeig*. Being a maritime nation, Catalonia takes its winds very seriously, assigning names to them all and often naming a street after the wind that blows along its length.

General Álvarez
Mariano Álvarez de Castro (1749–1810), military officer. Commander of the heroic but ultimately unsuccessful defence of Girona when besieged by the French in 1809. Died in Figueres as a prisoner of the French in 1810.

Gregal
North-east wind.

Jaume I
Count of Barcelona and king of Aragon (1208–1276). Expansionist king, enlarging considerably the Catalan-Aragonese empire and warring with the Moors. Sponsor of Catalan literature. Born in Montpellier, France.

Jaume Balmes
Jaume Lucià Balmes i Urpià (1810–1848), priest, writer and philosopher. Defended Catholicism and attacked Protestantism. Born in Vic, Osona.

Joan Maragall
Poet (1860–1911), leading member of the Catalan modernist movement. Born in Barcelona. His grandson, Pasqual Maragall, was mayor of Barcelona during the 1992 Olympic Games.

Josep Palau i Fabre
Poet and writer (1917–2008). Born in Barcelona. Apart from his poems and novels, he wrote many non-fiction works on Picasso and was recognised as a leading expert on the Spanish artist.

Josep Tarradellas
Politician (1899–1988), president of Catalonia in exile during the Franco years and on re-establishment of the Generalitat in 1977. Born in Cervelló, El Baix Llobregat.

Llebeig
South-west wind. Also called the *garbí*.

Llevant
Eastern, usually referring to an east wind.

Lluís Companys
Lawyer and politician (1882–1940), president of Catalonia during the civil war. Executed on the orders of Franco.

Major
Main, as in Carrer Major (main street) or Plaça Major (main square).

Méndez Núñez
Casto Secundino María Méndez Núñez, naval officer (1824–1869), commander of the Spanish Pacific fleet. Born in Vigo, Galicia.

Mestral
North-west wind.

Migjorn
Midday, usually referring to a southern wind.

Narcís Monturiol
Engineer (1819–1885), inventor of the first submarine driven by a combustion engine, a replica of which can be seen in Barcelona's Maritime Museum. Born in Figueres.

Navas de Tolosa
Battle won by the Christians in 1212 during the *Reconquista* of Muslim Spain. Named after the town of Las Navas de Tolosa, Andalusia, where it took place.

Països Catalans
The 'countries' or territories where Catalan or dialects of Catalan are spoken: Catalonia, the Valencian Community,

the Balearic Islands, Roussillon, Andorra, part of Sardinia...
arguably it's a matter of opinion rather than fact.

Pau Casals
Cellist (1876–1973), more widely known outside Catalonia
as Pablo Casals. Born in El Vendrell, Tarragona.

Pau Claris
Pau Claris i Casademunt, churchman and politician (1586–
1641), president of Catalonia at the start of the Reapers'
War/Catalan Revolt. Born in Barcelona.

Pep Ventura
Josep Maria Ventura, musician (1817–1875), populariser of
the *sardana*, the Catalan national dance. Born in Alcalá la
Real, Andalusia.

Pi
Plaça del Pi, Carrer del Pi, etc. are nothing to do with
mathematics. A *pi* is a pine, the dominant tree type in
Catalonia.

Picasso
Artist (1881–1973). Born in Málaga. It's just as well for
the size of the street sign that he's not commemorated
by his full name: Pablo Diego José Francisco de Paula
Juan Nepomuceno María de los Remedios Cipriano de
la Santísima Trinidad Ruiz y Picasso. This twenty-word
leviathan beats even Franco!

Pizarro
Francisco Pizarro y González (1471/76–1541), conquistador
in the Americas. Born in Trujillo, Extremadura.

Ponent
West wind.

Pujada
Rise. Therefore usually a steep street, probably with steps.

Rambla (or Rambles)
Pedestrianised street, or part of street, usually tree lined.

Ramon Borrell
Aristocrat (972–1017), count of Barcelona 992–1017. First count of Barcelona to mint his own coinage.

Ramon Llull
Writer and philosopher (1232–1315). Born in Palma de Mallorca. At first sight, his surname may seem to be unusual, having four out of its five letters the same; but LL is counted as a single consonant.

Ramon Muntaner
Soldier and writer (1270–1336), commander in the Catalan Company (see Roger de Flor). Born in Peralada, near Figueres.

Roger de Flor
Soldier and adventurer (1267–1305), leader of an army of mercenaries called the Catalan Company, but most active in the eastern Mediterranean. Born in Italy.

Roger de Llúria
Knight and admiral (1245–1305), commander of the fleet that captured Sicily for the Aragonese-Catalan Empire in

the thirteenth century. Born in Italy, but exiled to Barcelona as a young man.

Ronda
Ring road.

Rosselló
Catalan for Rousillon, over the border in the Catalan part of France.

Sant Jordi
Saint George.

Sant Pau
Saint Paul.

Sant Pere
Saint Peter.

Tramuntana
North wind.

Xaloc
South-east wind.

Statto Corner

My route distances were calculated from maps and signposts rather than an odometer.

Day	From	To	Km	Mi	Comment
1	Cerbère	Llançà	21	13	Hilly. The first 6 km were from Cerbère railway station to the Spanish border at Portbou, where this book starts.
2	Llançà	Cadaqués	37	22	Some tough off-road sections.
3	Cadaqués	L'Escala	43	27	Tough to Roses, then easy.
4	L'Escala	Sant Antoni de Calonge	43	27	Easy.
5	Sant Antoni de Calonge	Malgrat de Mar	57	35	Tough: Tour de France route.
6	Malgrat de Mar	Barcelona	63	39	Easy, if you stay off the beach.
7	Barcelona	El Prat de Llobregat	29	18	Easy. Includes diversion of 10 km to Platja del Prat.

8	El Prat de Llobregat	Calafell	69	43	Some tough, busy roads.
9	Calafell	Cambrils	51	32	Easy.
10	Cambrils	Sant Carles de la Ràpita	62	39	Mostly easy.
11	Sant Carles de la Ràpita	Ulldecona	24	15	Easy.
		Sub-total	499	310	= Catalan Coast
12	Prat de Comte	Tortosa	41	25	Easy: Vía Verde de la Terra Alta and Vía Verde del Baix Ebre.
13	Cal Rosals	Cal Rosals	11	7	Easy: Vía Verde del Llobregat.
14	Ripoll	Ripoll	24	15	Easy: Vía Verde del Ferro i del Carbò.
15	Olot	Girona	54	34	Easy: Vía Verde del Carrilet I.
16	Girona	Sant Feliu de Guíxols	40	25	Easy: Vía Verde del Carrilet II.
		Total	669	416	

Bike (Benny): sixteen-year-old Mercier VTT Light from Carrefour, France.

Bike (Tetley): three-year-old Triban Trail 7 from Decathlon, England.

Best day's cycling: Day 11, Sant Carles de la Ràpita to Ulldecona.

Worst day's cycling: Day 10, Cambrils to Sant Carles de la Ràpita, only because I went on too long.

Best stretch: Llançà to Cadaqués (Day 2).

Worst stretch: Barcelona to El Prat de Llobregat (Day 7).

Rainy days: two.

Rainy days while cycling: nil.

Punctures: nil (Thanks, Spokey).

Best deal accommodation: Ca l'Àngels, Prat de Comte (Day 11/12).

Best quality accommodation: Castillo de la Zuda (*parador*), Tortosa (Day 12/13).

Oddest accommodation: Hotel Planamar, Malgrat de Mar (Day 5/6).

Worst accommodation: None. Regardless of minor complaints, they were all fine.

Julie's Golden Grouting Award: Hotel Borrell, Olot (Day 14/15).

Best meal: 'Crisis menu' at La Trobada Hotel, Ripoll (Day 13).

Worst meal: Frazzled chicken and cardboard pizza at Sant Antoni de Calonge (Day 4).

Oddest dish: (Joint winners) sausage and mash at Malgrat de Mar (Day 5) and wild mushroom, green bean and shrimp sauce at Ca l'Àngels, Prat de Comte (Day 11).

Railway Access

For railway services throughout Spain, visit www.renfe.com.

The coastal route is served by regular railway stations, with the exception of the territory between Llançà and Blanes. Consequently there is no railway access to the end of Day 2 (Cadaqués), to either end of Day 3 (Cadaqués to L'Escala), to either end of Day 4 (L'Escala to Sant Antoni de Calonge) nor to the start of Day 5 (Sant Antoni de Calonge).

As for the Vías Verdes, since they are all railway routes that have closed, it's not surprising that in some cases access by train nowadays is not easy. Except where they are physically joined, we drove from one to the other with our bikes in the car. Where you can reach them by train, it is only to one end. Here are the details:

Vía Verde de la Terra Alta (Tarragona province)
From near Arnes to near El Pinell de Brai. No railway at either end, but one end joins the Vía Verde de la Val de Zafán in Aragon (also no railway access) and the other joins the Vía Verde del Baix Ebre (see below).

Vía Verde del Baix Ebre (Tarragona province)
From near Pinell de Brai (no railway access) to Tortosa (regular services to Barcelona). Note that a bus service run by Grupo Hife (www.hife.es) from Tortosa does call at a number of locations close to this Vía Verde and does carry bicycles.

Vía Verde de la Vall Fosca (Lleida province)
From near Estany Gento (no railway access) to Espui (no railway access). This Vía Verde is way up in the Pyrenees beyond Tremp. Access is by cable car only, operating just in July, August and September – not in spring, when we made this trip. For information, visit www.trenscat.com/funis/gento_ct.html.

Vía Verde del Llobregat (Barcelona province)
From near Cal Rosals (no railway access) to La Baells (no railway access). Nearest station: Ripoll (regular services to Barcelona).

Vía Verde del Ferro i del Carbò (Girona province)
From near Ripoll (regular services to Barcelona) to Ogassa (no railway access). From San Joan de les Abadesses near Ogassa there is now, since this trip, a Vía Verde link to Olot, so that you can take Vías Verdes all the way from Ripoll to Sant Feliu de Guíxols.

Vía Verde del Carrilet I (Girona province)
From near Olot (no railway access) to near Girona (regular services to Barcelona).

Vía Verde del Carrilet II (Girona province)
From Girona (regular services to Barcelona) to Sant Feliu de Guíxols (no railway access).

Selected Sources

Books

Ford, Richard *A Handbook for Travellers in Spain* (1845, John Murray)

Lewis, Norman *Voices of the Old Sea* (1996, Picador)

Hughes, Robert *Barcelona* (1992, Alfred A. Knopf)

Macaulay, Rose *Fabled Shore* (1986, Oxford University Press)

O'Callaghan, Joseph F. *A History of Medieval Spain* (1975, Cornell University Press)

Read, Jan and Manjón, Maite *Catalonia: Traditions, Places, Wine and Food* (1992, The Herbert Press)

Articles

Bons, Paul and Druguet, Elena 'Cap de Creus Lighthouse Excursion' (at www.docstoc.com)

Cerrillo, Antonio 'Paisajes bajo control' (*La Vanguardia* newspaper, 2 May 2010). Feature on the measures proposed at Cap de Creus, as discussed on Day 2.

Websites

www.costabrava.org.

www.gencat.cat. The informative government website of the Generalitat de Catalunya.

www.iberianature.com. Nick Lloyd's vast and fantastic guide to the geography and natural history of Spain.

www.renfe.com. Information on Spanish railways. Partly translated into English.

www.viasverdes.com. The definitive guide to Spain's 'Green Ways', abandoned railways converted to cycle tracks. Partly translated into English.

www.trenscat.com/funis/gento_ct.html. Information on the cable car that gives access to the Vía Verde de la Vall Fosca. Website in Catalan only.

Have you enjoyed this book?
If so, why not write a review on your favourite website?

Thanks very much for buying this Summersdale book.

www.summersdale.com